IMAGES
of America

PAMPA

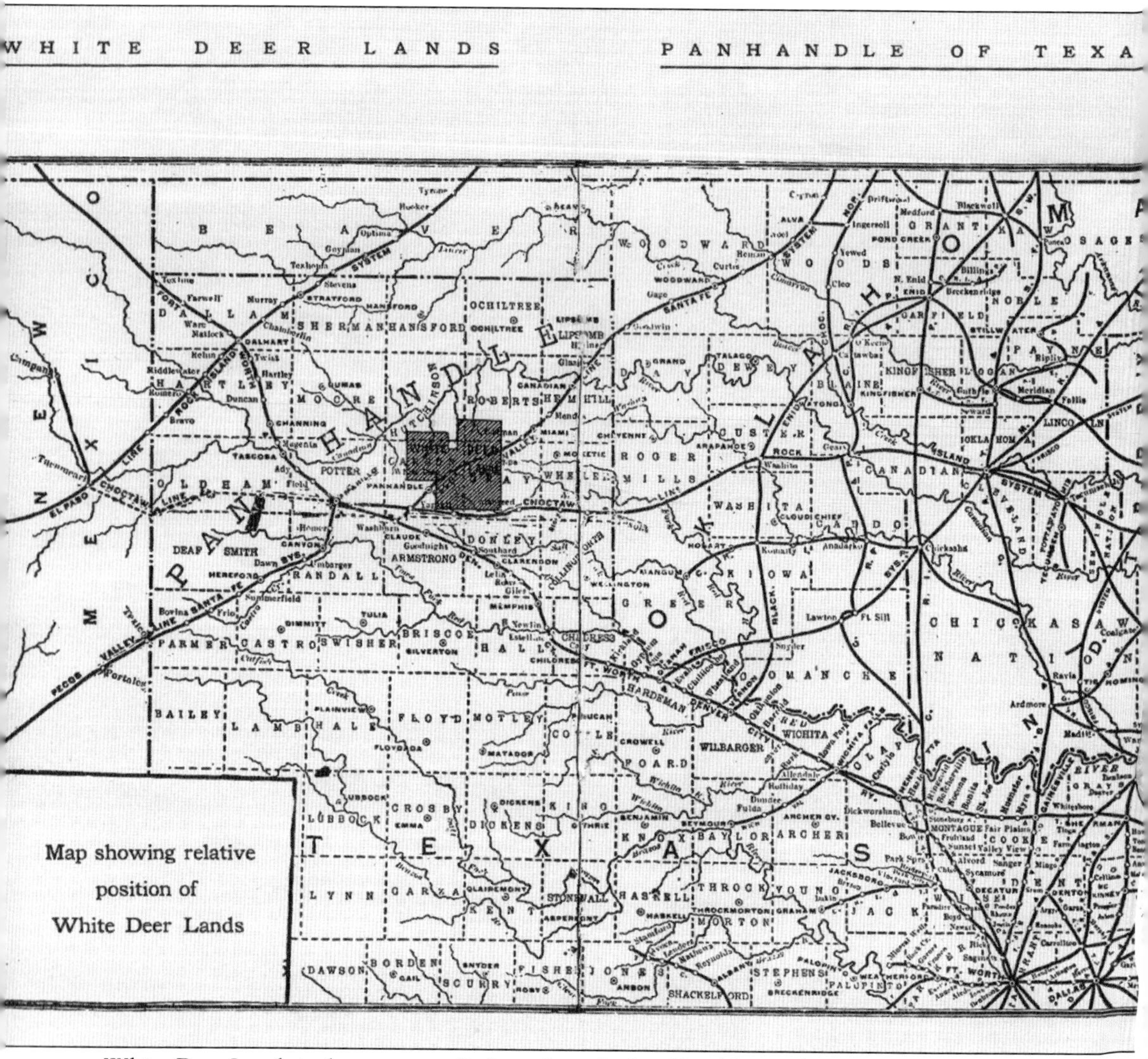

White Deer Lands is the name applied to a large body of land located in the counties of Carson, Gray, Hutchinson, and Roberts in the state of Texas and consisting of block numbers 2, 3, 4, 5, and 7 of the International and Great Northern Railroad. Notice the word "Panhandle" stretched across the top of the map, which referred to the top portion of the state, according to T. D. Hobart, manager. The White Deer Lands would eventually sell more than 631,000 acres before they closed the business. (Photograph courtesy of the White Deer Land Museum.)

On the Cover: This was Gray County's 1907 celebration of the Fourth of July under the tent. One of the fun pastimes of the day was horse racing, and these folks were waiting for the races to begin. The county seat was at Lefors in 1907, so they were celebrating there. (Photograph courtesy of the White Deer Land Museum.)

IMAGES
of America

PAMPA

White Deer Land Museum
Anne Davidson and Deborah Chambers

ARCADIA
PUBLISHING

ISBN 978-0-7385-8555-0

Published by Arcadia Publishing
Charleston SC, Chicago IL, Portsmouth NH, San Francisco CA

Printed in the United States of America

Library of Congress Control Number: 2009938751

For all general information contact Arcadia Publishing at:
Telephone 843-853-2070
Fax 843-853-0044
E-mail sales@arcadiapublishing.com
For customer service and orders:
Toll-Free 1-888-313-2665

Visit us on the Internet at www.arcadiapublishing.com

This book is dedicated to the pioneers who, with great courage, settled Pampa and Gray County. We are grateful.

Contents

Acknowledgments

This book would not have been possible without the rich archives of the White Deer Land Museum in Pampa. Since the late 1960s and 1970s, the people of Gray County and the surrounding area have brought priceless photographs and family stories in to be collected here. Now we have access to 40 years of good material from which to draw. The White Deer Land Museum excelled from its beginning in 1970. Now two additional buildings have been acquired, and the artifacts are still growing in number. We are grateful to the good folks who compiled our Gray County Heritage Book. We use it every day and much of what you read will have come from its pages. We are indebted to Darlene Birkes, chairman of the Gray County Historical Commission, for this printed history. She's also a great proofreader. Our thanks go to a special friend and board member Nancy Coffee.

I am so thankful for the help of my husband, Jim Davidson. He has copied, scanned, run errands, and cooked supper. I couldn't do this museum work without him. We are also grateful to the Gray County commissioners court, who backed us every step of the way. We thank the Lovett Library and the Chamber of Commerce. Our gratitude goes out to Eloise Lane, who is the Gray County historian and our friend. She taught us to love history.

We want to give a special thanks to Pauline Robertson for the information in her book, *Cowman's Country*. We also appreciate the use of material from the *Cable Tool Drilling* book by Delbert Trew.

The real thanks goes to the Gray County people who have donated priceless materials and photographs for 40 years. Thank you so very much.

And Luke Cunningham at Arcadia Publishing, you have been a blessing!

All photographs, unless otherwise designated, have been taken from the White Deer Land Museum archives.

INTRODUCTION

The Kiowa, Apache, Cheyenne, and Comanche Indians roamed this land before the white man's time. The Panhandle Plains region now consists of 26 counties that cover the most northern part of Texas. Coronado, in 1541, the first white man to enter the Panhandle area, is given credit for the term "Llano Estacado" (staked plains). It would be over 500 years before the first cattle were brought into the Western world. By 1820, Maj. Stephen Long became a trailblazer of this harsh land. Long was followed by Josiah Gregg, Lt. James Abert (1845), and Capt. Randolph B. Marcy (1849–1852) along with Capt. George B. McClellan.

Modern Texas cowboy traditions grew from the vaquero culture to Texas. Many ranchers were kept out of the panhandle by two factors: Native Americans and buffalo. By now, the Plains Indian had acquired Spanish horses and had become accomplished riders and hunters. Then, for nearly a quarter century, the cowboy culture took over the Great Plains' unfenced grasslands, rangy longhorns, and long trail drives.

In the mid-1800s, as more white settlers moved into Texas, military posts were being built. The military established a cantonment in Gray County in 1875 but later moved it to Sweetwater Creek and named the camp Fort Elliott. It was to be the only fort ever established in the panhandle. The Llano Estacado was becoming a dangerous place because of the tension between the Native Americans and the settlers. The buffalo-hunting settlers were taking all the meat, and the Native Americans were raiding and killing the white men. A buffalo hide was bringing in $3 in Dodge City, and an experienced hunter with a high-powered rifle could kill 100 to 150 animals a day and keep several skinners working to keep up. This situation was to bring about the Red River War of 1874–1875.

Three known skirmishes took place in the future Gray County area. On September 9, 1872, Col. Ronald S. Mackenzie routed a 262-tepee Comanche village in a surprise attack east of present-day Lefors on the North Fork of the Red River. That night, the Comanche Indians recaptured their horses, which taught Mackenzie a crucial lesson and helped prepare him for the 1874–1875 Red River War. The Farnsworth skirmish on November 6, 1874, involved a patrol of 28 soldiers ambushed by about 100 well-armed Cheyenne warriors. The soldiers were blocked three times before they broke loose and escaped. Two were killed. The largest battle in the area took place November 8, 1874.

After their defeat, the Native Americans were forced to move to Oklahoma reservations. With the land cleared and the arrival of trains, windmills, and barbed wire, settlers began to descend on the area. Gray County was organized in 1902, which brought an influx of more people.

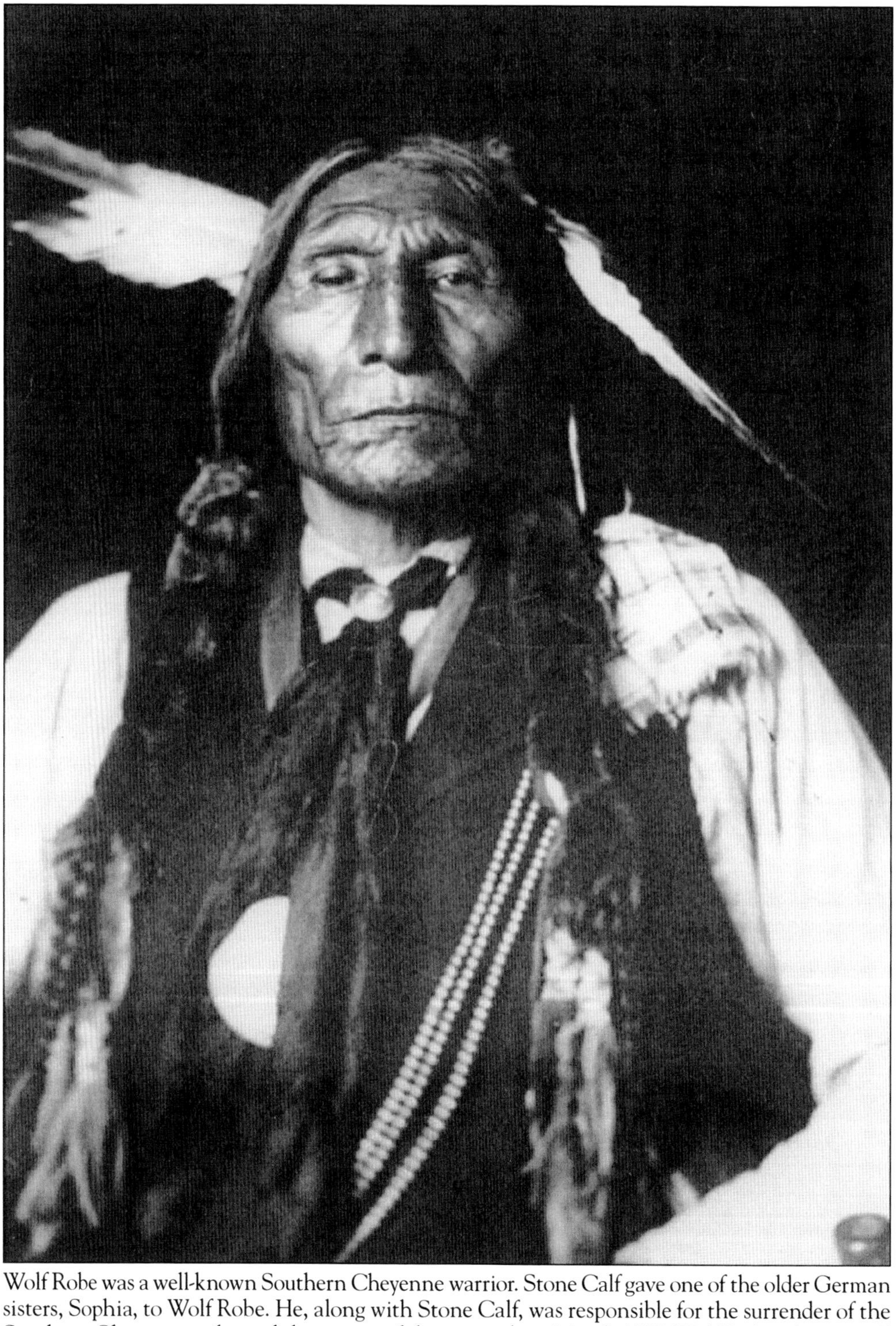

Wolf Robe was a well-known Southern Cheyenne warrior. Stone Calf gave one of the older German sisters, Sophia, to Wolf Robe. He, along with Stone Calf, was responsible for the surrender of the Southern Cheyenne tribe and the return of the two girls in March 1875. Wolf Robe's face is well known. His image is said to be the Native American on the Indian Head nickel.

One

The Red River War

About 1874, the final period of struggle between the Native Americans and the Anglos for control of the area took place. Desperate because of the great buffalo slaughter—some have estimated that millions of buffalo were killed—the Native Americans increased raids on the white settlers. The Red River War began in the Texas Panhandle with a raid at Adobe Walls in 1874, led by the Comanche chief Quanah Parker. It was the beginning of 25 skirmishes, and three of those were in Gray County, Texas.

The largest battle in Gray County took place about 12 miles south of Pampa at McClellan Creek. In November 1874, Lt. Frank Baldwin's troops camped in a cottonwood grove. Baldwin had 23 empty supply wagons. Early the next morning, one of Baldwin's scouts reported Cheyenne Indians on the creek about a mile away; they suspected the camp of Grey Beard. There were 110 lodges. Baldwin surprised the Native Americans by loading infantrymen into the 23 wagons, with cavalrymen on each side pulling a howitzer. They ran, and Baldwin's troops lost them after a 12-mile chase.

When the soldiers returned to the deserted camp, they found two girls, cold and emaciated. Julie and Addie German, seven and five years old, along with their two older sisters, Catherine and Sophia, had been carried off by Native Americans two months earlier.

The family of nine, the John Germans from Georgia, was camped in Kansas when they were attacked by a band of 19 on September 11, 1874. All were killed except the four girls. The Native Americans burned the wagon and left with the girls. They rode into the village of Grey Beard and Stone Calf. After two weeks, Grey Beard abandoned the two small girls where they were later picked up by another band of Cheyenne. The U.S. troops found the German camp and buried the bodies. Identification was made from the family Bible, which had escaped the fire.

It was not until Ronald S. Mackenzie defeated a large force of Native Americans in Palo Duro Canyon that Anglo-Americans could make permanent settlement in the area. Charles Goodnight moved 1,800 head of cattle to Palo Duro Canyon in 1876 and, in partnership with John G. Adair, founded the JA Ranch. The establishment of Fort Elliott guaranteed settlement in the eastern Panhandle.

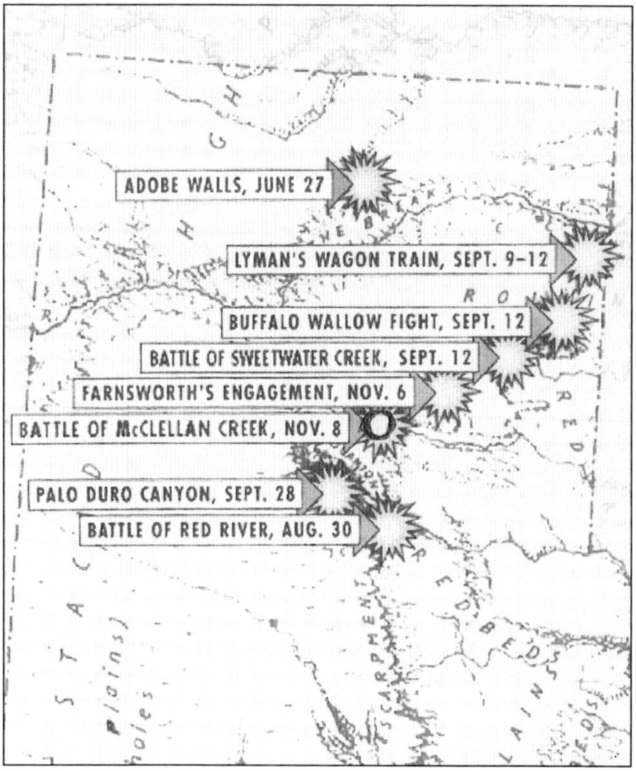

This map shows the 1874 battles of the Red River War. Circled in black on this map is the location of Baldwin's charge about 12 miles south of Pampa. This was where the German sisters were rescued. The war ended when the last holdouts, Quanah Parker and his Kwahadi Comanches, surrendered at Fort Sill, Indian Territory, in June 1875.

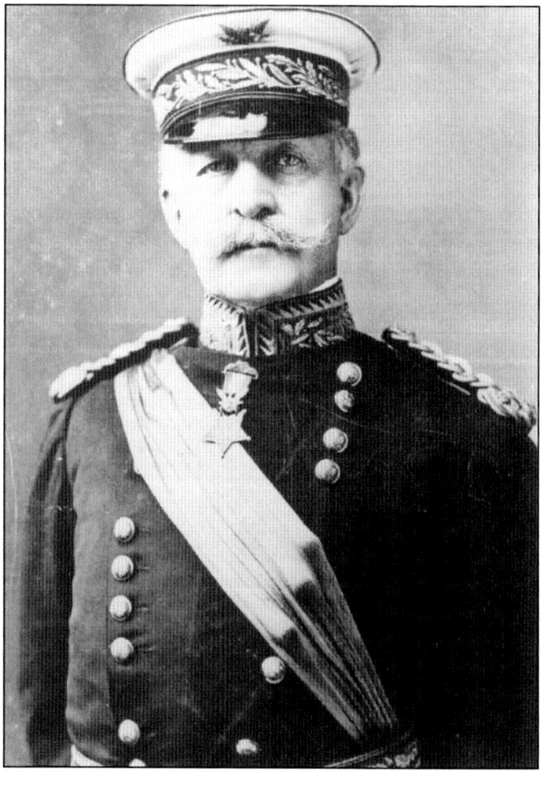

Col. Nelson Miles was in charge of four companies of the 5th Infantry, eight companies of the 6th Cavalry, Indian scouts, Gatling guns, and howitzers. He came from Fort Dodge in August 1874. At Fort Dodge, his mission was to engage large groups of Cheyenne in the area of the Red River and the Washita.

November 8, 1874, Lt. Frank D. Baldwin was escorting a group of 20 empty wagons to the supply camp. Scouts reported a large camp of Cheyenne Indians. Infantry soldiers loaded into the wagons with howitzers on each side. Grey Beard's Cheyenne were forced to run. Soldiers quickly discovered the two younger German girls wrapped in buffalo robes. Baldwin was awarded the Congressional Medal of Honor for this rescue.

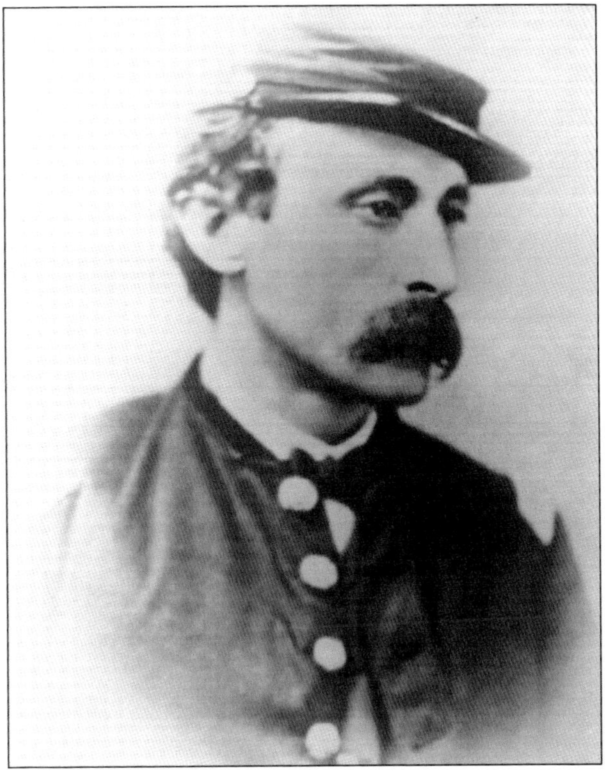

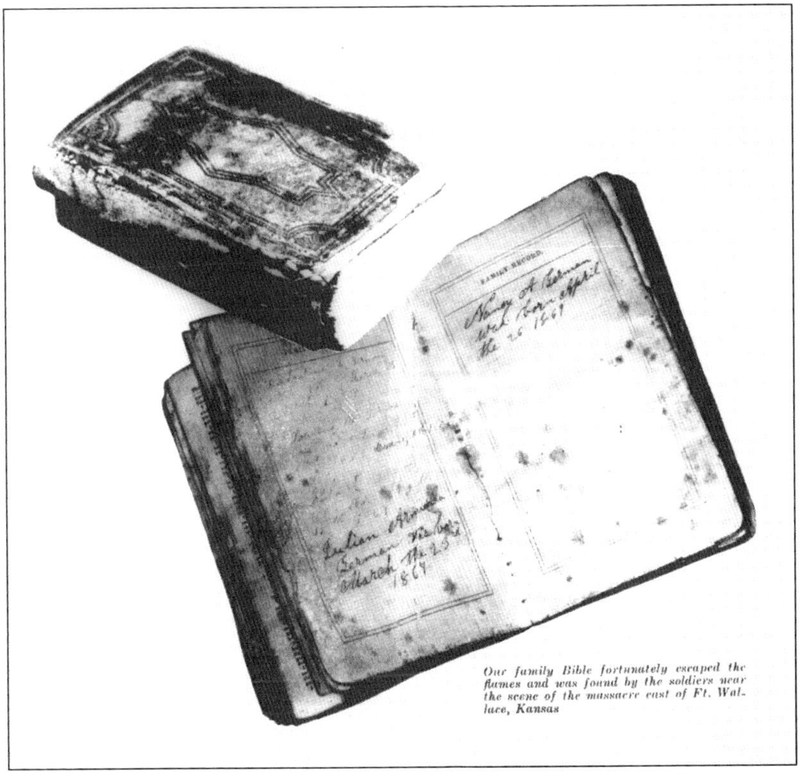

This is the German family Bible found at the attack site, close to Fort Wallace, Kansas.

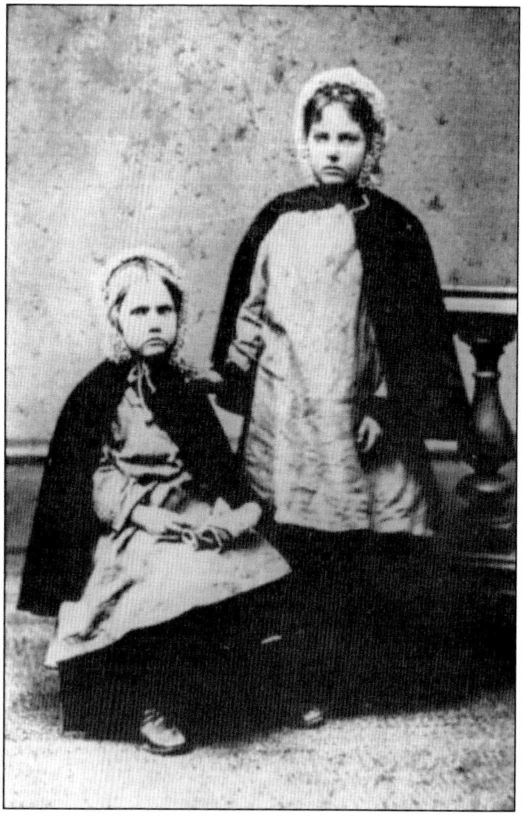

At the time of this photograph, Adelaide German was five and Julia German was seven. These were the two younger girls captured by the Cheyenne September 11, 1874, in Kansas and rescued November 8, 1874, by Lt. Frank D. Baldwin south of Pampa at present-day Lefors, Texas.

This is a photograph of an unidentified family who might resemble any family in the 1800s moving west. It was a very dangerous and tiring journey. This could have been the John German family coming from Georgia across the plains.

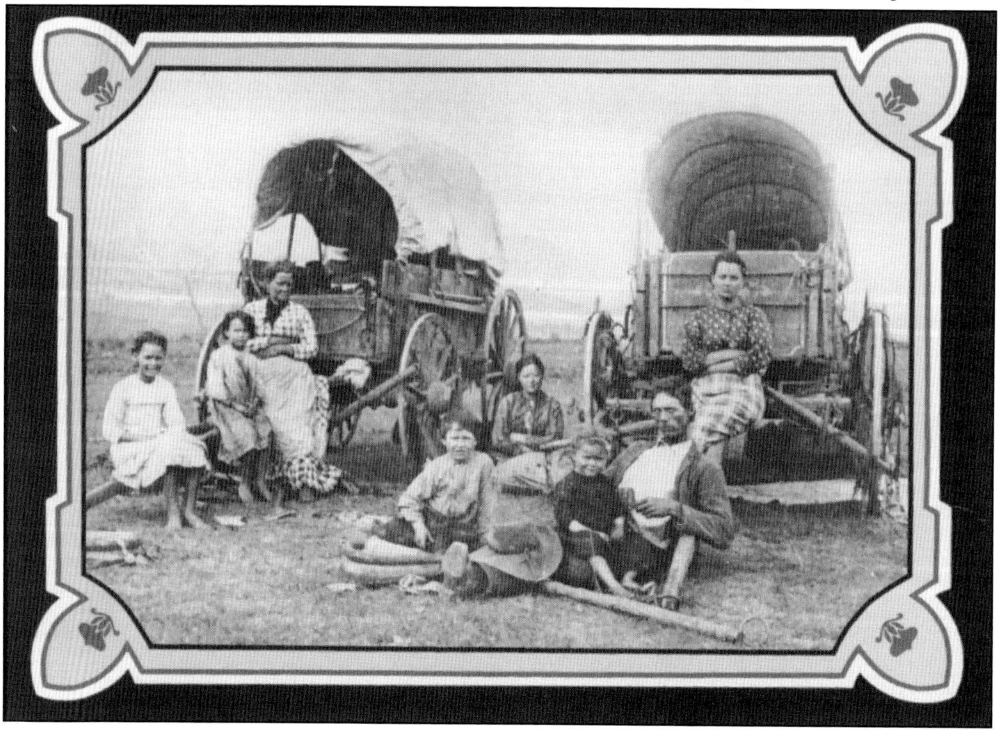

Maj. Joel Hawarth Elliott fought for the Union army, 7th U.S. Cavalry, during the Civil War. After the war, he served under the command of Lt. Col. George A. Custer in Kansas. In 1867, Major Elliott took 150 men from the 7th U.S. Cavalry to meet with five major Plains Indian tribes. Their mission was to get the tribes to sign a peace treaty at Medicine Lodge Creek in Kansas. Over 500 Native Americans from different tribes were present, and their leaders signed the Medicine Lodge Treaty. One year later, November 27, 1868, when Custer's 7th Cavalry lead a surprise attack along the banks of the Washita River, Indian Territory, Maj. Joel Elliott was killed in battle. This river is 36 miles from Pampa. There was much discussion later in army circles as to whether Chief Black Kettle, who was also killed in the battle, was trying to surrender on that day. Maj. Joel Elliott is buried at Fort Gibson National Cemetery in Fort Gibson, Oklahoma, in Muskogee County. The fort named after Elliott opened in 1975.

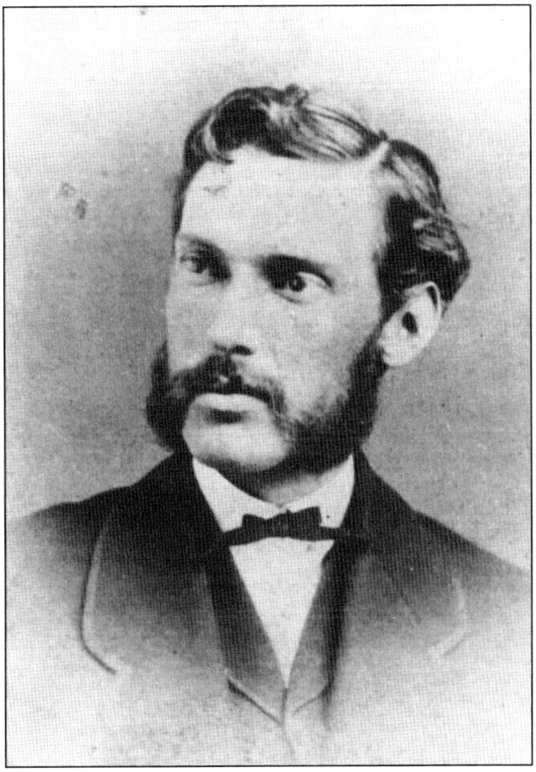

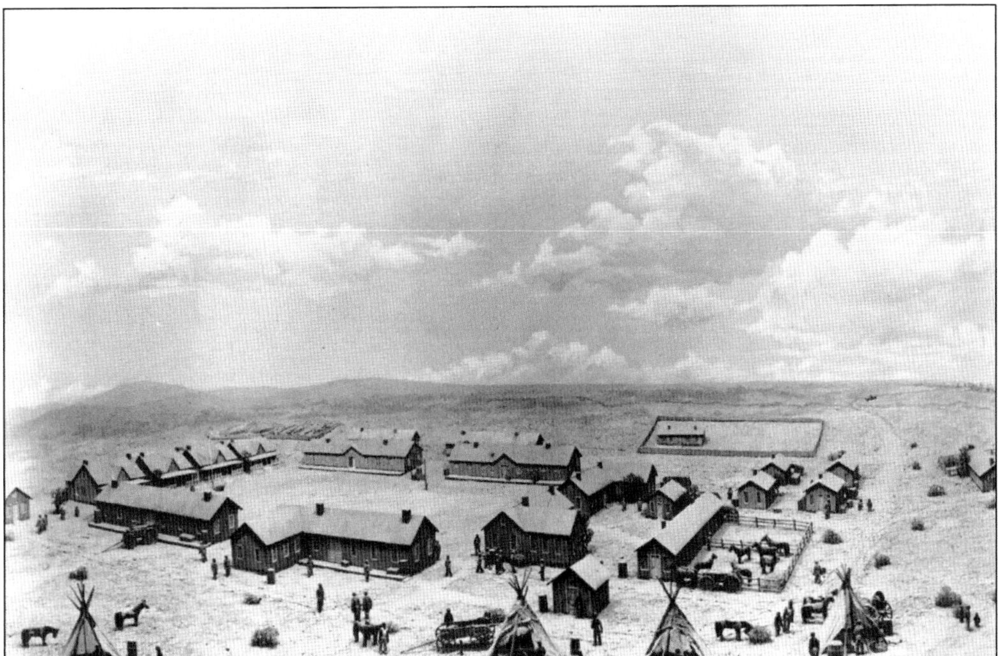

Fort Elliott was first a cantonment and was located 12 miles from Pampa. In 1874, the army moved the cantonment back 12 miles to the east and named it Fort Elliott. The fort served the area until 1890.

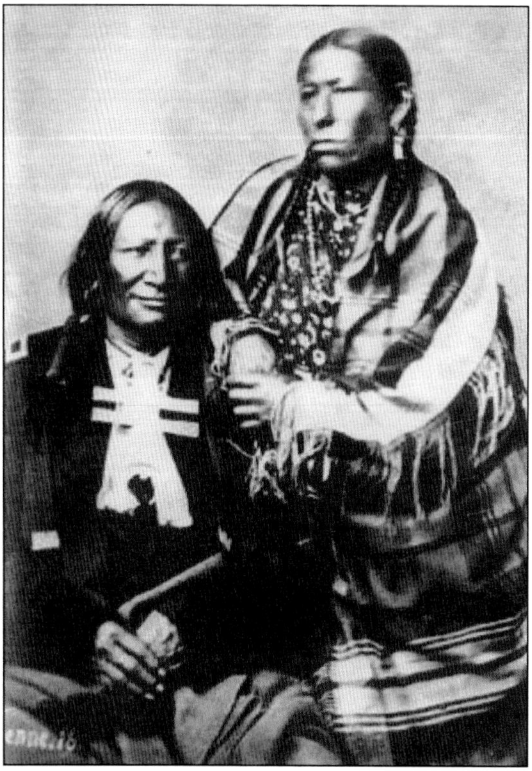

This is the Southern Cheyenne chief Stone Calf and his wife. They received the two older German sisters from Grey Beard and, soon after, headed south to the Llano Estacado. Gen. Nelson A. Miles insisted that they surrender with the understanding that the two female captives were alive and unharmed. Because they were out of provisions in a brutal winter, Stone Calf agreed. They surrendered on March 1, 1875. The two younger girls had already been rescued on the McClellan Creek in Gray County, Texas. The four sisters were reunited soon after that. The girls would later say that Stone Calf had treated them better than many of the other Cheyennes.

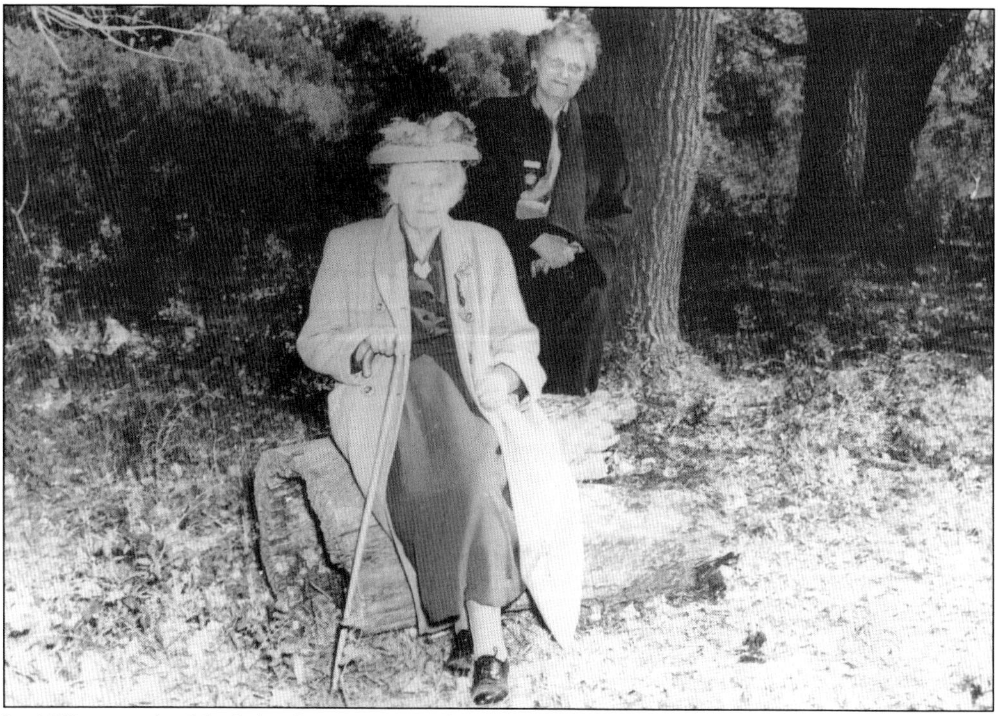

In 1952, a much older Julia German came back to Pampa to see the site where she was rescued 78 years earlier. Julia German is seated and the other lady is her driver.

Lydia German was the mother of the captive girls. She and her husband, John, were killed when the wagon was attacked.

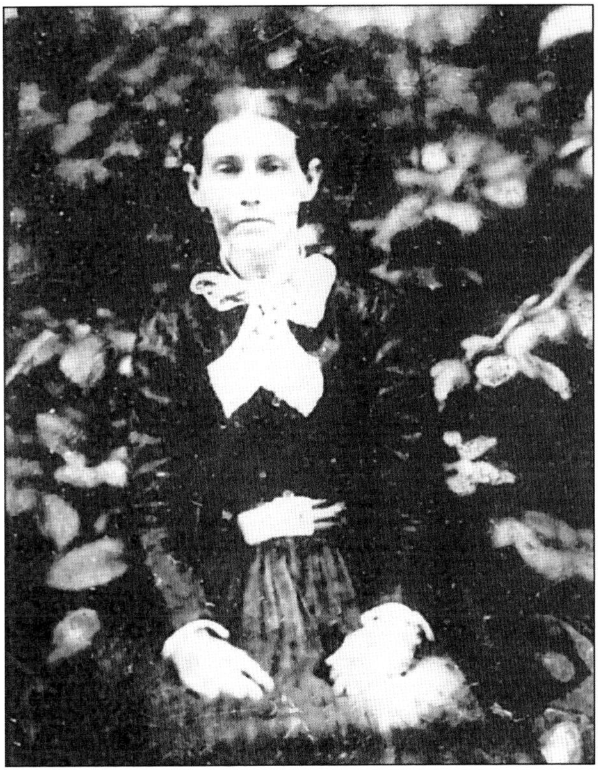

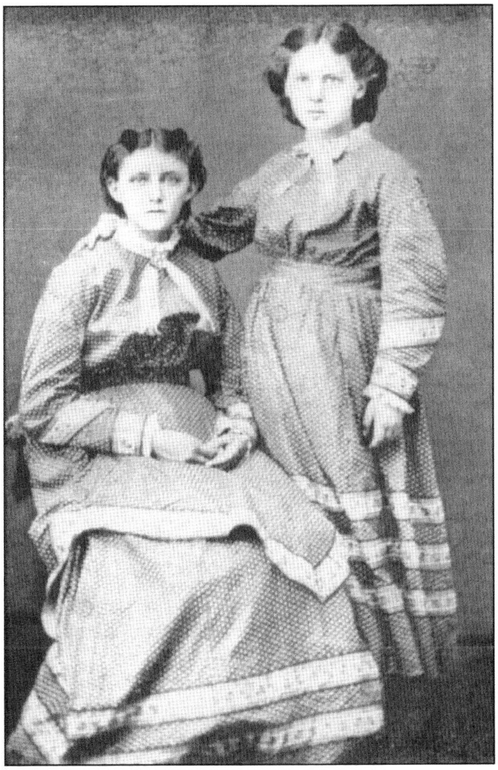

The two older girls were Catherine and Sophia. They are shown here after the army took them to Fort Sill. This was in 1875.

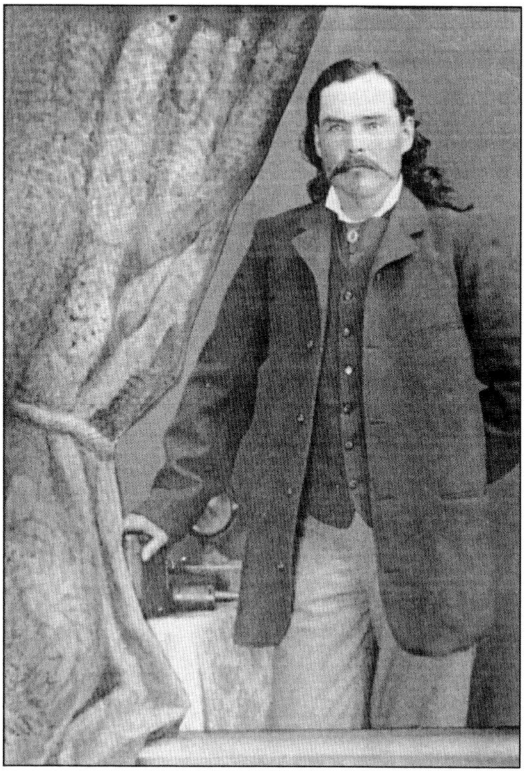

Scout William "Billy" Dixon fought at the McClellan Creek battle with Baldwin. He was awarded the Congressional Medal of Honor for his valor at the Battle of Buffalo Wallow ("Waller").

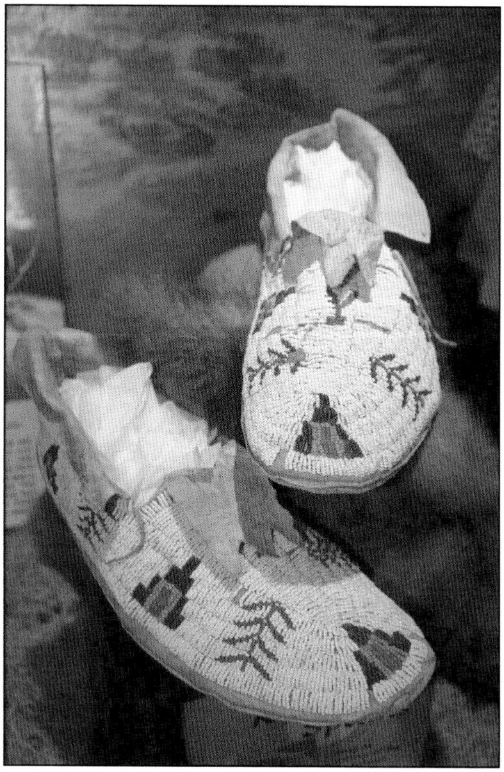

These Cheyenne moccasins are on display at the White Deer Land Museum in Pampa. They are reproductions of the moccasins that the older German sisters might have been wearing when they were rescued. The beading is more elaborate, but the buckskin style is the same.

Two

The White Deer Lands

Pampa's beginning dates back to the Santa Fe Railroad in 1888. Pampa is located on the territory that comprises a part of what is known as the White Deer Lands, belonging to an English syndicate controlled by Foster and Cuyler of New York. This became part of the White Deer Land Corporation, which encompassed Carson, Gray, Hutchinson, and Roberts Counties. George Tyng was the first manager. He had difficulty finding a name for this new dot on the plains. He finally settled on Pampa, from the Spanish word *pampas*, which means plains.

Pampa was an unpretentious place in 1888. In 1892, Tyng built the first building in the town. A portion was later used as part of the old Schneider Hotel.

The first wheat crop came in the fall of 1891. It was 20 years before abundant farming was done. For the next 60 years, the annual output of wheat was about 1.2 million bushels. In 1902, an election put the county seat at Lefors, 16 miles south of Pampa.

T. D. Hobart was managing the White Deer Lands in 1903. That year, and in 1905, two Englishmen came to work for the company. They were M. K. Brown and C. P. Buckler, who were to become comanagers. They sold land for $10–$15 per acre. Prospective land buyers came on trains, so the land company built an exhibit house near the train tracks to display some of the farm produce. They also printed brochures. Ultimately, the White Deer Land Company would sell over 631,000 acres of land. The managers were well respected leaders of the community and sensitive to farming conditions. When drought or hail destroyed crops, the managers worked with farmers, sometimes allowing them to postpone payments. The White Deer Land Company was dissolved in 1957 by comanagers Brown and Buckler.

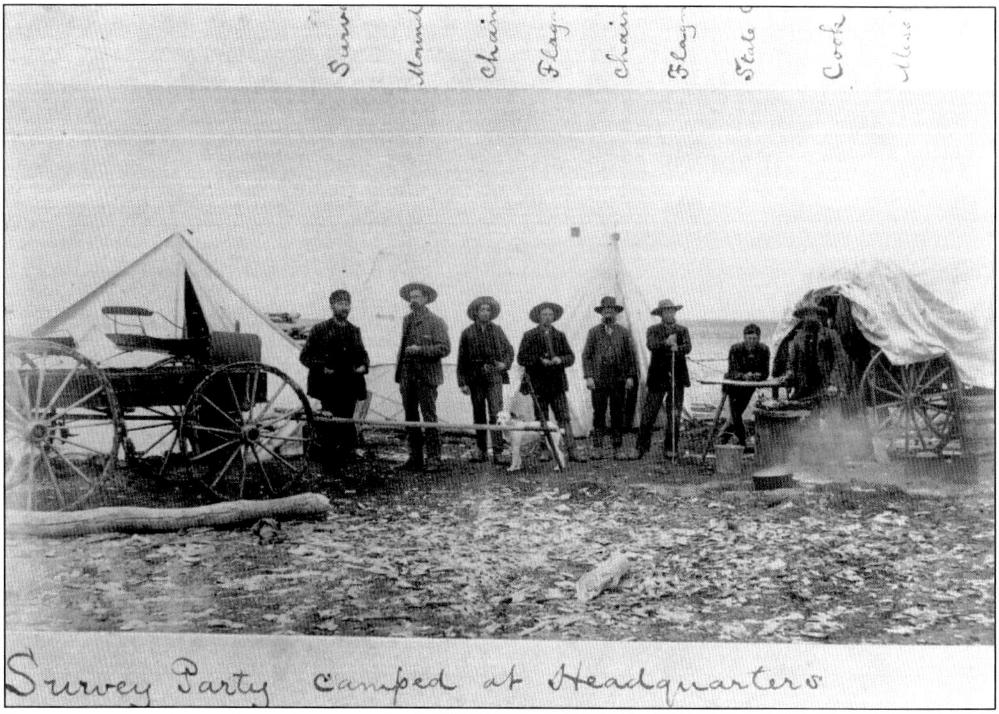

This is one of the earliest photographs of the White Deer Lands, or "White Deer Pasture," as they called it. This surveying party was camped at the headquarters on White Deer Creek. This could have been as early as 1887.

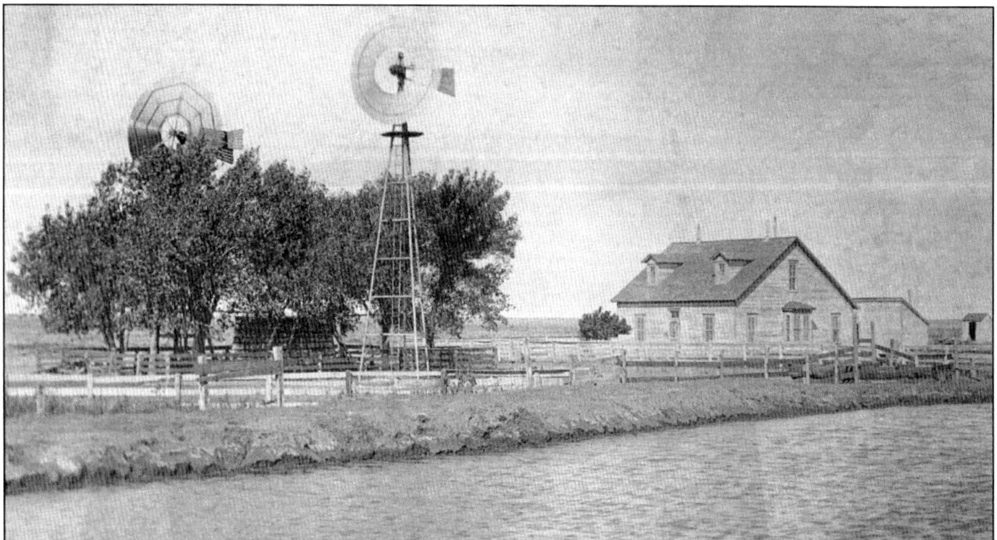

The first headquarters house of the White Deer Lands was 14 miles west of Pampa at White Deer.

George Tyng (rhymes with sing) was the first manager of the White Deer Lands. He came to the Pampa area in 1886. He had been hired by two New York lawyers, Frederick de Peyster Foster and Cornelius C. Cuyler. Tyng divided the property into 18 large pastures where he leased land, built fences, and drilled water wells. He first called Pampa "Glasgow," then "Sutton," and finally Pampa. Tyng had spent time in Argentina and thought our grasslands looked like theirs. The word *pampas* means plains in Spanish. The bottom picture shows pampas grass growing in Pampa. George Tyng hired T. D. Hobart in 1903 to manage the land company. To be closer to his silver mining interests, Tyng moved to Utah, where he was killed in a snow avalanche in 1906.

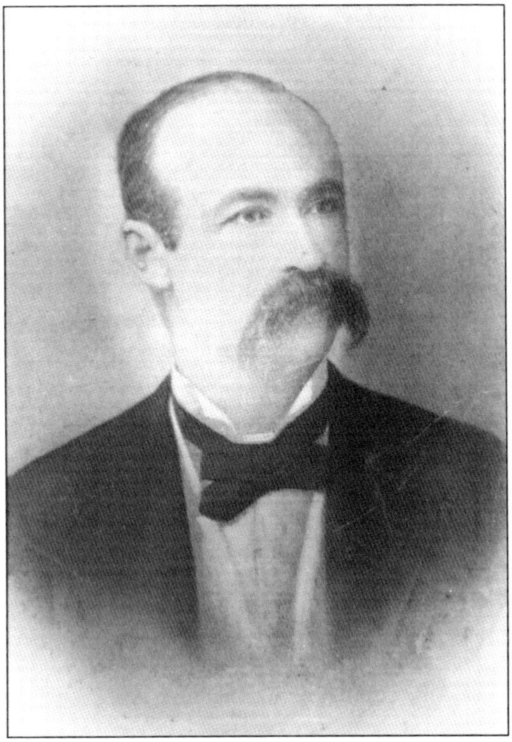

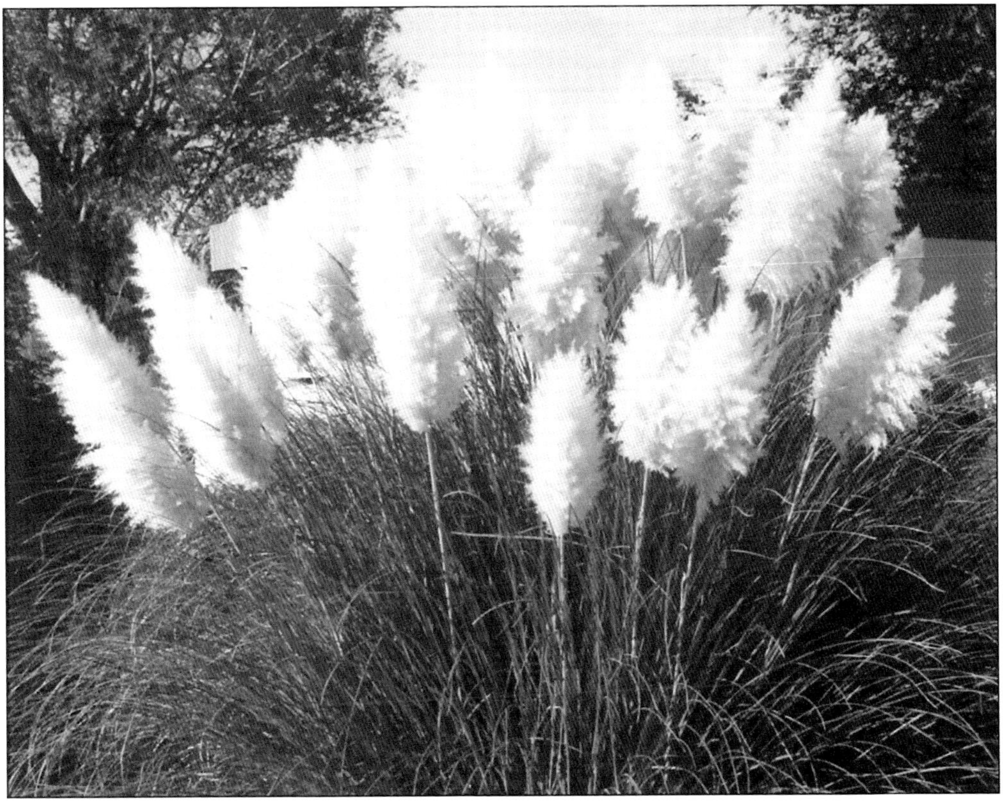

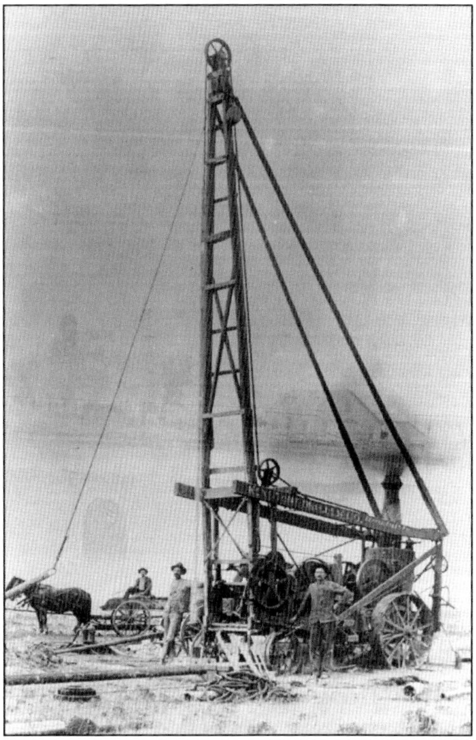

George Tyng was the first to get water into the Pampa area. This horse-drawn steam rig was brought into Pampa in 1886.

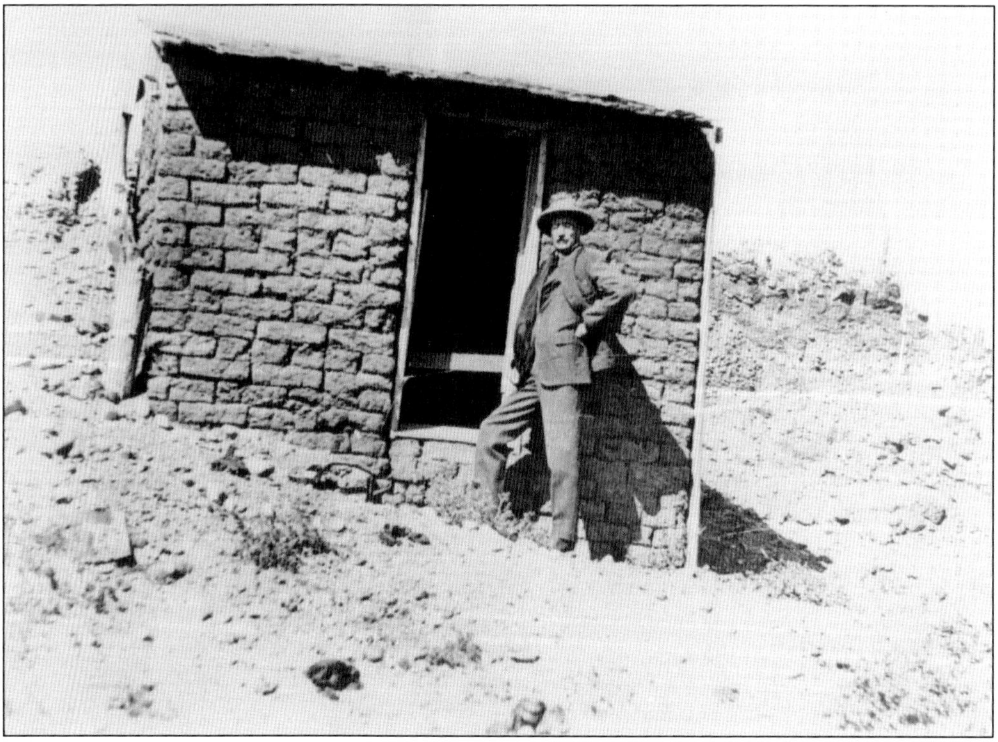

This was called the Rider Camp house. It was built on the north section of the White Deer Lands for the workers to live in, and M. K. Brown is visiting there.

The first post office in Gray County in 1886 is marked by this Texas Historical Commission marker. It is 18 miles south of Pampa and was called Eldridge. Later, when it was moved south to the railroad, it became Alanreed.

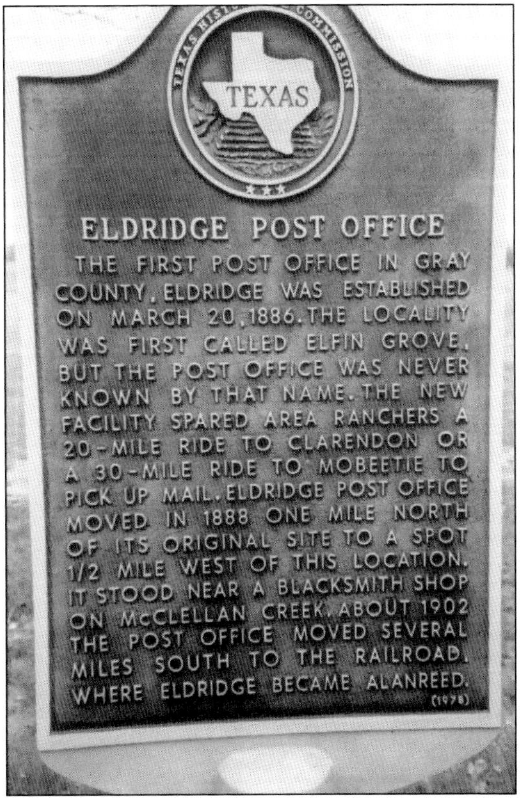

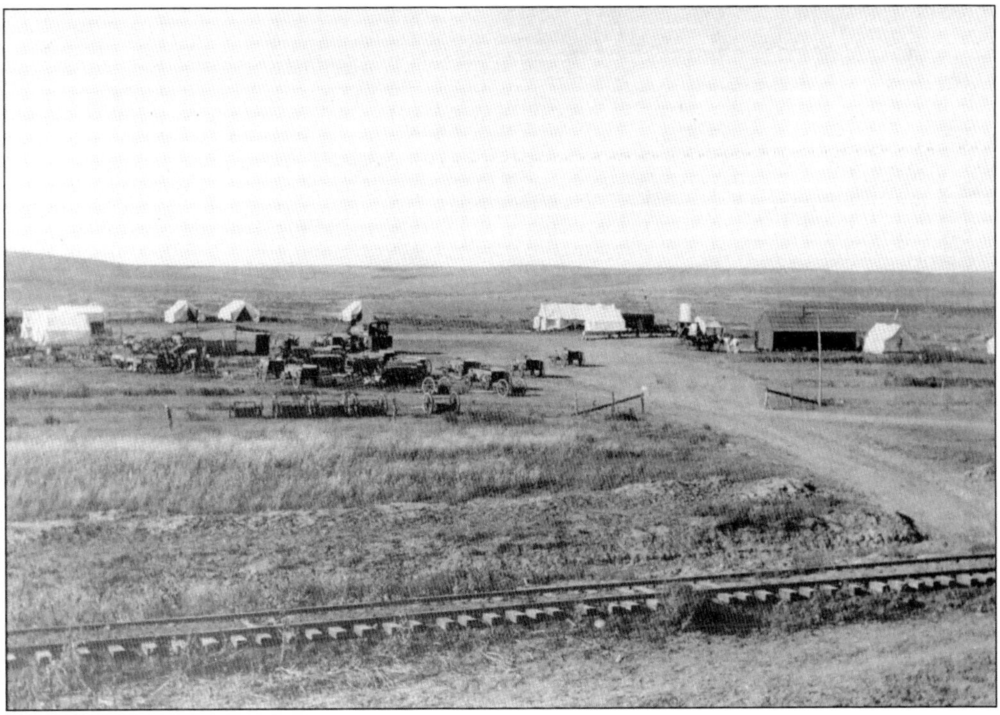

The Santa Fe Railroad camp east of Pampa was built in 1887 or 1888.

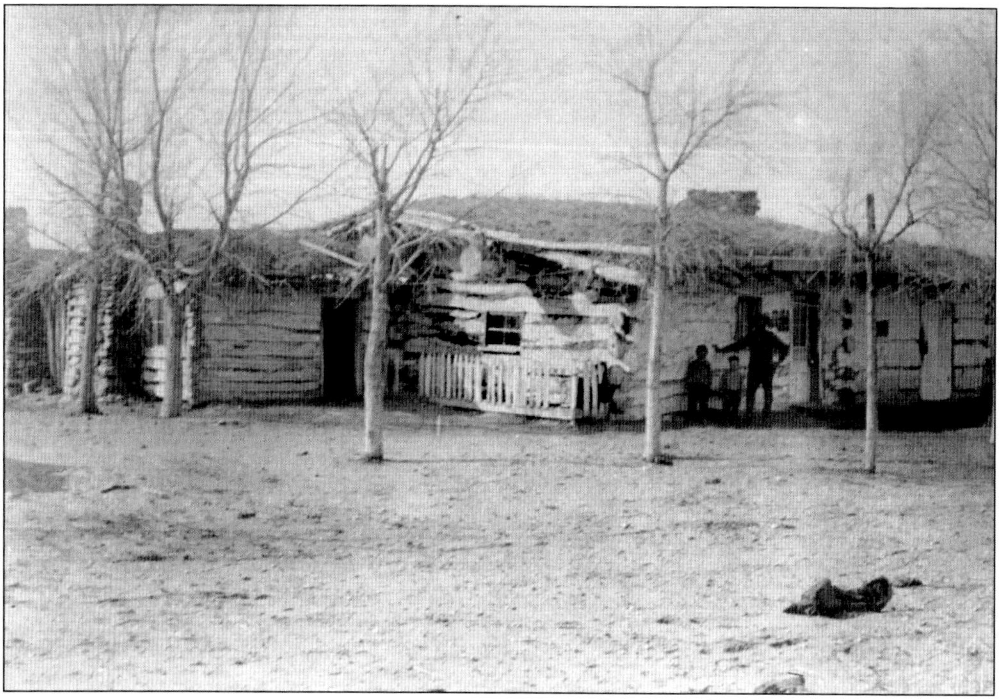

This is the first headquarters of the White Deer Lands in 1886. It was a log cabin on the White Deer Creek.

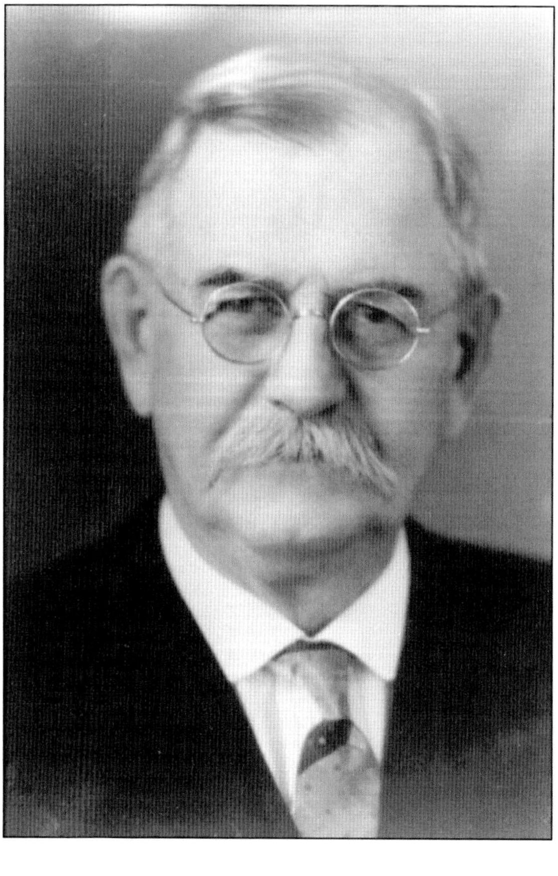

T. D. Hobart was the longest manager of the White Deer Lands, coming to Pampa in 1903. He was Pampa's first mayor. He brought settlers in and helped Pampa adjust to the oil boom that came in the 1920s. Hobart went to work for Cornelia Adair and the JA Ranch, overseeing huge herds of cattle until his death during the Depression.

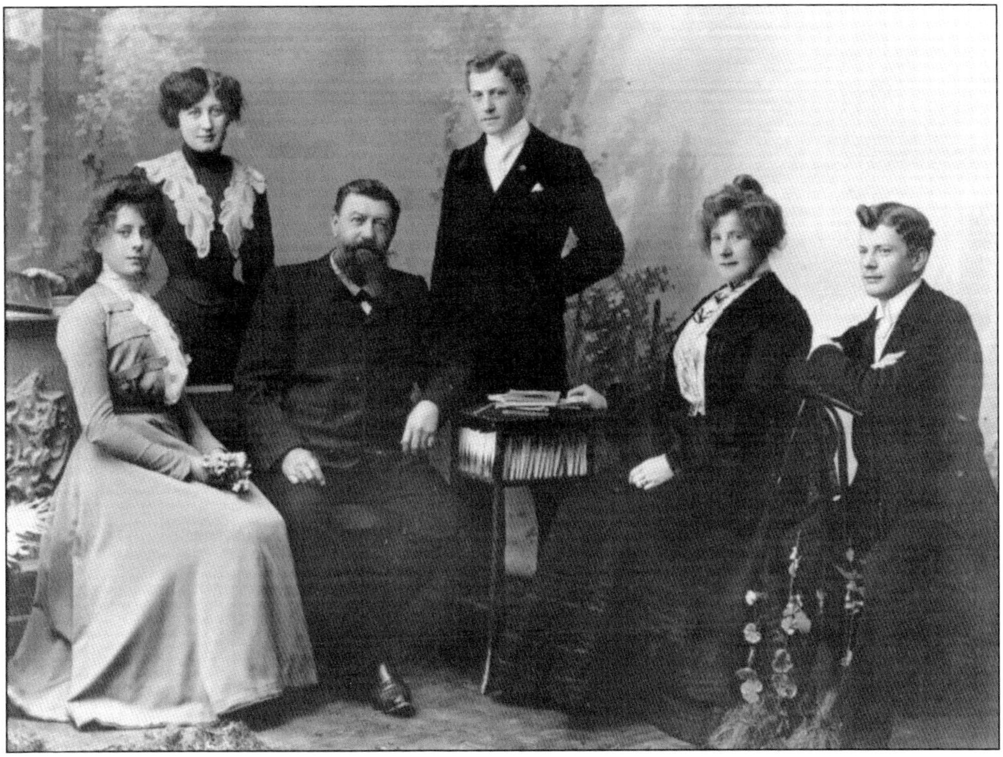

The Alex Schneider family, immigrants from Switzerland, came to Pampa in 1912. They bought the Holland Hotel and changed its name to the Schneider Hotel. This photograph was taken in Biel, Switzerland, in 1902.

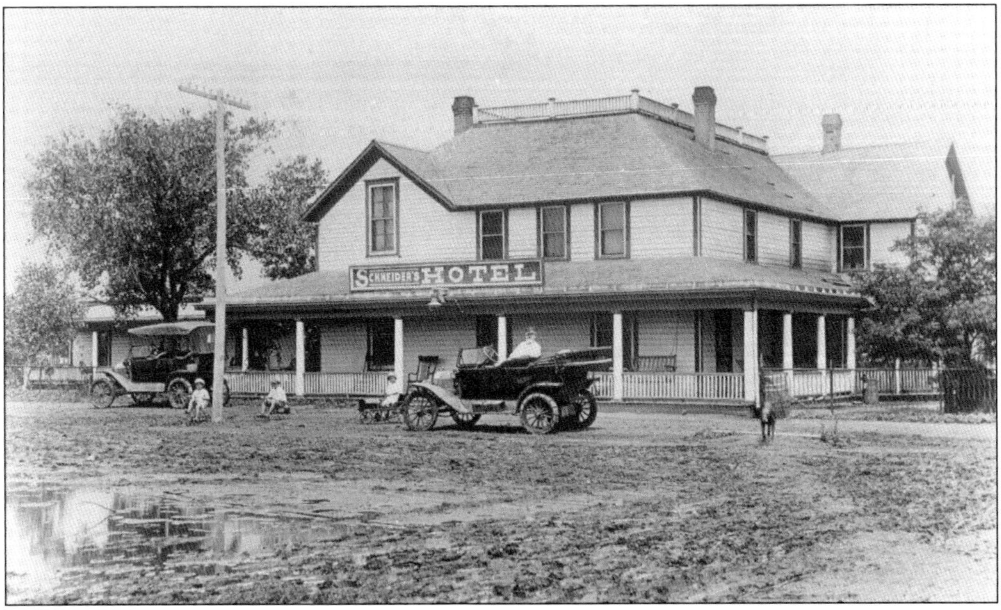

Alex Schneider is shown sitting in his new car at the Schneider Hotel. Schneider had come to this country in 1886, worked for the White Deer Lands with his brother-in-law Henry Thut, and then returned to Switzerland. He came back to the United States permanently in 1912.

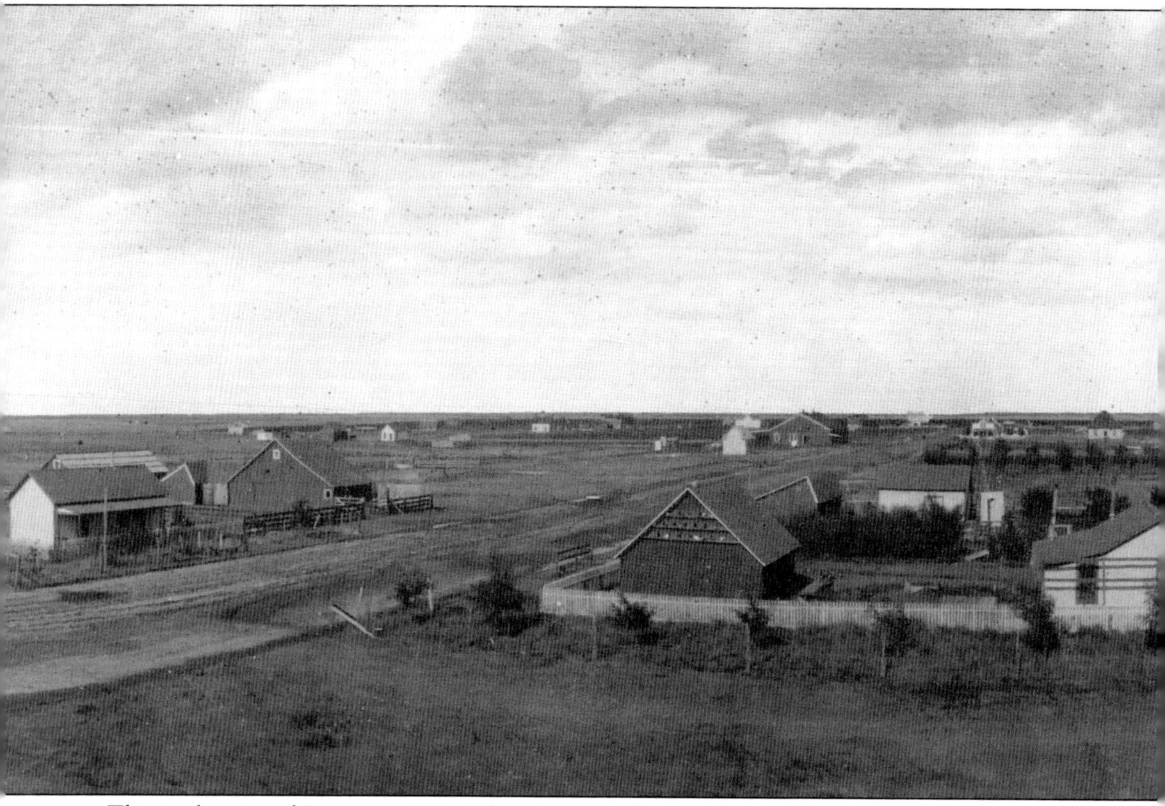

This is the city of Pampa in 1907. The white building in the middle is the White Deer Lands

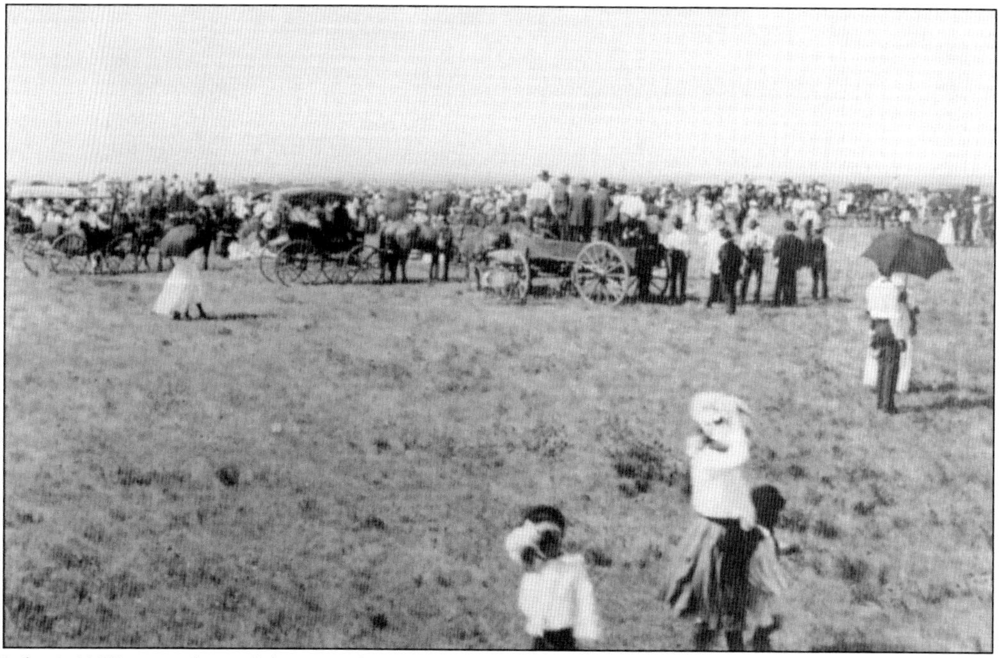

July 4, 1907, was a big celebration day in Lefors. These people were waiting for the horse race to begin. They had picnics and swimming before the races started.

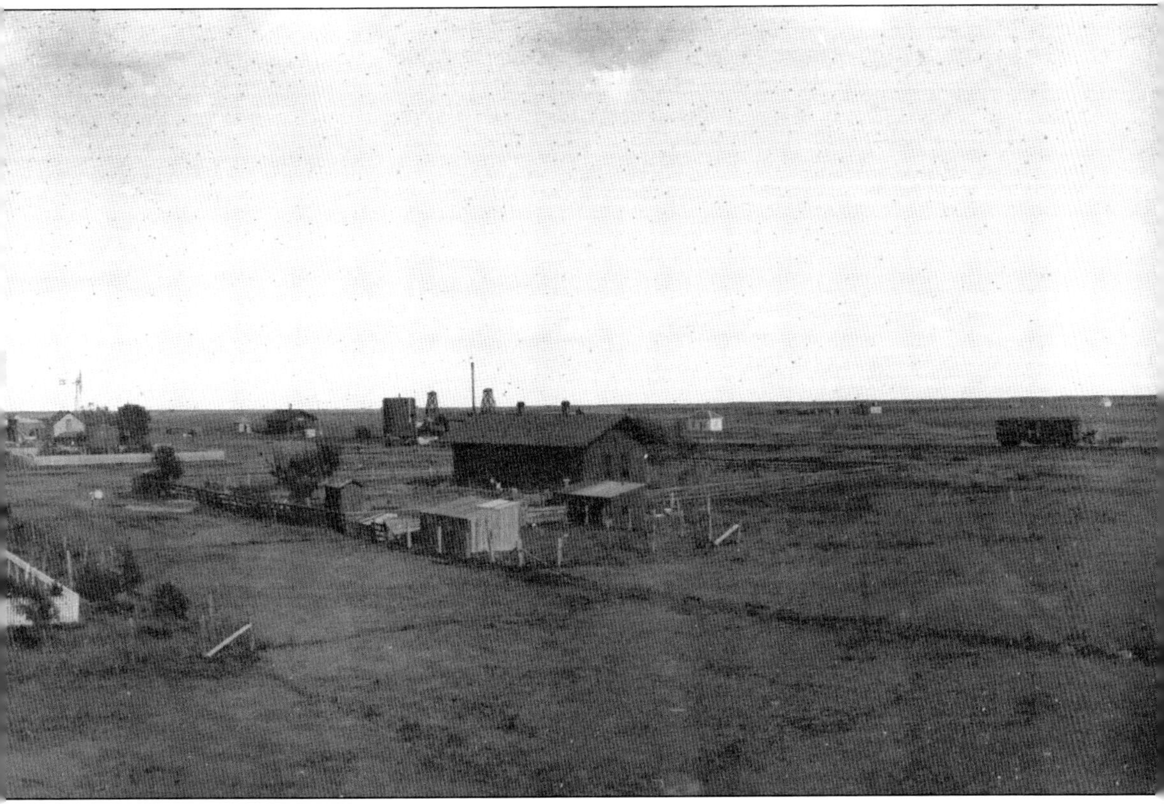

office, and the railroad section house at the right is still standing in a different location.

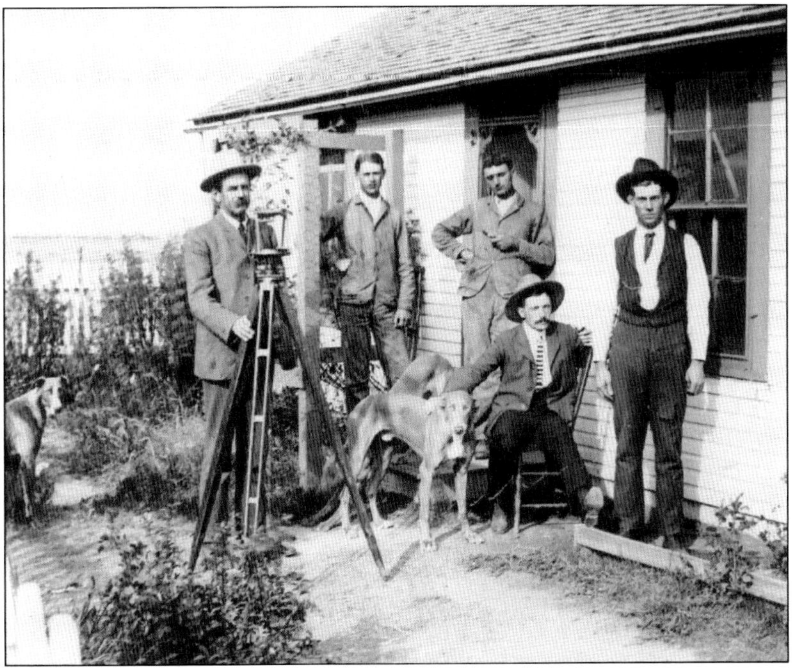

These five men are the White Deer Land employees. T. D. Hobart is holding what appears to be a surveying tripod. The hounds were used by the company for hunting.

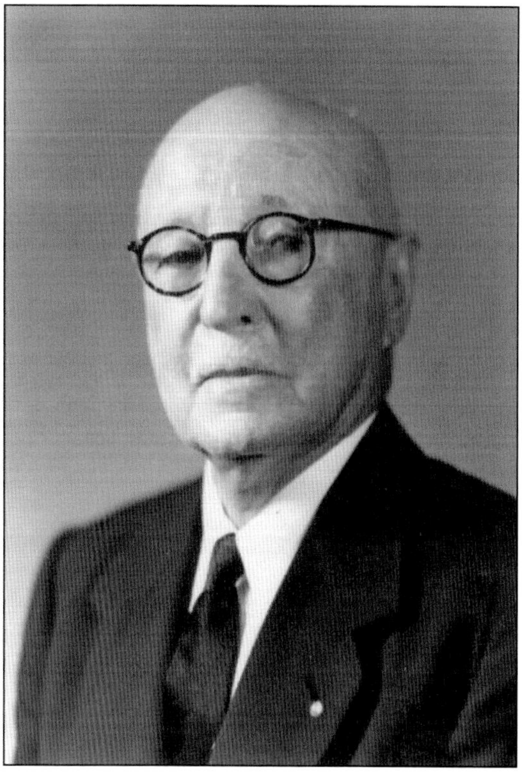

These are the last two comanagers of the White Deer Land Company. On the left is Montagu Kingsmill "M. K." Brown, born in Middlesex County, England, in 1878. He fought in the Queen's Army in the Boer War and came to America in 1903. Brown became a naturalized citizen of this country in 1915. After starting as a bookkeeper, he later helped Hobart in managing the JA Ranch. Below is Cecil Payne "C. P." Buckler. Buckler was also born in England and came to this country in 1905. When there was no Episcopal church in Pampa, they met in the Buckler home until one was built. Brown and Buckler closed the White Deer Land Company in 1957. Brown bought the building, and it now houses the White Deer Land Museum.

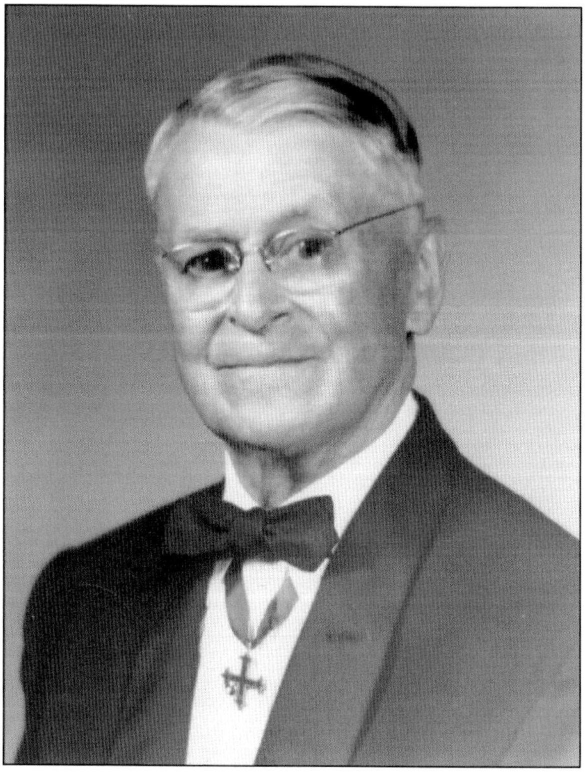

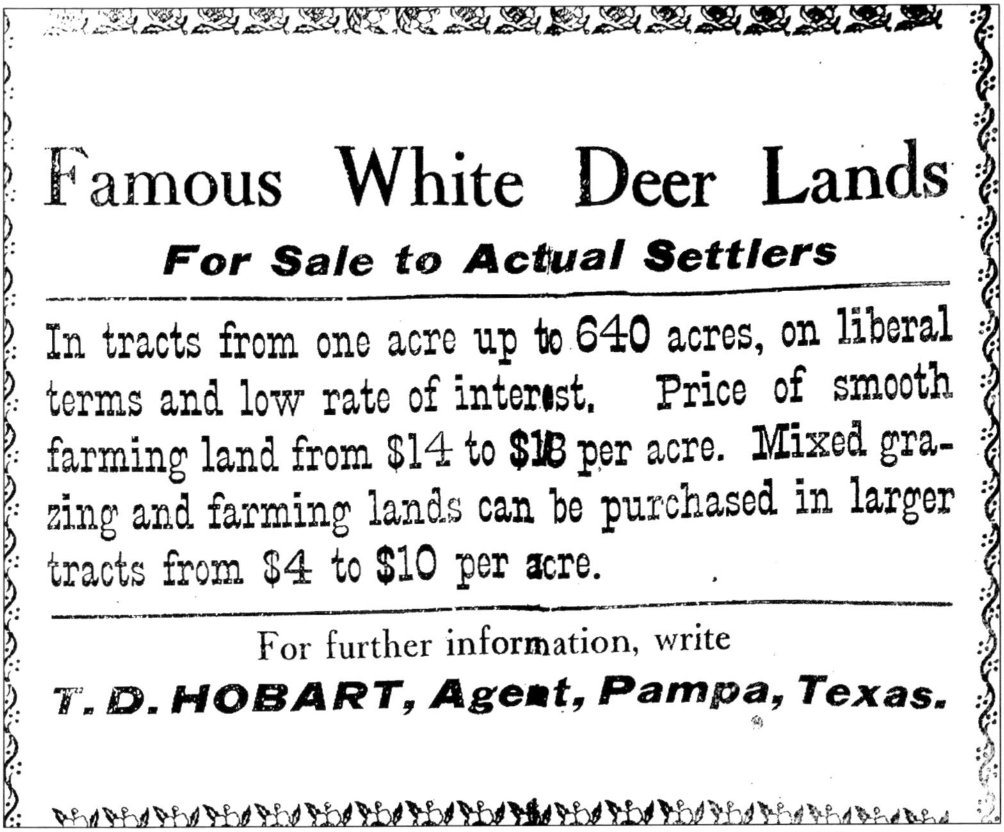

Famous White Deer Lands

For Sale to Actual Settlers

In tracts from one acre up to 640 acres, on liberal terms and low rate of interest. Price of smooth farming land from $14 to $18 per acre. Mixed grazing and farming lands can be purchased in larger tracts from $4 to $10 per acre.

For further information, write

T. D. HOBART, Agent, Pampa, Texas.

This is the sales advertisement that T. D. Hobart ran in the White Deer Lands brochure.

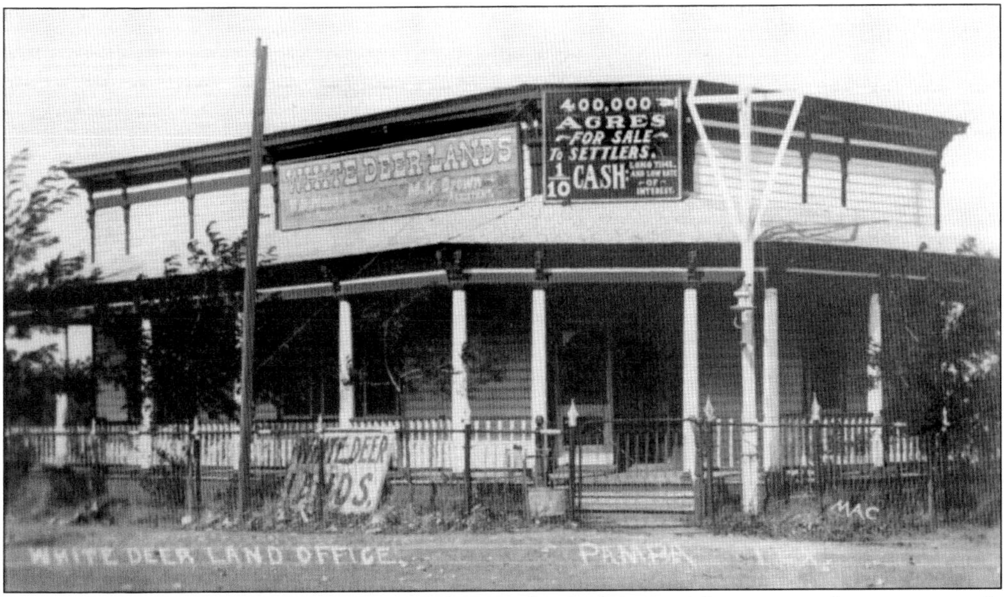

The second office of the White Deer Lands (pictured), which housed the company for approximately 13 years, was located on the corner just south of the site where the third office, a brick building that would eventually become the home of the White Deer Land Museum, was later constructed.

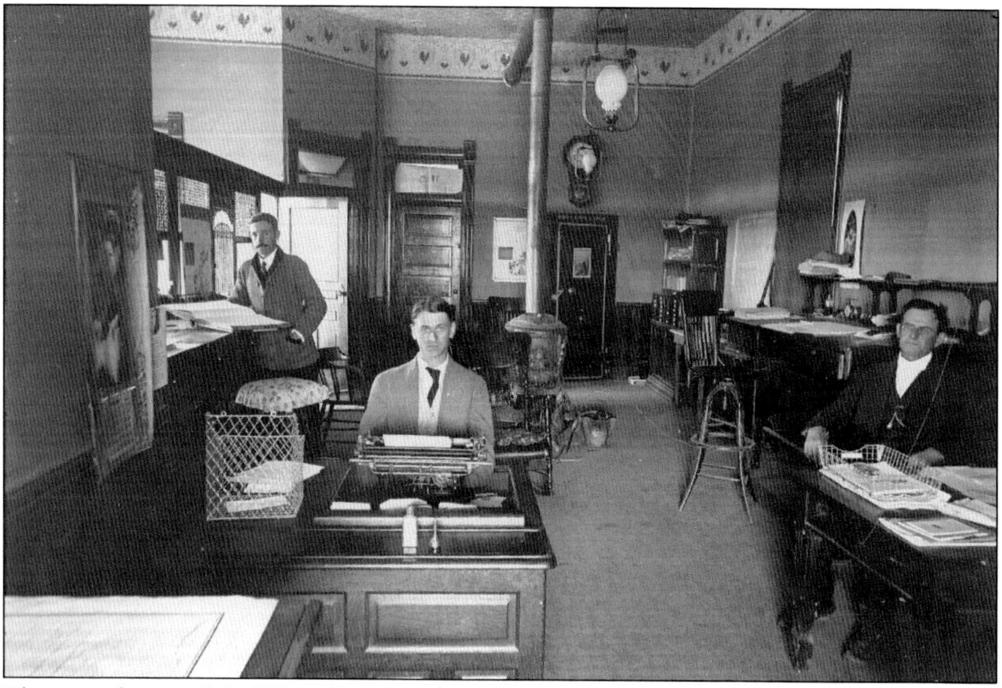

These employees of the White Deer Land Company are in the second Pampa office. The first office was a frame house built in 1887. This picture was taken in 1905. This museum displays the furniture that these men are using, which was moved to the present location in 1916. From left to right are M. K. Brown, C. P. Buckler, and T. D. Hobart, manager of the company.

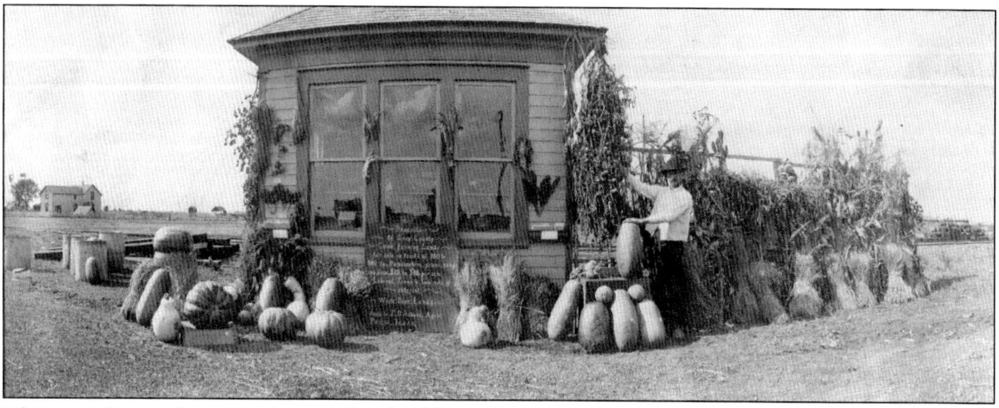

This was the produce stand set up by the White Deer Lands in the early 1900s beside the railroad tracks. All passengers and prospective buyers could see what was grown on the farmland. They were showing wheat, tomatoes, watermelons, pumpkins, and grain sheaves. The sign in front is explaining the tracts of land and the sale prices.

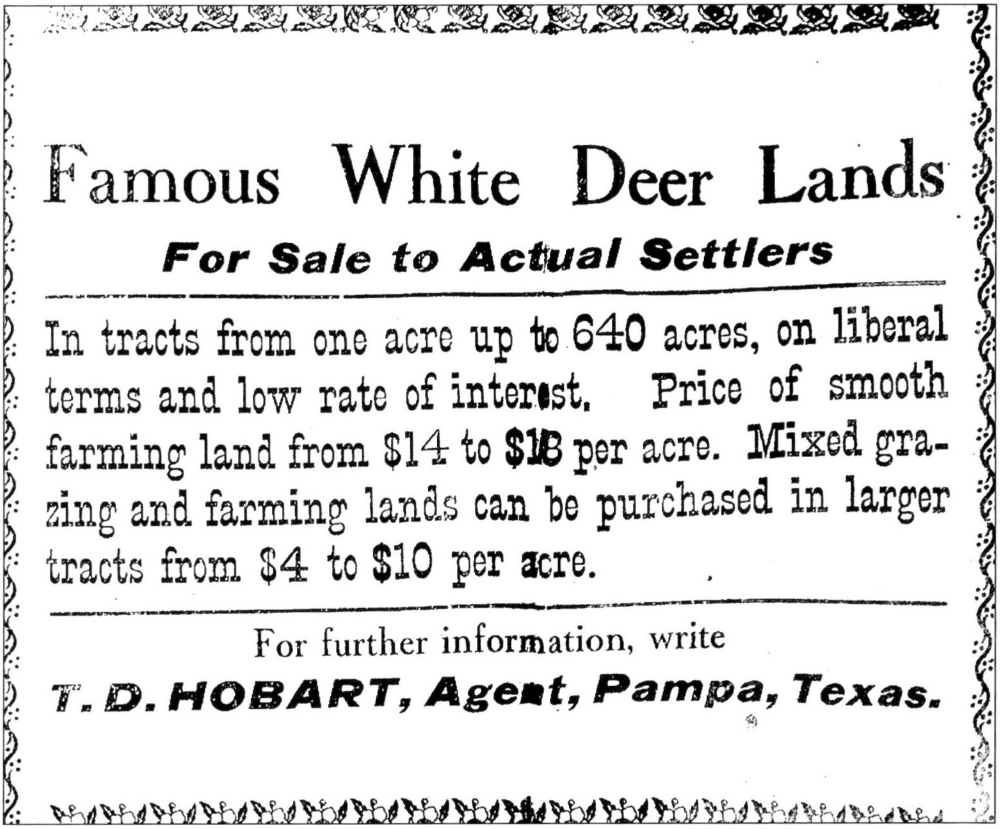

Famous White Deer Lands

For Sale to Actual Settlers

In tracts from one acre up to 640 acres, on liberal terms and low rate of interest. Price of smooth farming land from $14 to $18 per acre. Mixed grazing and farming lands can be purchased in larger tracts from $4 to $10 per acre.

For further information, write

T. D. HOBART, Agent, Pampa, Texas.

This is the sales advertisement that T. D. Hobart ran in the White Deer Lands brochure.

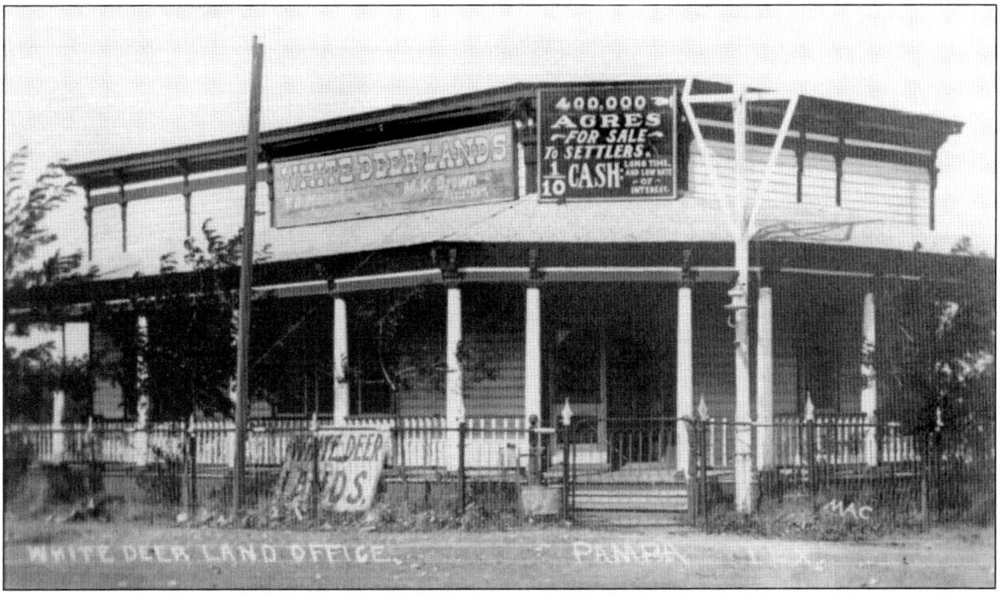

The second office of the White Deer Lands (pictured), which housed the company for approximately 13 years, was located on the corner just south of the site where the third office, a brick building that would eventually become the home of the White Deer Land Museum, was later constructed.

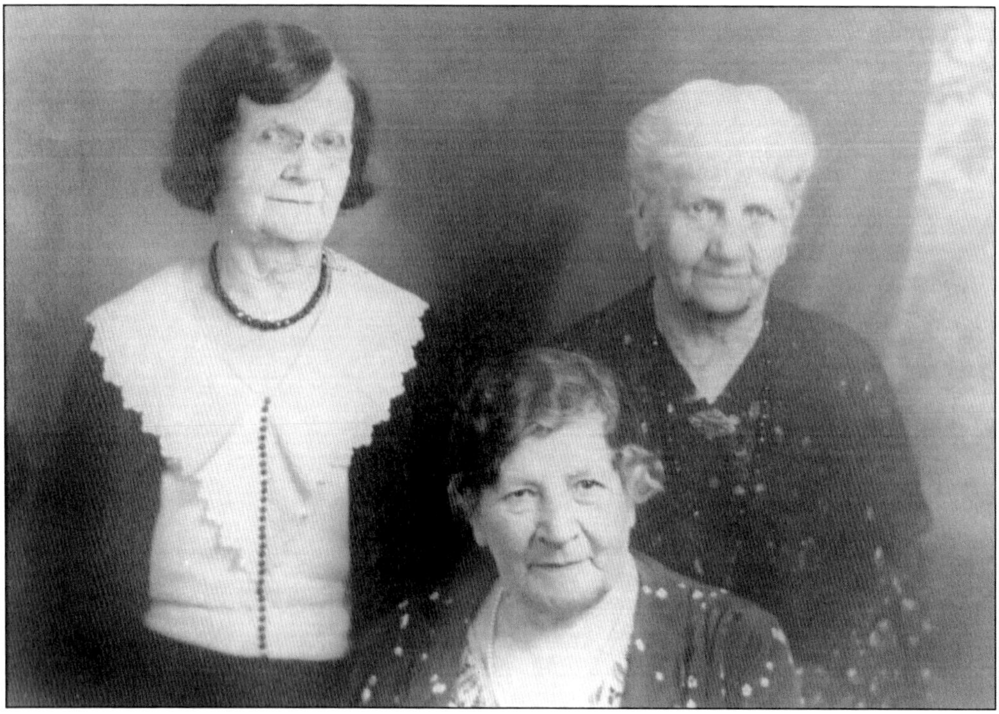

The word *tante* is French for aunt. These three French-speaking sisters came to America from Switzerland between 1880 and 1884 and married three important area settlers. Tante Emma (left) married Perry Lefors, Tante Lena (center) married Alex Schneider, and Tante Anna married Henry Thut. Their maiden name was Lang.

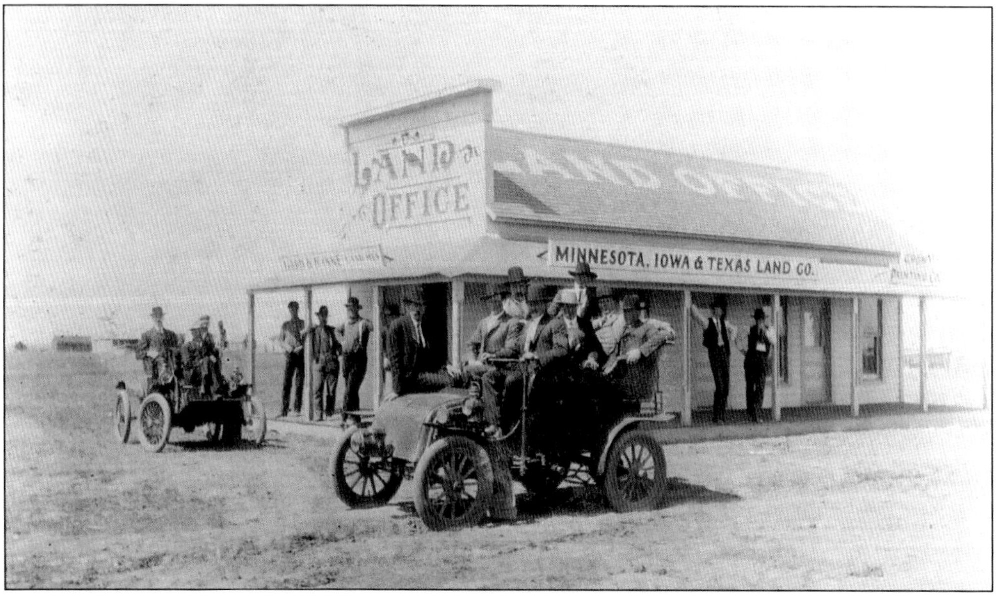

These were the first two cars that came into Pampa in 1908. The first one, on the left, belonged to Pampa's first doctor, Vittorio von Brunow. The second car purchased, seen in the foreground, belonged to Charlie Thomas. Later the White Deer Land Company bought a car to show the land to prospective buyers.

Pampa's first doctor was V. E. von Brunow. The photograph was taken in 1939. He was of German descent, although he was born in this country. He came to Pampa in 1903.

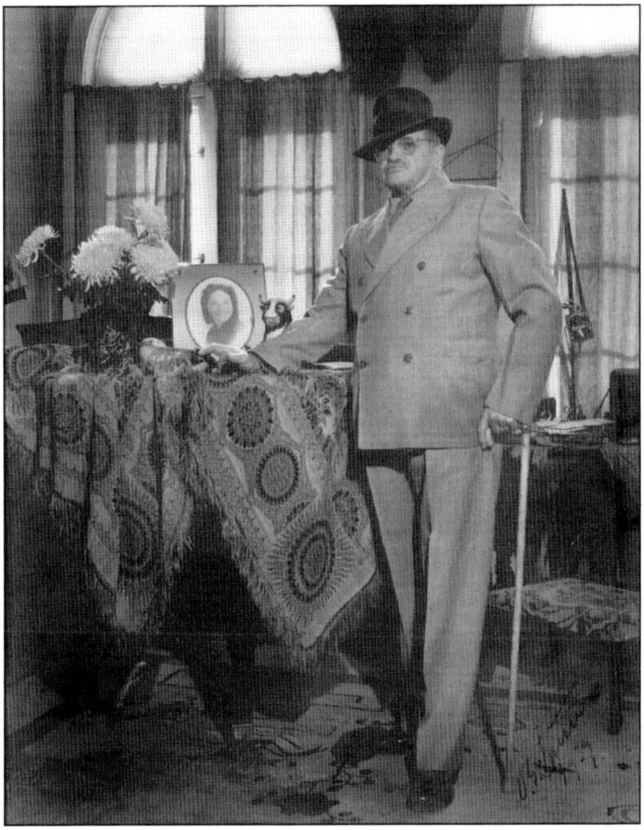

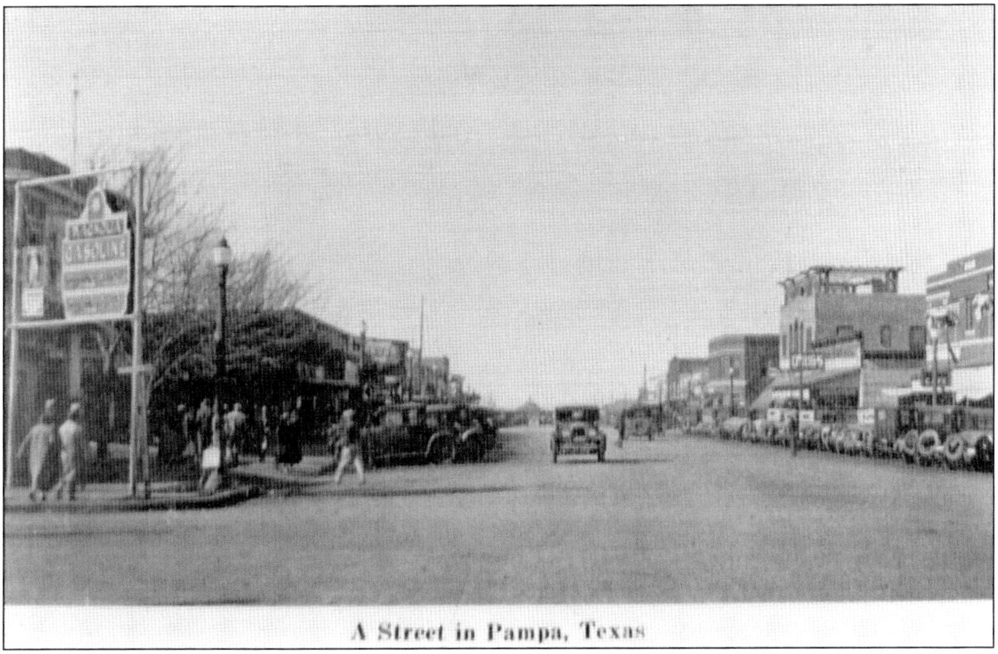

This street scene shows Dr. Brunow's office on the right. It is the building with the atrium-style roofline. The doctor grew a beautiful garden on top of his building.

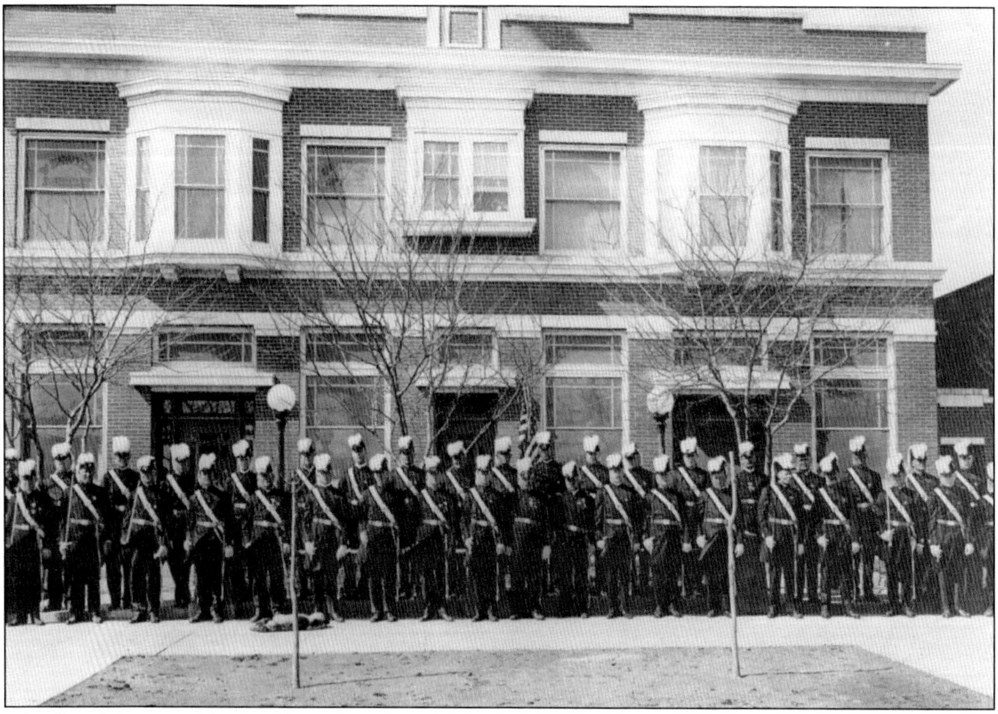

The local Pampa Shrine chapter is standing in front of the new White Deer Land Company building. The structure was completed in 1916, and the trees were very young. Judging by the building and uniforms, we have dated the photograph as 1917.

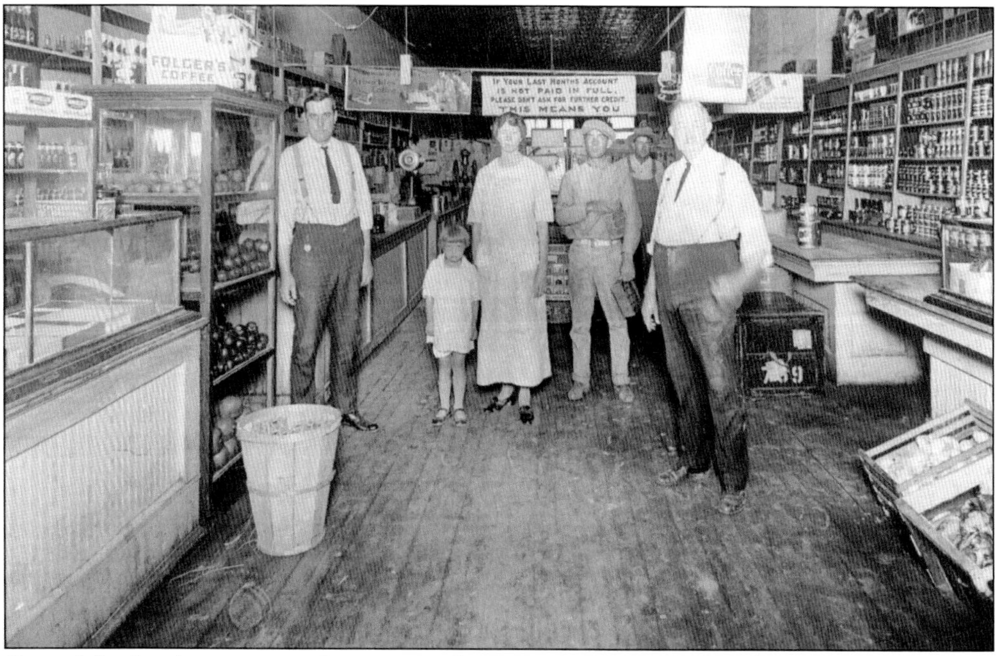

One of the first businesses in Pampa was this grocery store, Woodward-Lane, owned by C. P. Woodward and T. V. Lane. It was built on the main street in 1925. Notice the produce on the shelf to the left.

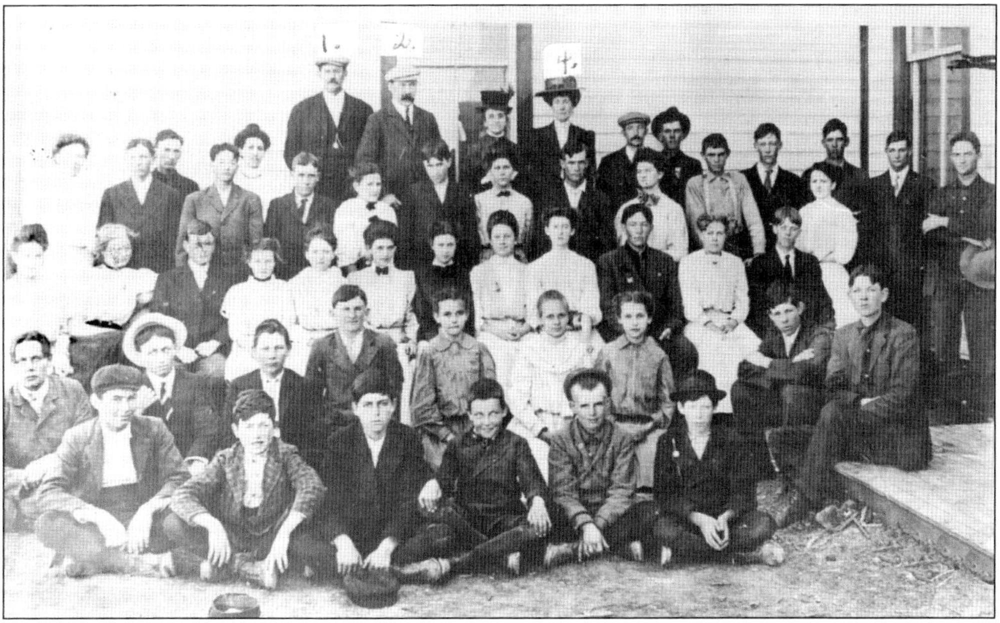

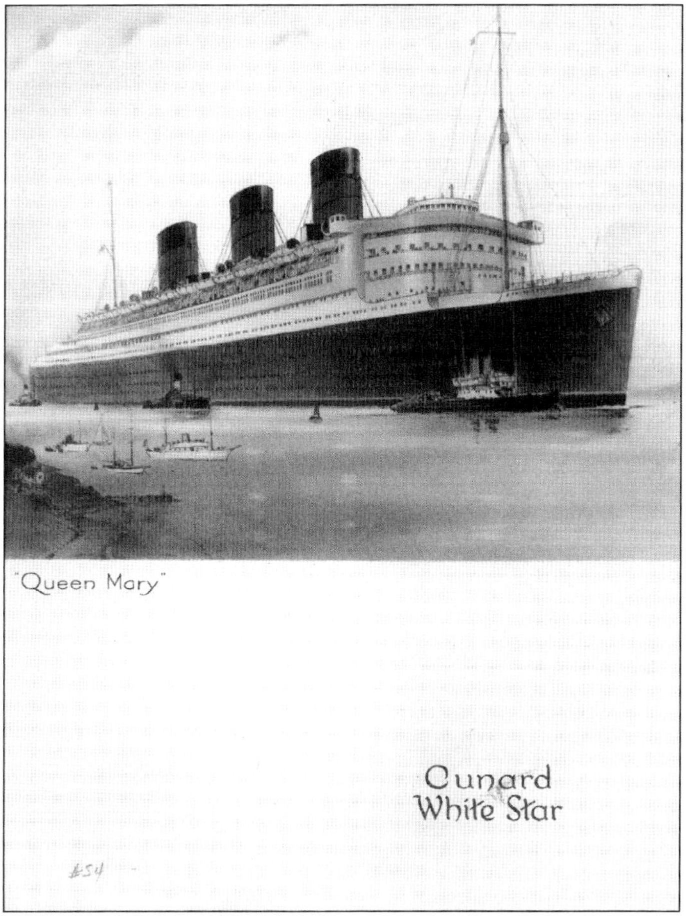

In 1908, the Gordon Cunards of the English shipping lines came to Pampa to visit. They were early stockholders in the White Deer Lands. The students and teachers at the school, built by the White Deer Lands, turned out that day to have their picture taken with the influential visitors. In the back row is T. D. Hobart (1), Sir Gordon Cunard (2), and Lady Cunard (4). They were driven around the holdings of the land company in a newly purchased Buick. The picture at right is a menu from the *Queen Mary* that was placed on the dining tables. The menu names the guests in the dining room, including "M. K. Brown, Pampa, Texas, USA."

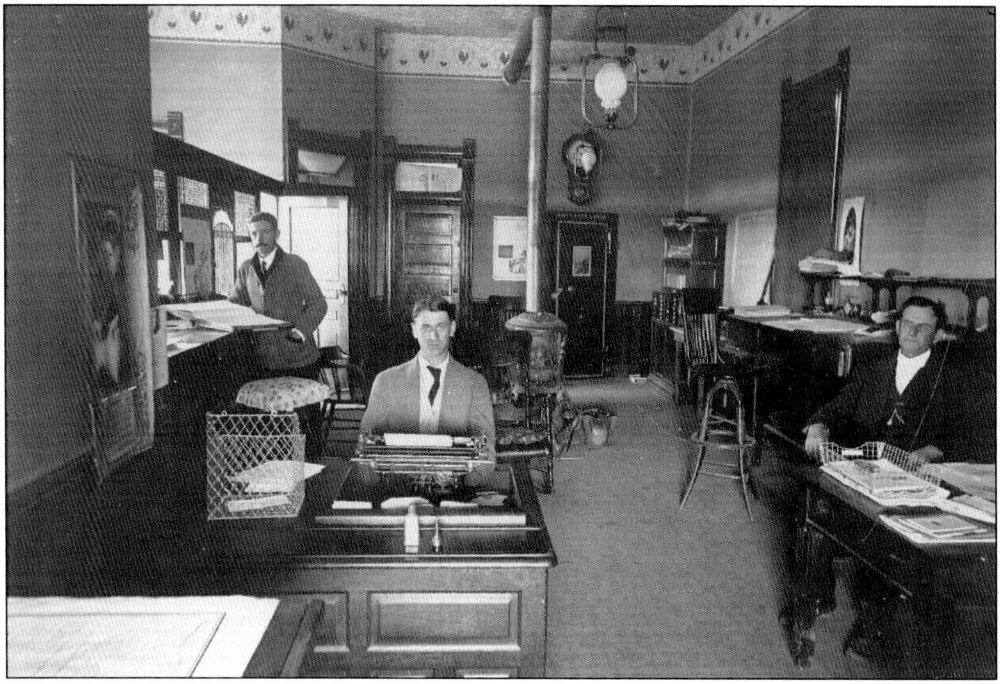

These employees of the White Deer Land Company are in the second Pampa office. The first office was a frame house built in 1887. This picture was taken in 1905. This museum displays the furniture that these men are using, which was moved to the present location in 1916. From left to right are M. K. Brown, C. P. Buckler, and T. D. Hobart, manager of the company.

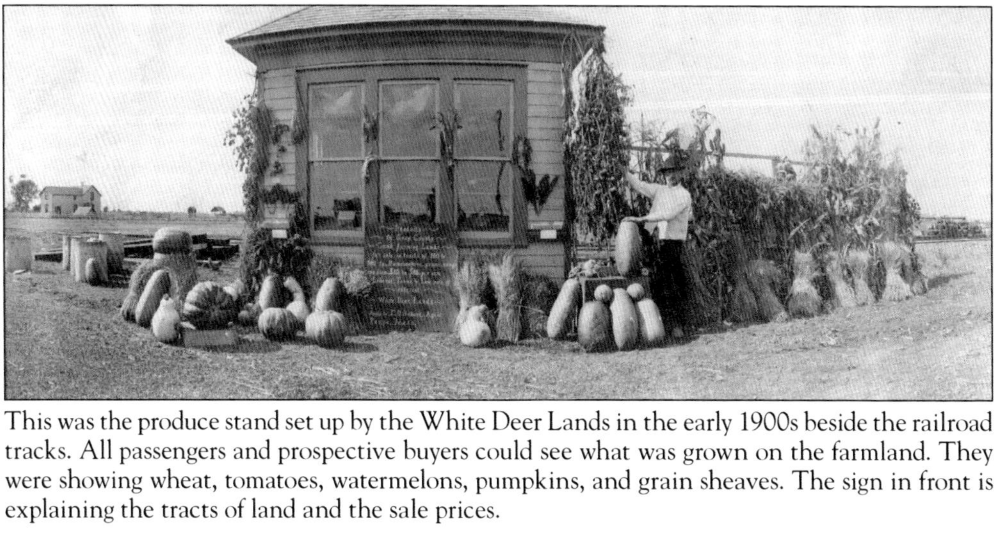

This was the produce stand set up by the White Deer Lands in the early 1900s beside the railroad tracks. All passengers and prospective buyers could see what was grown on the farmland. They were showing wheat, tomatoes, watermelons, pumpkins, and grain sheaves. The sign in front is explaining the tracts of land and the sale prices.

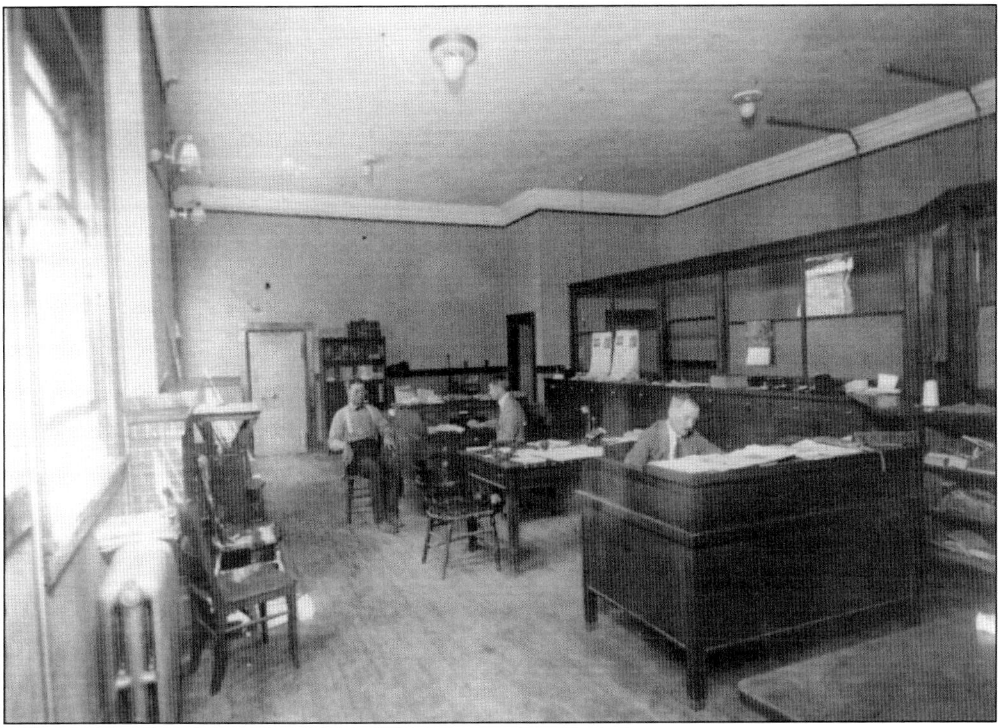

This is the inside of the third office of the White Deer Land Company in Pampa. This is almost the same now as it was then. The furniture is all intact, but the floor has been covered. The museum still uses the safe in back, and the desks and chairs are being shown as artifacts.

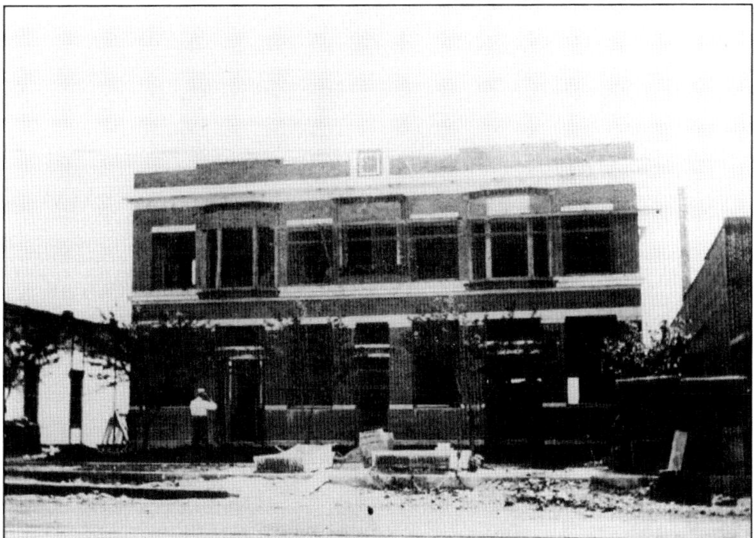

Construction of the White Deer Land Office Bldg.-1916

The bldg at the far right was probably built ca 1914-15. It is now the Holland Wing of the White Deer Land Museum. The address is 112 S. Cuyler & the museum building is 116 S. Cuyler.

This is a picture of the existing White Deer Land building under construction. The building at the right, which is barely visible, was purchased in 1995, and the museum offices were moved there. It is called the Holland wing and joins the original building.

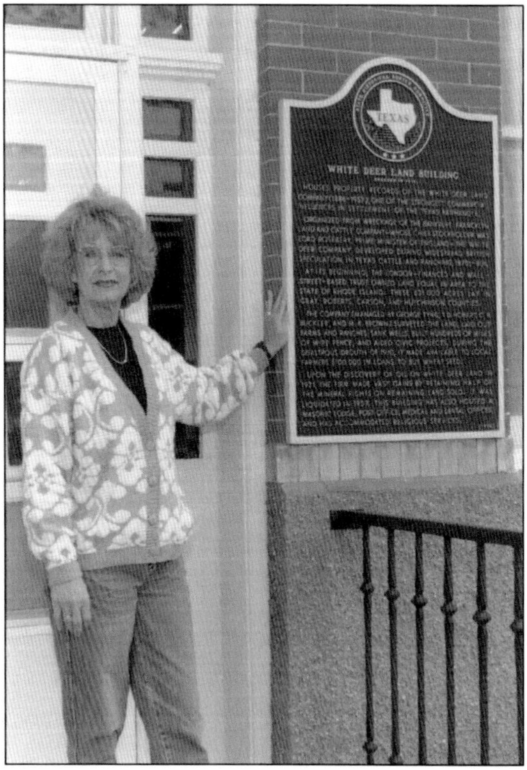

The museum director, Anne Davidson, is pointing out the Texas Historical Commission marker that was placed on the museum building in 1970 at its opening. The building also bears the seal of the National Register of Historic Places.

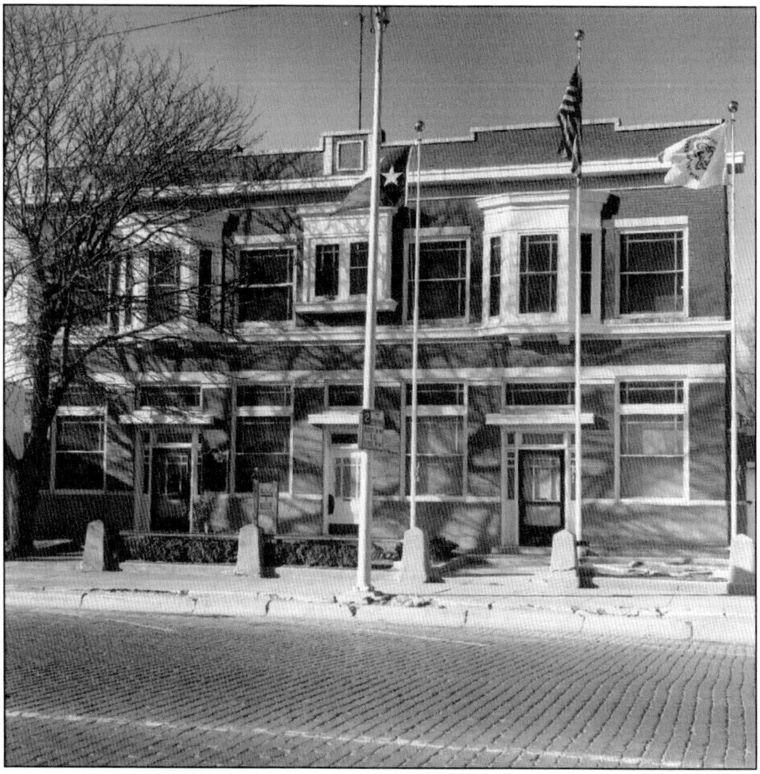

The last office of the White Deer Land Company is pictured here. It now houses the White Deer Land Museum. The land company was dissolved in 1957 because most of the land was sold. The White Deer Land Company had sold 631,000 acres of land since its inception. Notice the brick streets in front that were laid by Native American Jim Brown in 1927.

Three

Cowboys and Indians

Since the Plains Indians had been sent to various reservations, farmers and ranchers had access now to open range. After the severe winter and drought of 1886, the cattle industry suffered greatly. This experience forced the cattlemen to operate with more caution. By 1876–1888, the railroad was expanding and farm and rangeland was selling fast. The cattle industry was changing with the invention of the windmill and the barbed wire fence.

The first wheat crop came in the fall of 1891. Later Pampa would be called the "Wheat Capital of the World," producing over one million bushels annually. In the meantime, many ranches were being established: Z–Z, the Combs-Worley, N–N, the Quarter Circle Heart, the U–U, and the RO Ranch, which was purchased by the Englishman Alfred Rowe. He went down with the *Titanic* in 1912. He gave the land to the town now called McLean, 34 miles south of Pampa. The Bar N outfit was owned by the Niedringhaus brothers. Their headquarters were on White Deer Creek and were the largest land lease that the White Deer Lands ever had.

One of the largest of the Panhandle ranches was the JA Ranch, which is still a good working ranch. John Adair was a partner of Charles Goodnight, who kept herds of buffalo on his ranch. The offspring of those buffalo still roam the Palo Duro Canyon and elsewhere on the Texas plains.

Some of the great ranches of Texas are still in rural Pampa. Ranches such as the Gethings, the Combs-Worley, the Franklin, and the Saunders are some of the finest anywhere. They are located in the rolling pastures of central Gray County. Many of the ranchers raise grain sorghum and wheat crops to supplement winter feeding.

Life for the cowboy has changed. At first he had a team and wagon with a saddle horse tied to the side. Now the cowboy can sit in his pickup truck equipped with a C. B. radio, heater, and air conditioner and listen to the stereo.

But cattle and agriculture would soon share the economy of the plains with another industry.

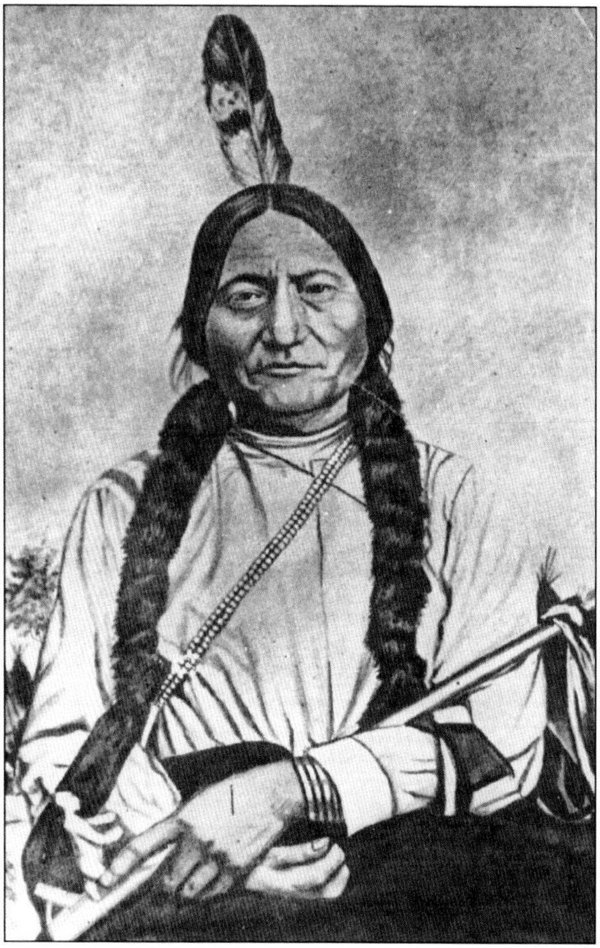

Chief Black Kettle was killed at the Battle of the Washita, about 35 miles from Pampa. It was this engagement that caused the uprising of the Sioux and the defeat of Custer.

Cheyenne and Arapaho Indians are pictured camped on the Washita. The exact date is unknown.

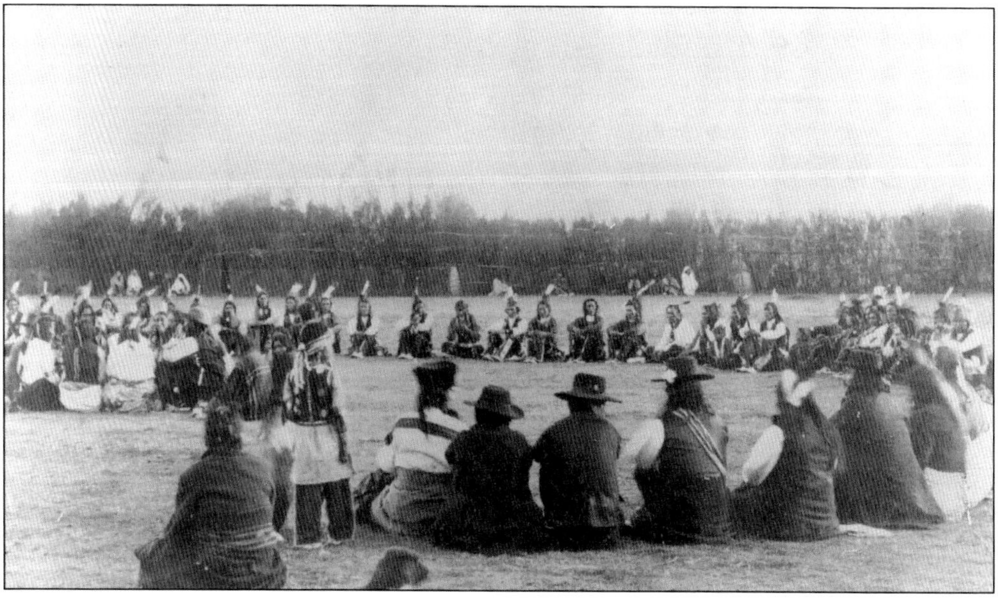

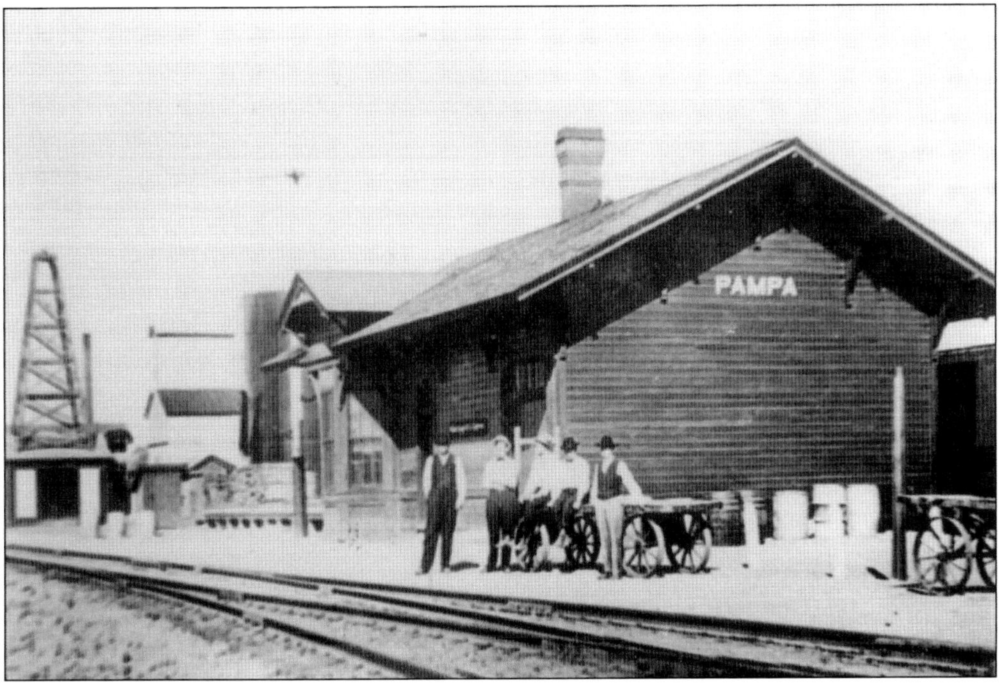

The earliest train depot was built in Pampa in 1905. It burned in 1914 and was rebuilt on the east end of the track.

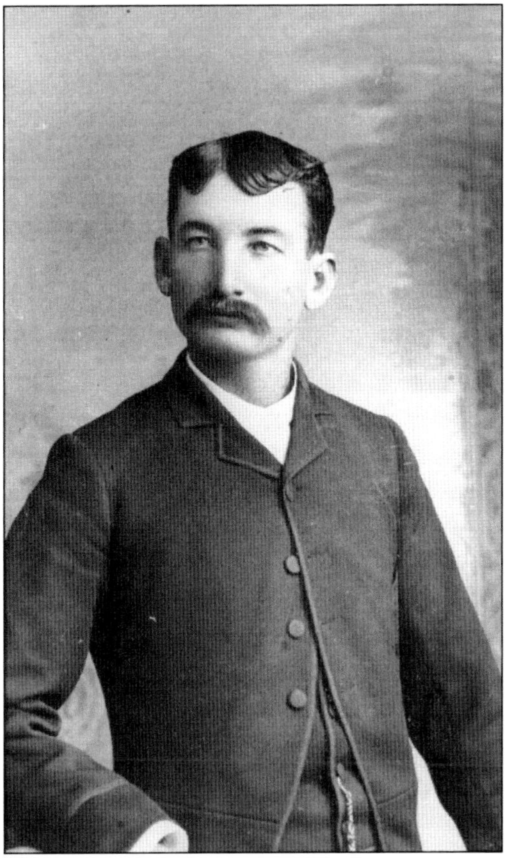

Tobe Odem owned the Z–Z Ranch. The ranch was located some 12 miles south of Pampa on the North Fork of the Red River. It was a good outfit, but the winter of 1886 virtually ruined this ranch and many other ranches of its size in the area.

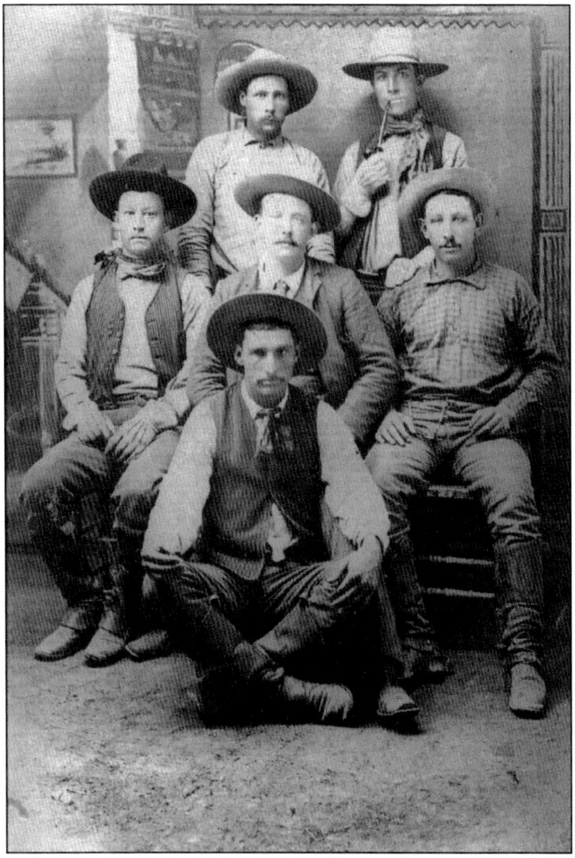

These six cowboys belonged to the Z–Z Ranch around 1881. The manager was George Saunders, who is not in this picture. Note the dirt floor.

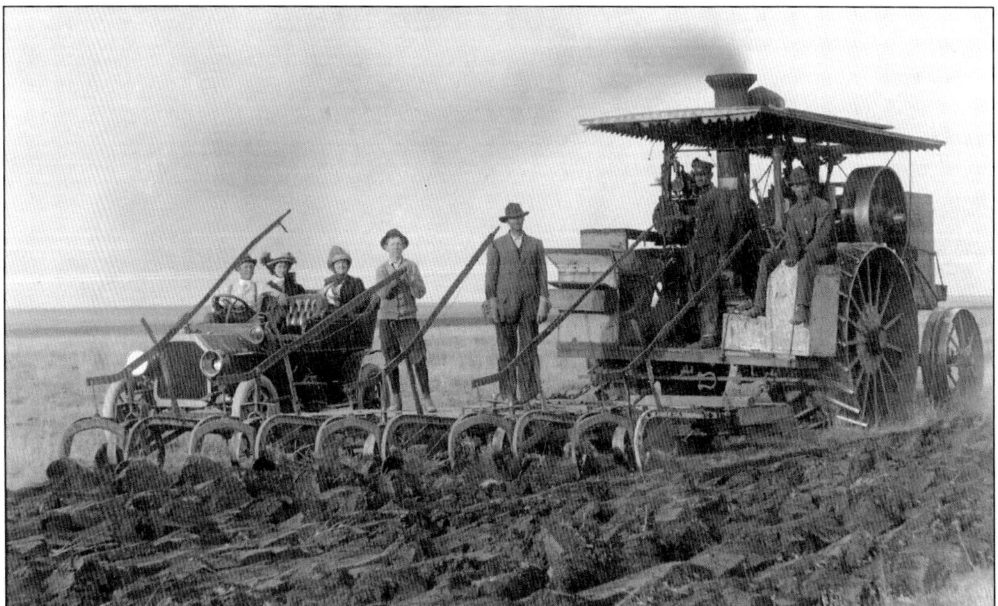

The ladies in the car are watching the men work the steam-grinding tractor, which was used on this farm in 1910.

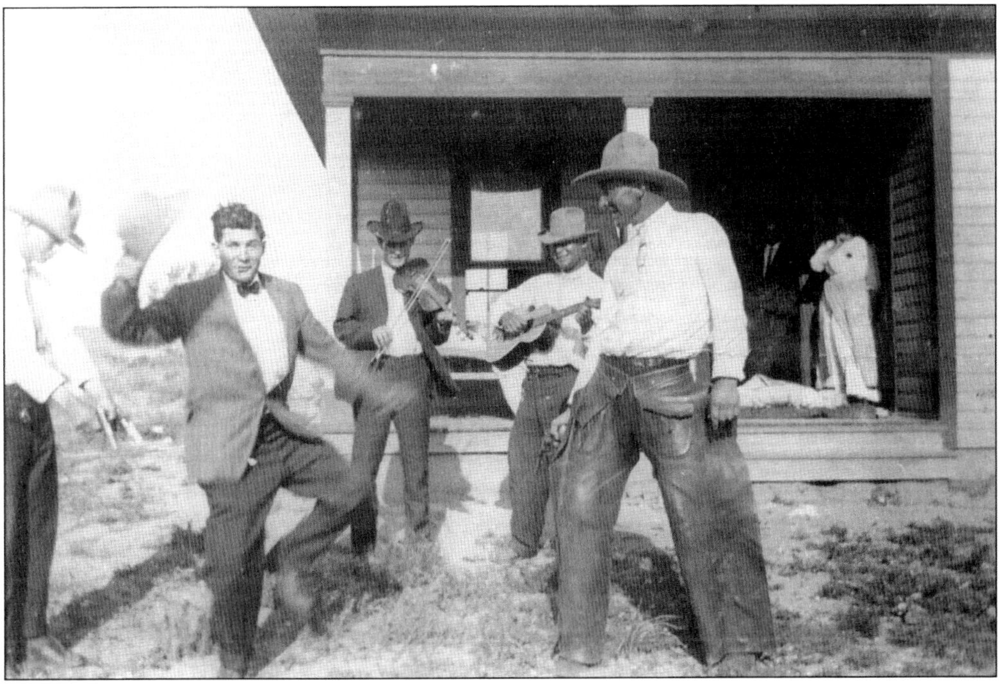

These are really happy cowboys! Maybe they are dancing because the man on the left is shooting two pistols.

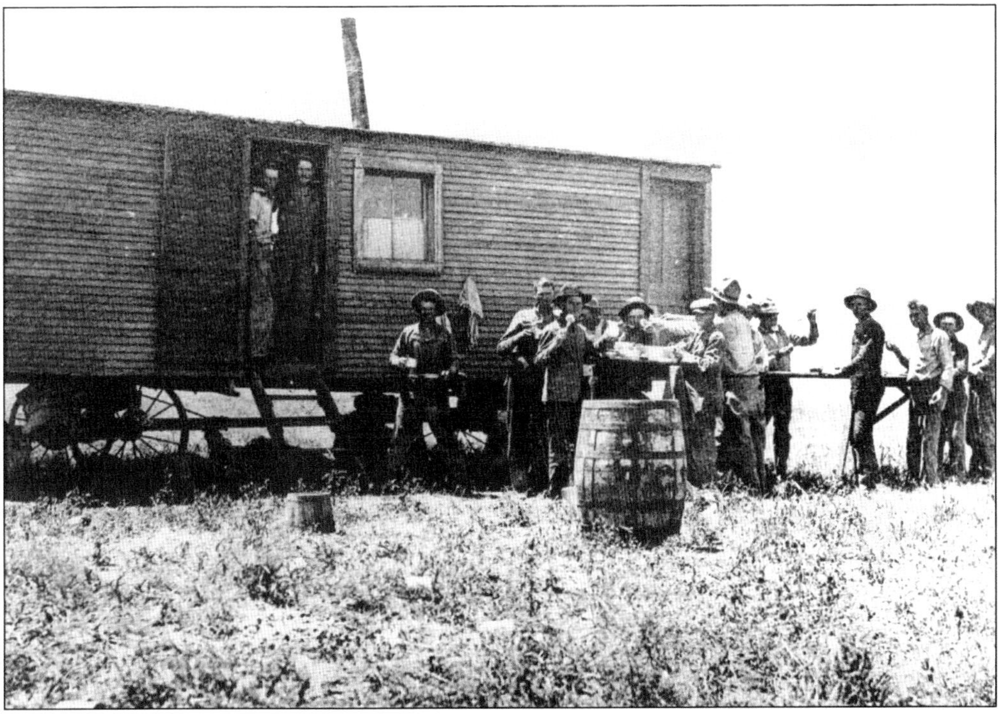

This is a wheat harvest crew eating lunch at a chuck wagon shack. This photograph was taken on the Earl Talley farm in 1915. The cook's name was Roberta.

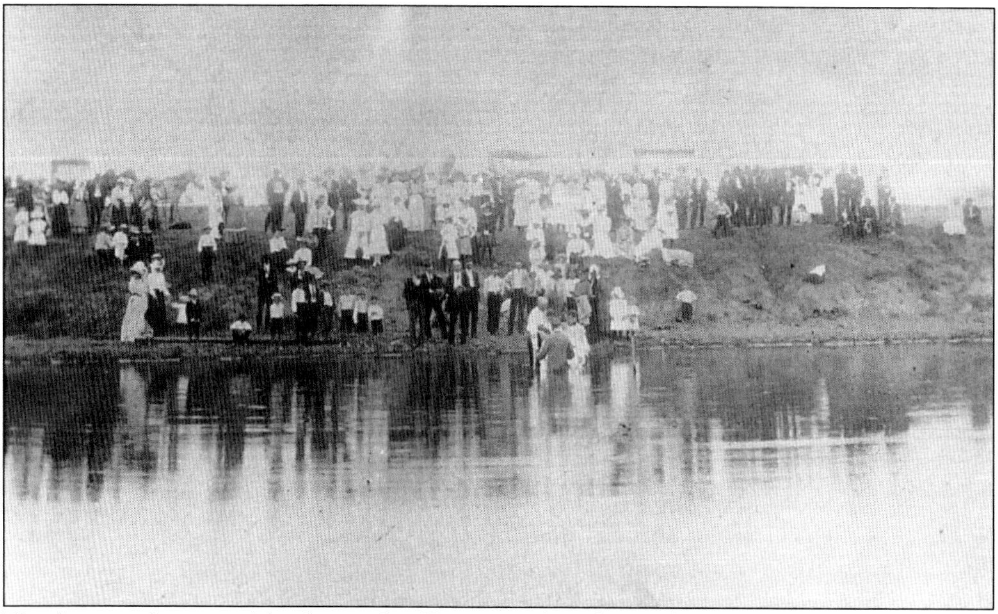

This baptismal scene is 16 miles south of Pampa at the Alanreed Spring Tank in 1888.

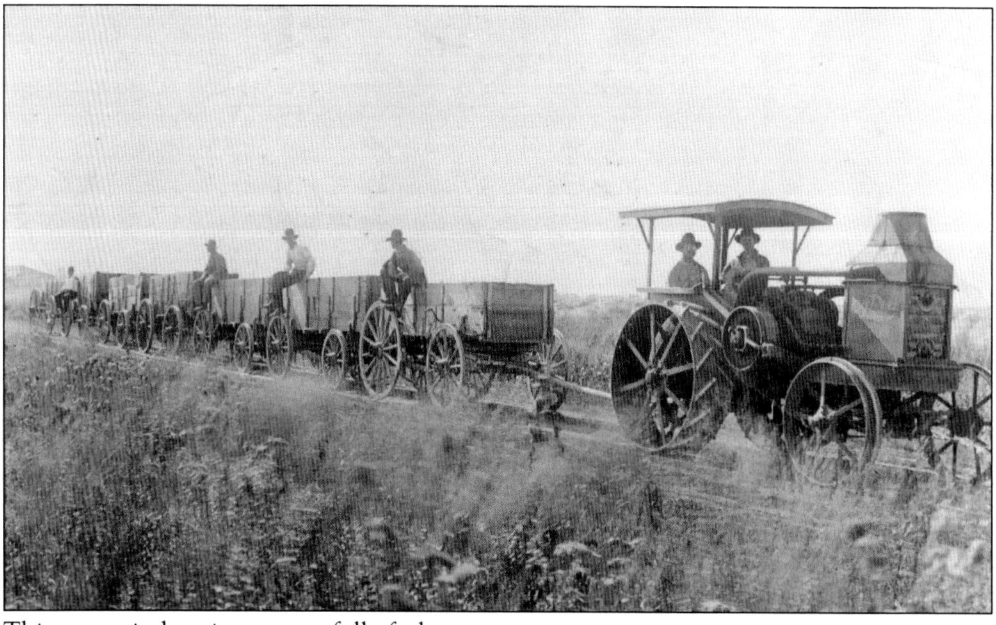

This tractor is dragging wagons full of wheat.

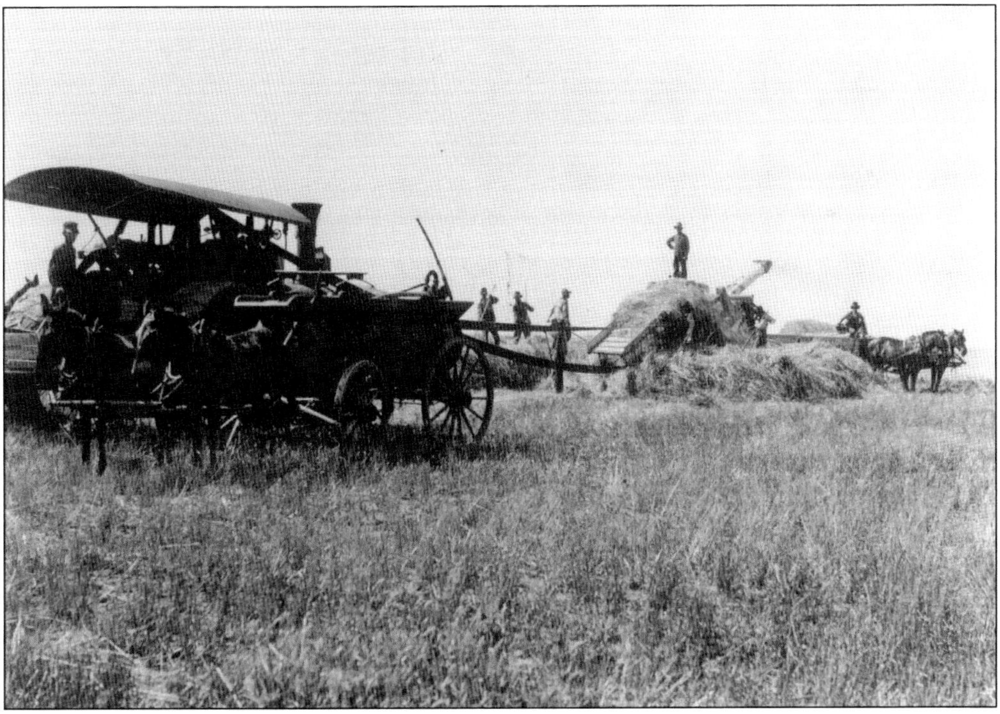

These men are baling hay in 1910 with horses and wagons.

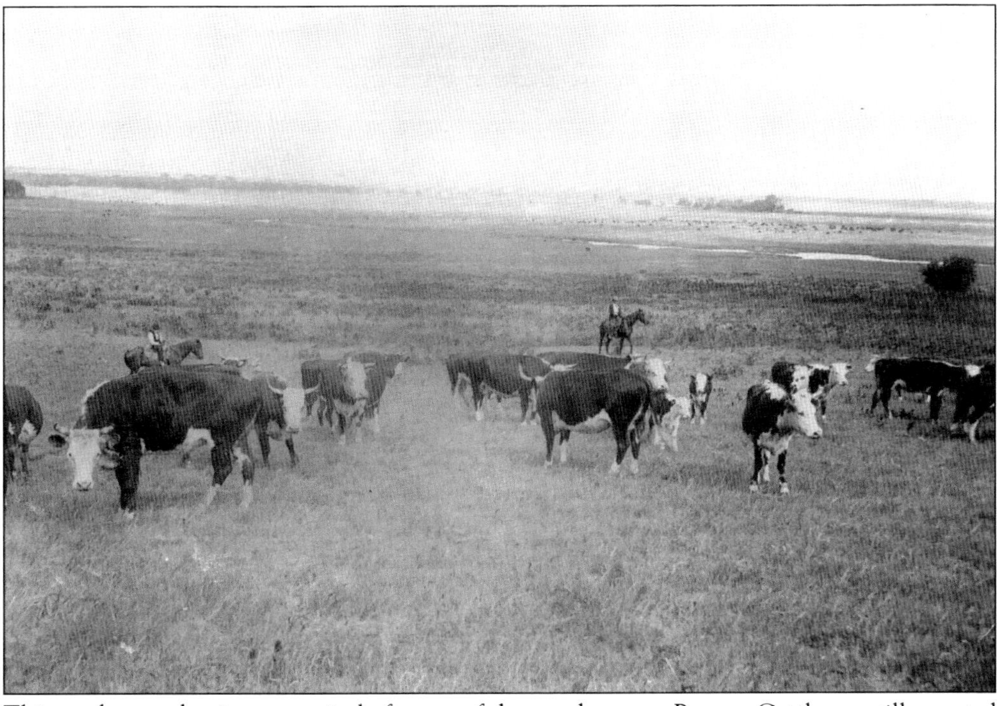

This cattle roundup is very typical of many of the ranches near Pampa. Cattle are still counted and moved by men on horseback.

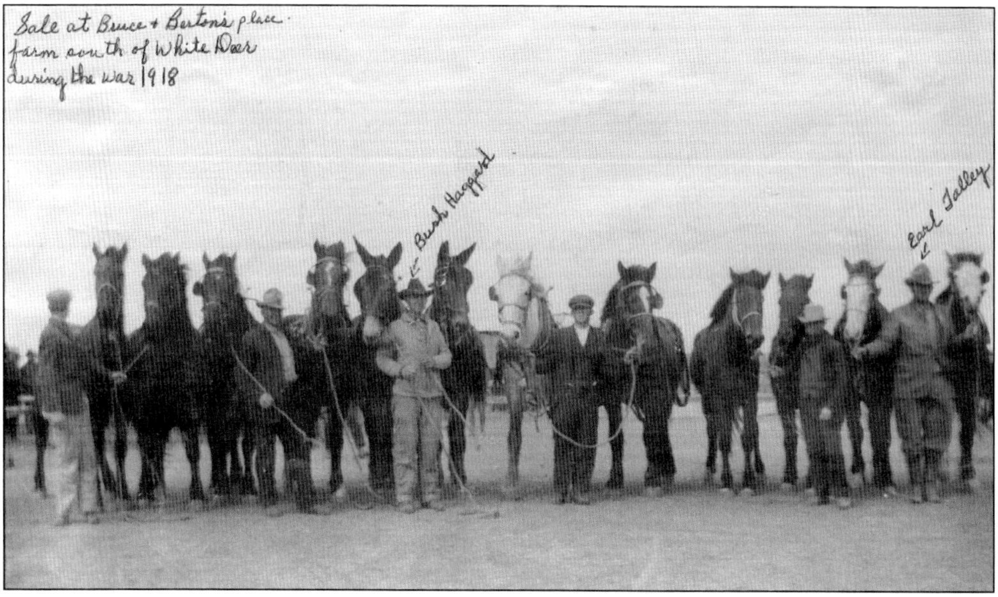

This horse auction was on the Martin farm about 16 miles west of Pampa. Most of the men were entering the army in 1918 and needed to get rid of the livestock. They were lined up waiting for the bids to begin.

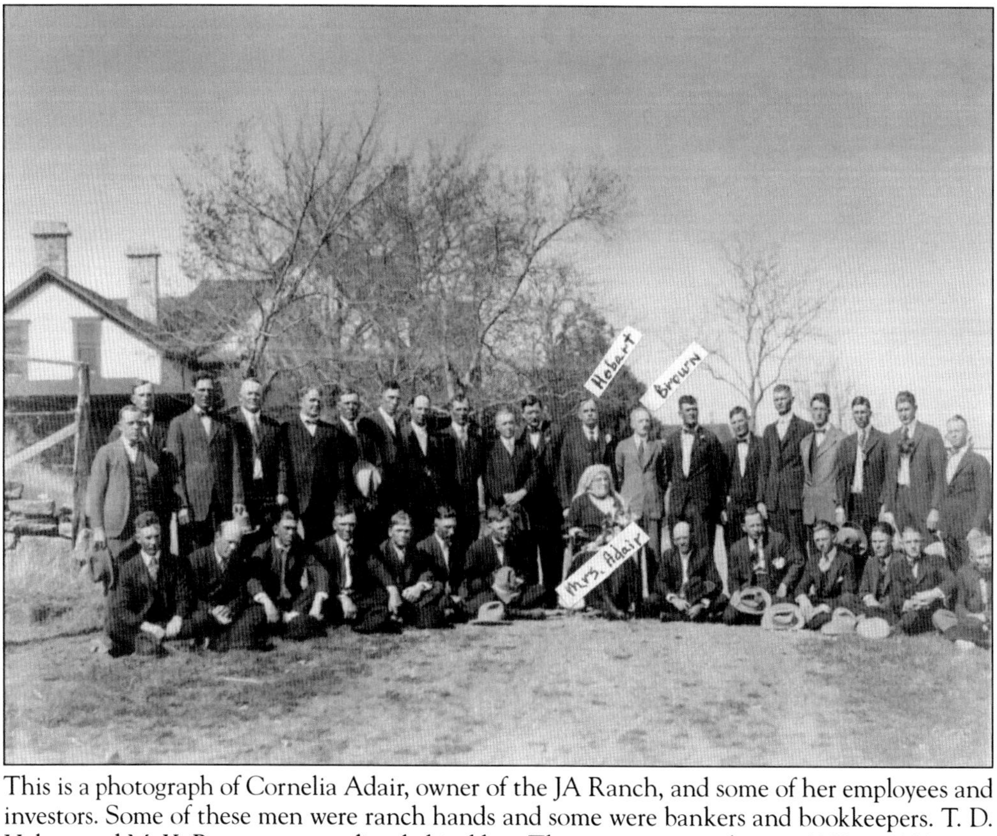

This is a photograph of Cornelia Adair, owner of the JA Ranch, and some of her employees and investors. Some of these men were ranch hands and some were bankers and bookkeepers. T. D. Hobart and M. K. Brown are standing behind her. This picture was taken in 1929 or 1930.

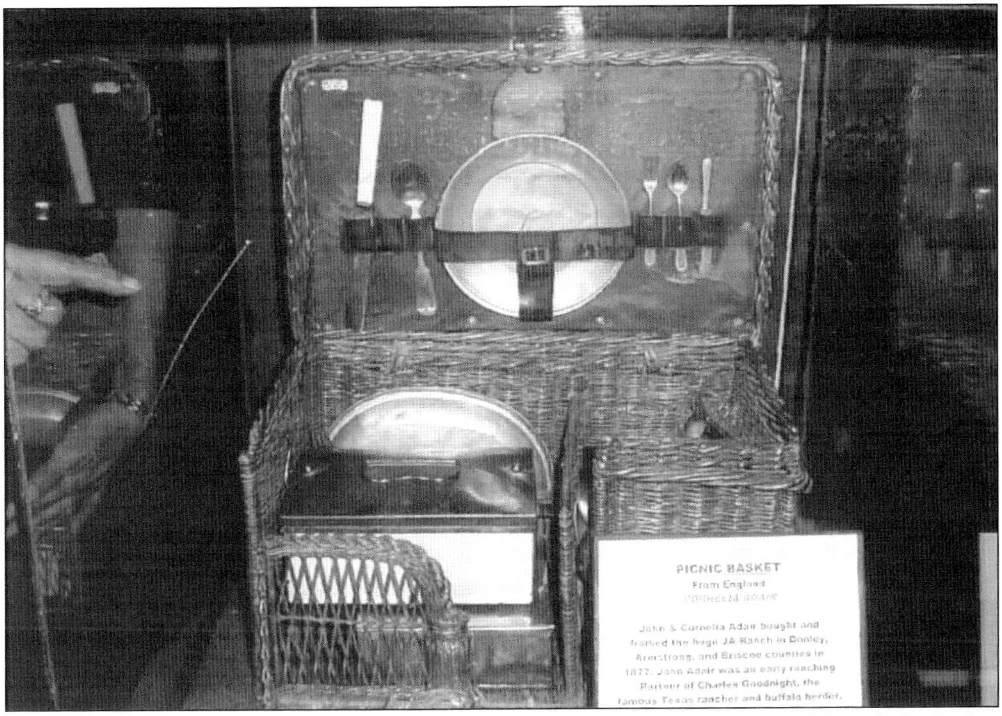

Cornelia Adair's picnic basket is on display at the White Deer Land Museum. Although the basket was made in England, she is believed to have brought it home from Philadelphia, Pennsylvania, c. 1877.

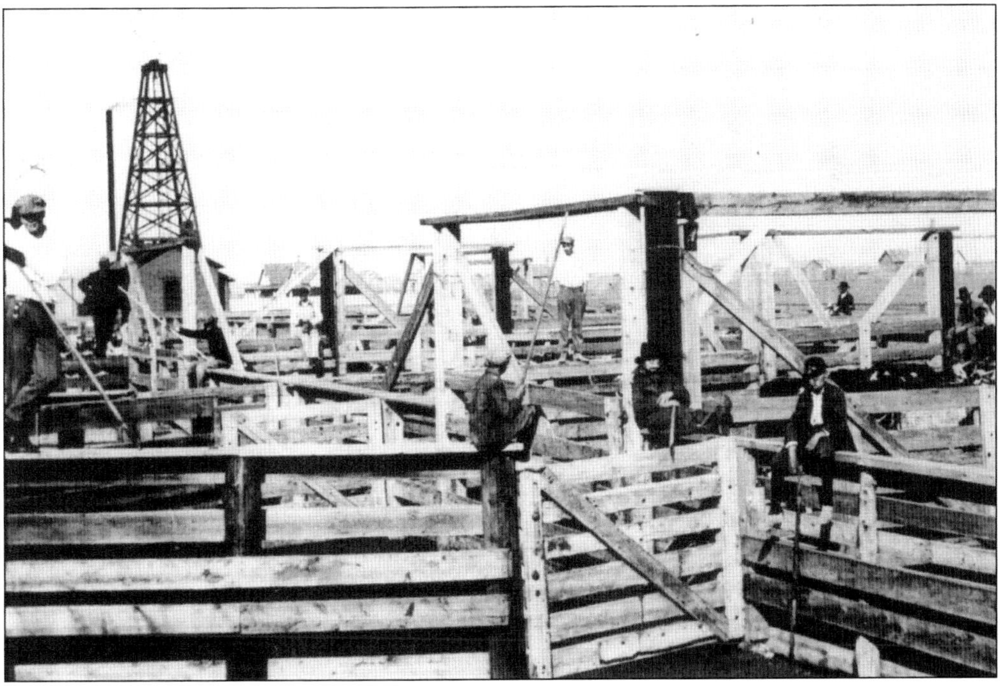

There are many loading pens in the Pampa area, such as this one. Note the oil rig in the background.

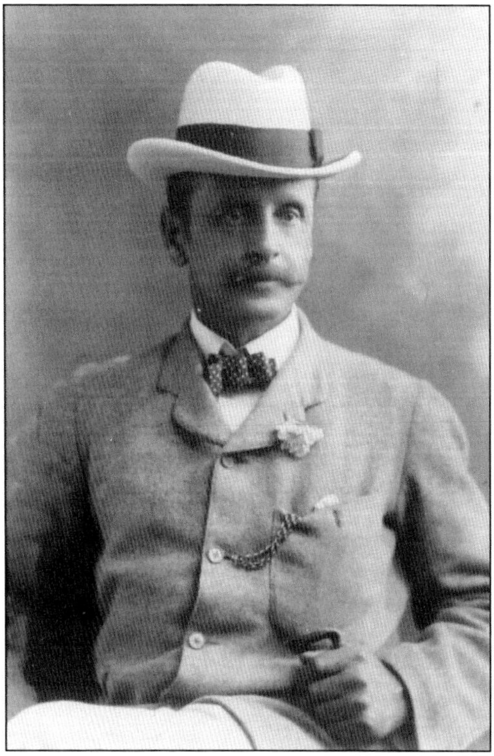

The English gentleman is Alfred Rowe. He donated the land for the town site of McLean, Texas, 34 miles southeast of Pampa. Rowe went down with the *Titanic* in 1912. The photograph below displays Alfred Rowe's brand, the "RO," usually placed on the animal's left hip.

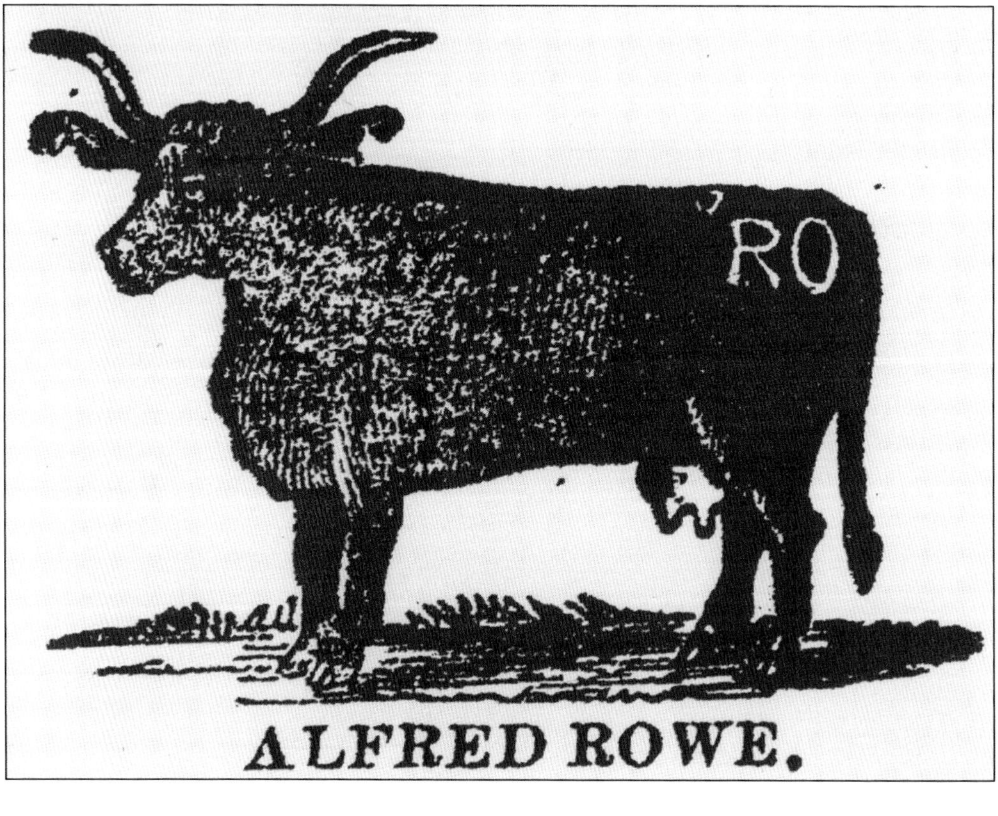

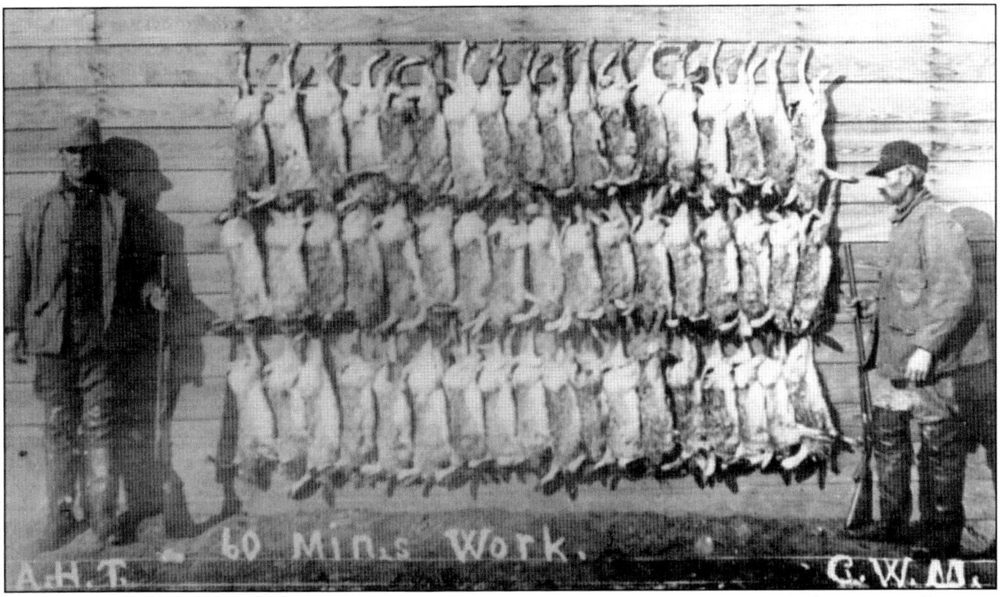

These farmers claimed to have killed these jackrabbits in 60 minutes. By 1910, there was a bounty paid for rabbits, coyotes, and eagles.

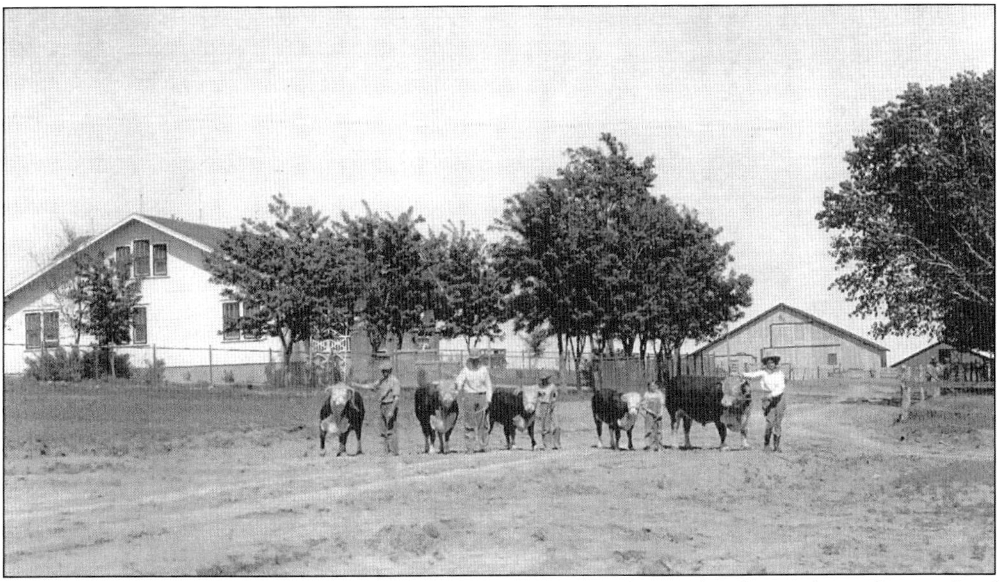
One of the longest-working ranches in Pampa is the Combs-Worley, located 4 miles south of Pampa. These folks are showing some prize Hereford show cattle after having won blue ribbons. This was the ranch where the first oil well was drilled in 1924. Phebe Worley helped finance a hospital and an office building in Pampa, completed in 1931, that both bear her name.

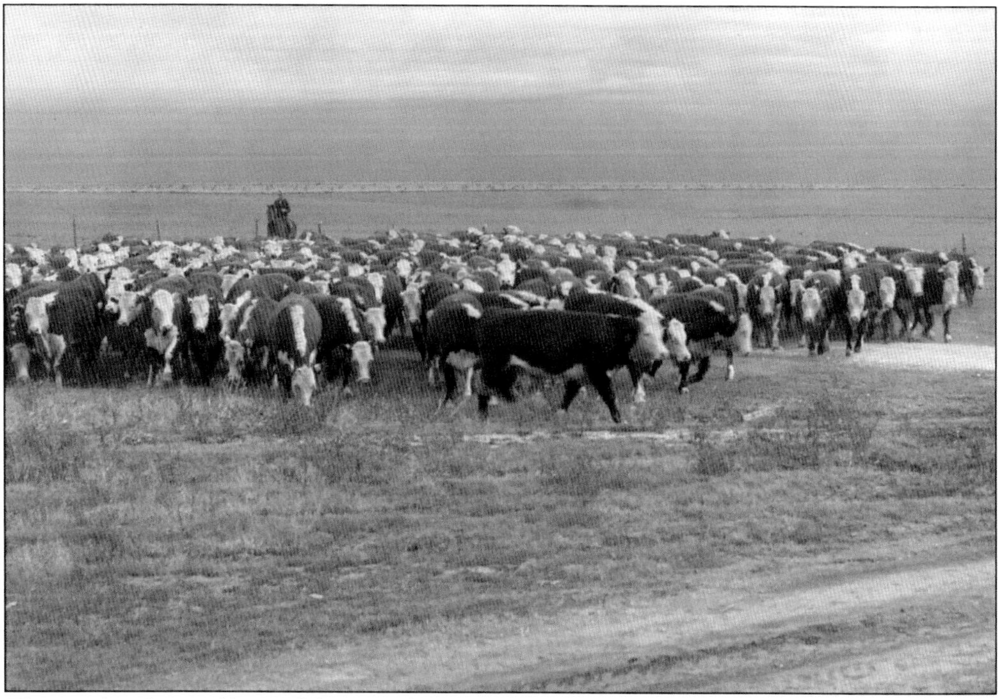

This is a familiar and beautiful scene of men working herds of Hereford cattle on the grasslands of Gray County.

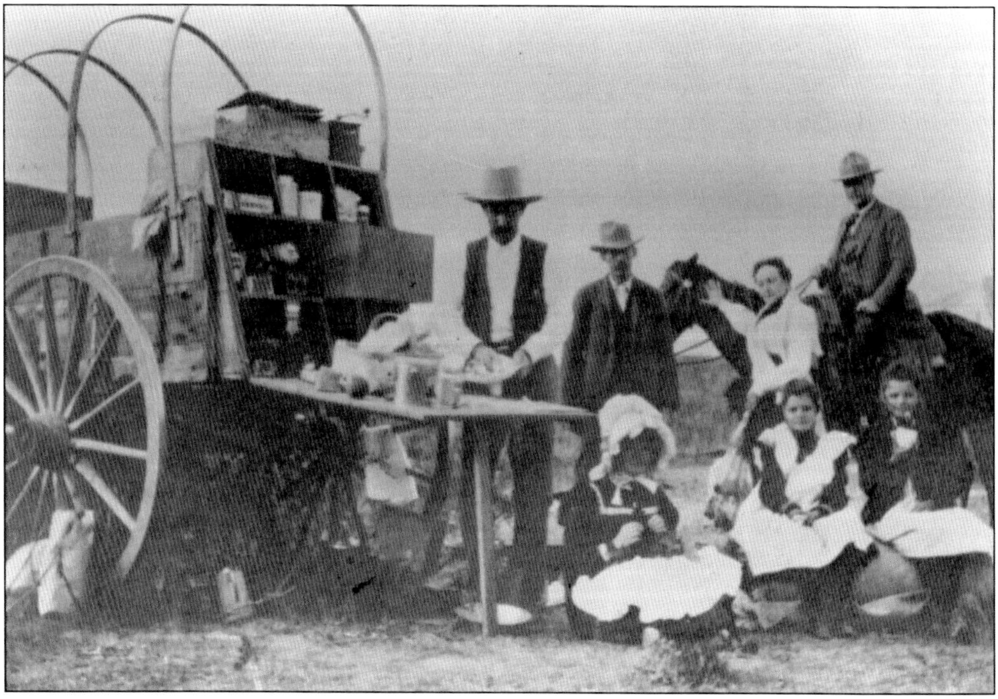

This group is eating lunch on White Deer Creek. Serving is Tom Crawford, and White Deer Lands manager George Tyng is on horseback. The visiting Jess Wynn ladies are seated on the ground.

This is one of the cowboy stories of Matthew "Bones" Hooks. He was the son of freed slaves and had worked for many cowboys, including Charles Goodnight. He was working on the Santa Fe Railroad in 1911. At a stopover in Pampa, some men bet $25 that he could not ride a certain horse. Bones rode him to a standstill and collected his money. This sketch depicts the Pampa ride.

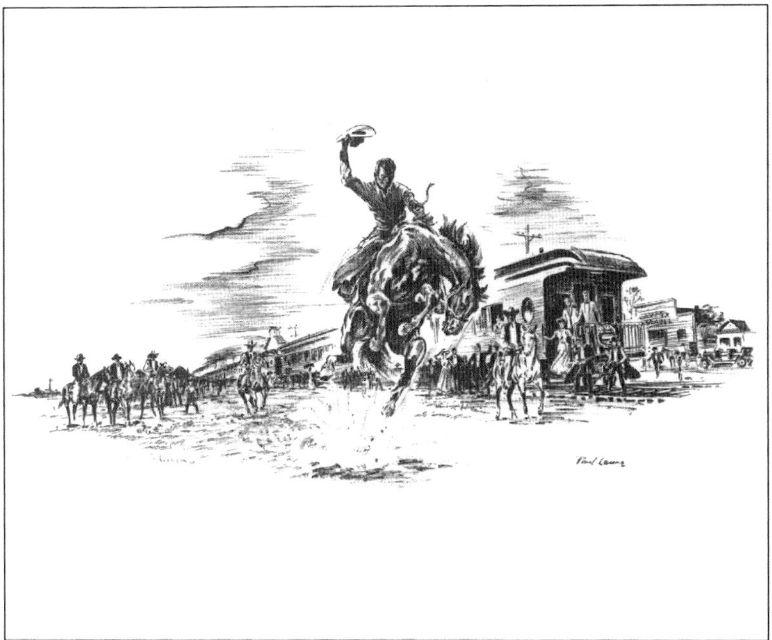

"Bones" Hooks rides a bad one during a train stop at Pampa, Texas, 1911

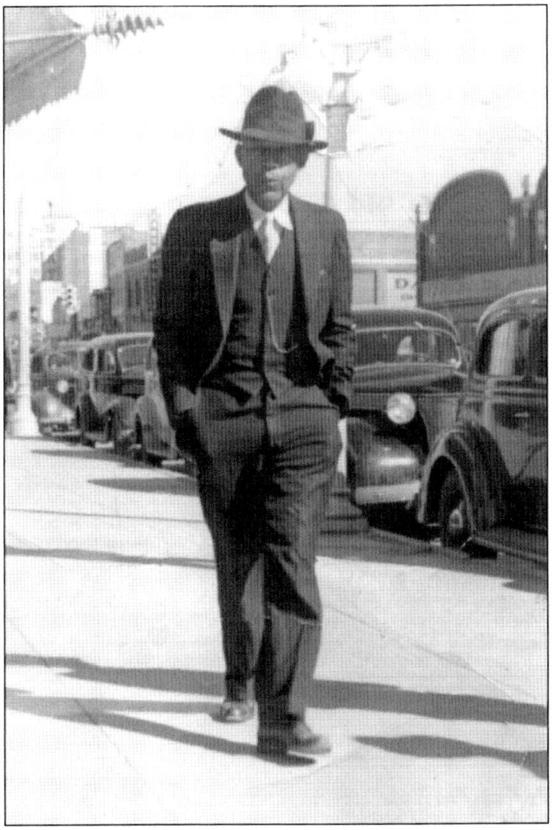

Bones later moved to Amarillo, Texas, where he became very instrumental in the black community. He started one of the first black grade schools in the North Heights section of Amarillo. He was the first black man to serve on a Potter County grand jury and is credited with starting the first black church in the Panhandle at Clarendon. (Photograph courtesy of the Amarillo Public Library.)

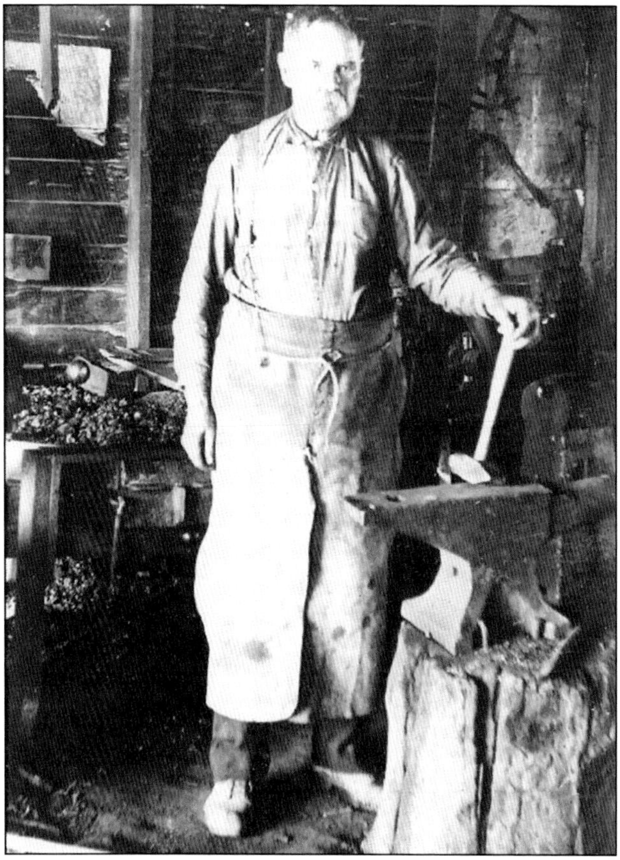

This blacksmith is John C. Noel. His shop was on Pampa's main street in 1910.

Hamp Brown (left) and Mel Davis, below were clearly having a wonderful time.

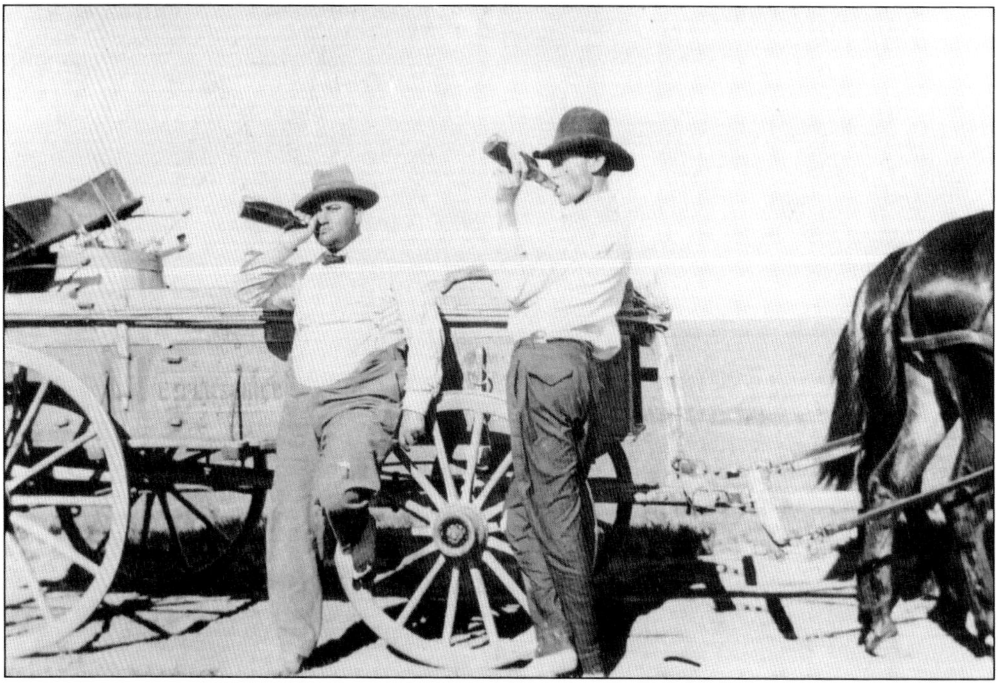

Four

Growing Pains

The settlers were coming to buy grass and farmland in this area. This called for local government, schools, and churches. At one time, there were over 27 rural schools in Gray County.

In April 1902, one-hundred-and-fifty-three qualified voters in unorganized Gray County filed for petitions to hold an election for organizing the county. This was granted by the Roberts County commissioners court.

According to a law passed in 1881, the seat of a Texas county was to be at "no point more than 5 miles from the geographical center of any county in the State unless by two-thirds vote of all electors voting on the subject of said county." The seat of Gray was located at Lefors, the center of the county. Salaries were set and supplies were ordered: coal, oil, two lamps, and two brooms.

All stayed relatively calm until April 1915, when Judge F. P. Greever was entering the yard of the Thut Hotel after a noon recess and was shot in the back by a man named A. E. Hume. The judge had granted the man a divorce, and Hume had not agreed to the division of property, so he took his revenge on the judge. When Hume was found, he had died of an apparent suicide.

Because the rail lines came through growing Pampa, the county seat was moved—after two elections—back north to Pampa, in 1928, where it remains today. The city streets were bricked by an Oneida Indian named Jim Brown. In 1928, a park called Albert Square became known as "Million Dollar Row." It covered three city blocks and included a new courthouse, city hall, fire station, and the Schneider Hotel. Together with the Combs-Worley building, these buildings all comprise the National Register of Historic Places District.

The Panhandle oil and gas field that ran through Pampa was one of the largest in the United States. It would become the largest economic boom to ever hit Pampa.

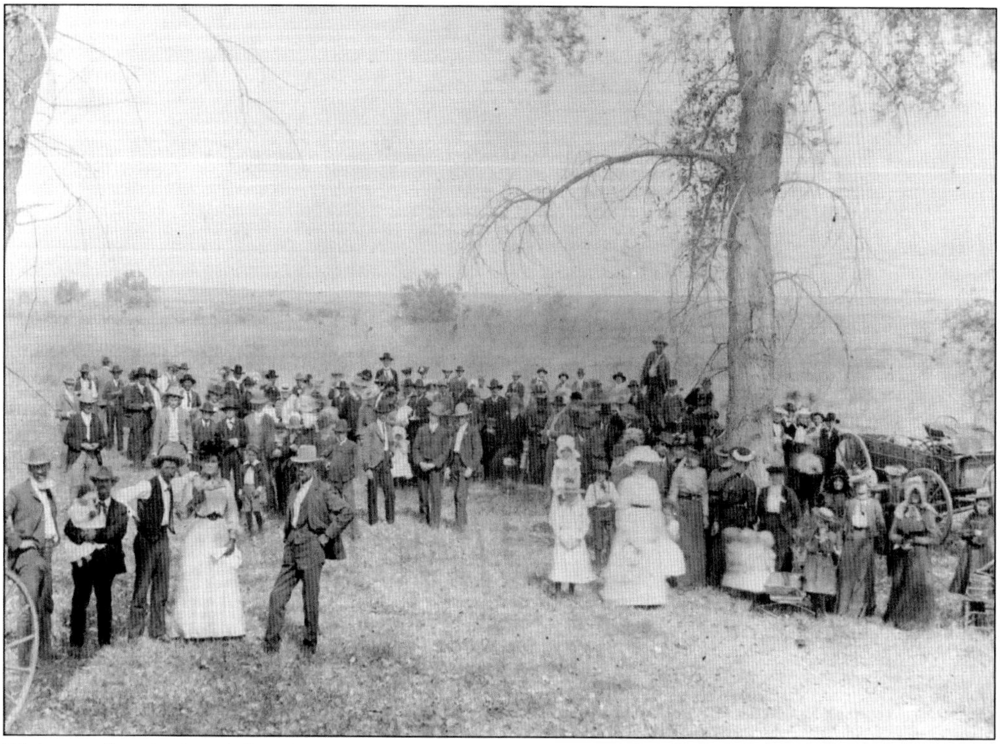

This was the picnic celebrating a new county organization and a new courthouse at Lefors, Texas. This great day was October 18, 1902. Lefors is 12 miles south of Pampa. The county seat was moved in 1928 to Pampa.

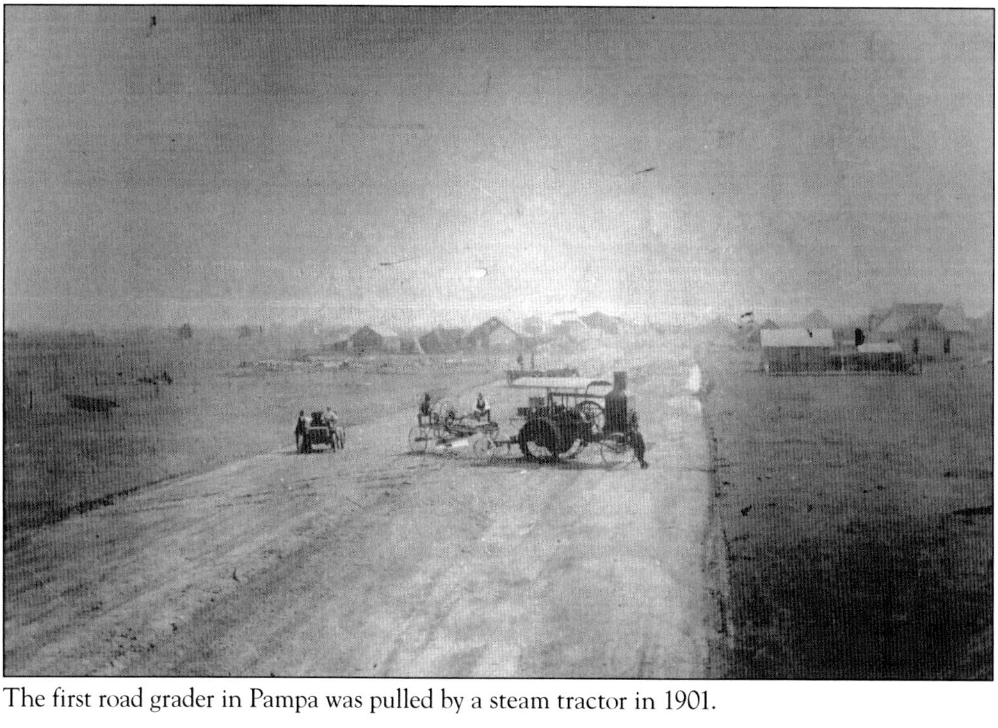

The first road grader in Pampa was pulled by a steam tractor in 1901.

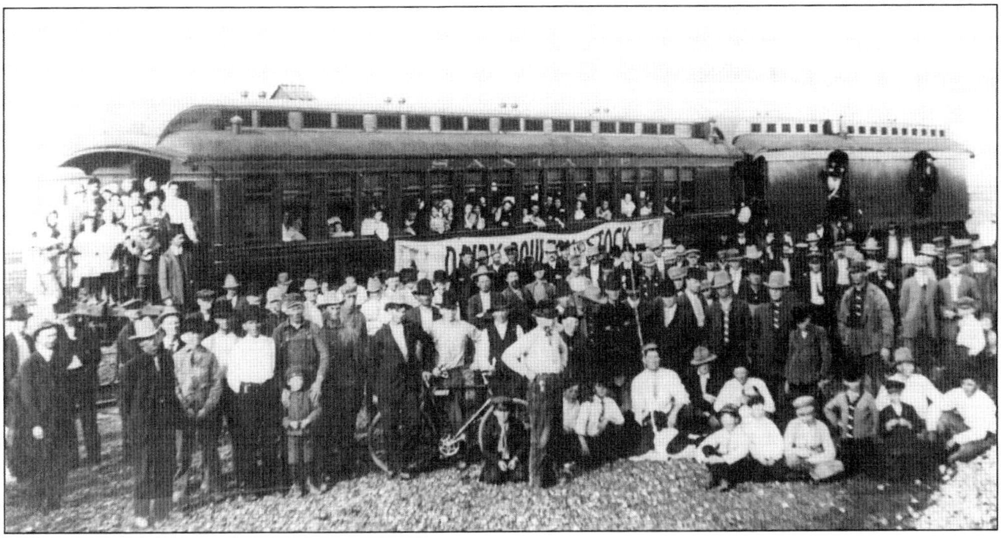

This Santa Fe passenger train was coming through Pampa in 1905. The ladies must all be in the train.

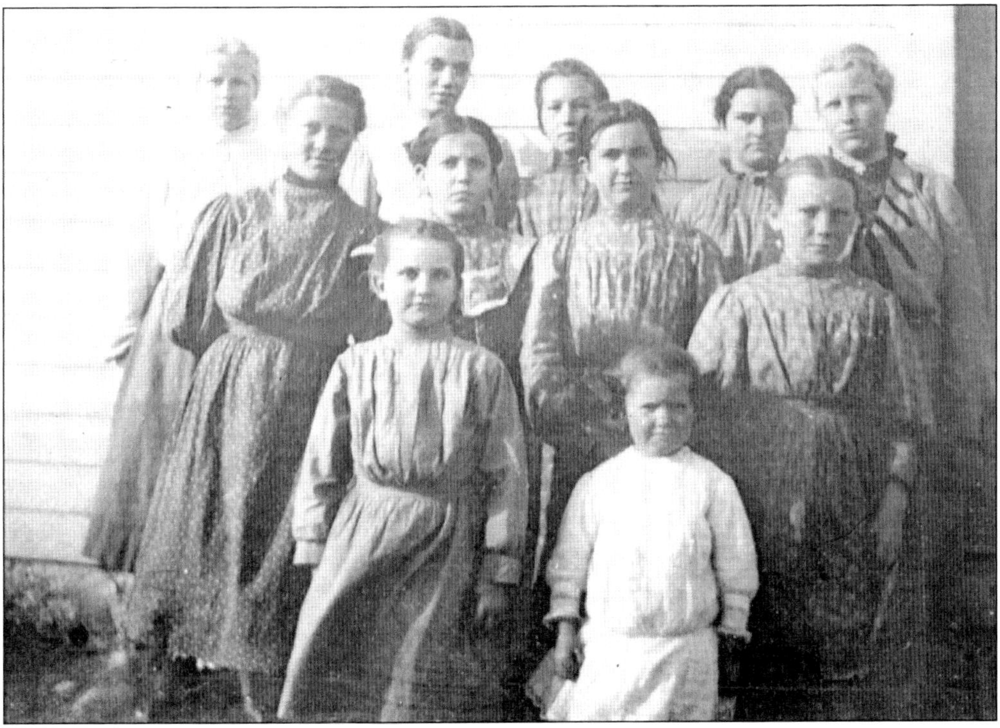

These girls went to the first school in Gray County. It was called Highwindy, for obvious reasons. The dresses these girls are wearing were all made of flour sacks.

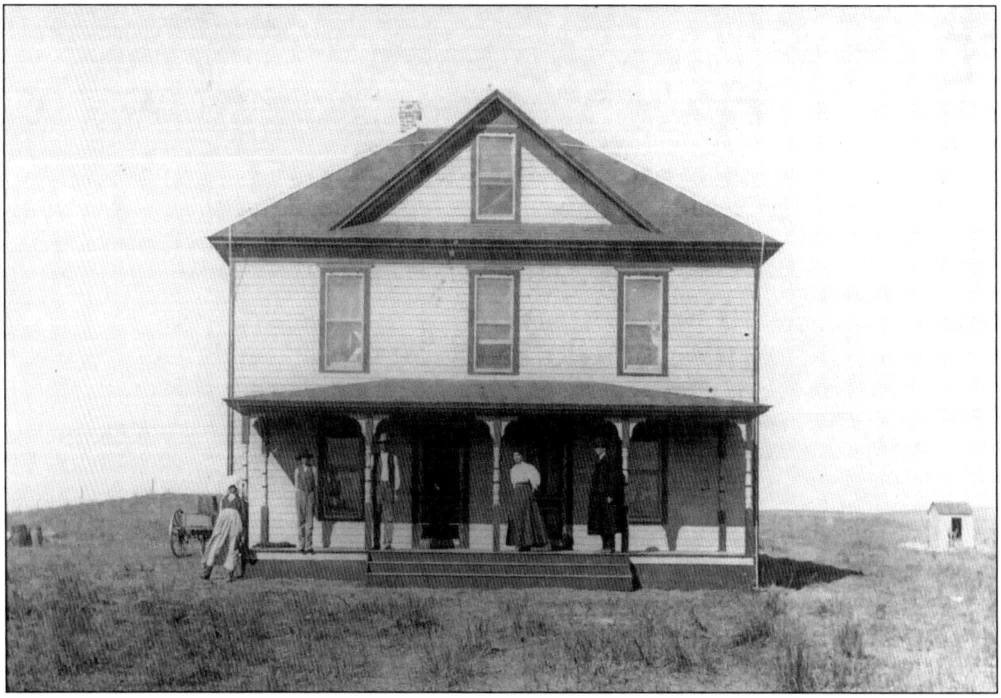

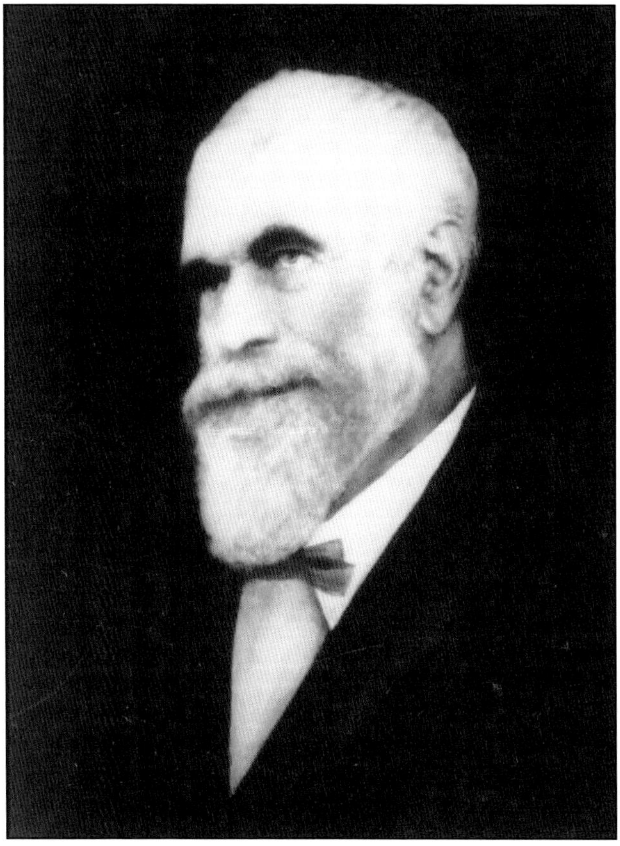

This is the Thut Hotel in Lefors. Henry Thut came from Switzerland when the state of Texas began to lease public lands to cattlemen. He filed for land along the North Fork of the Red River, for which he paid $1 an acre. Henry's sod house became the first house in Lefors, Texas. In 1892, the post office was established in the Thut home. Henry was the postmaster for 30 years. In 1902, Gray County was organized with the county seat at Lefors, prompting Thut to build this hotel.

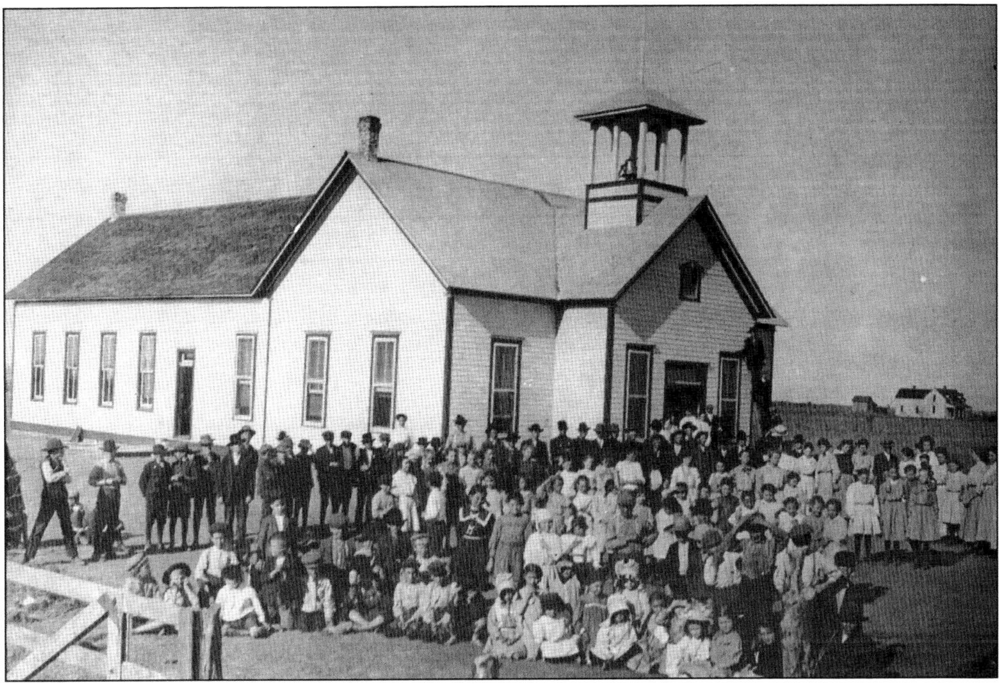

The White Deer Land Company built the first school in Pampa in 1903. Everyone came out to have their pictures taken. The building was remodeled in 1907.

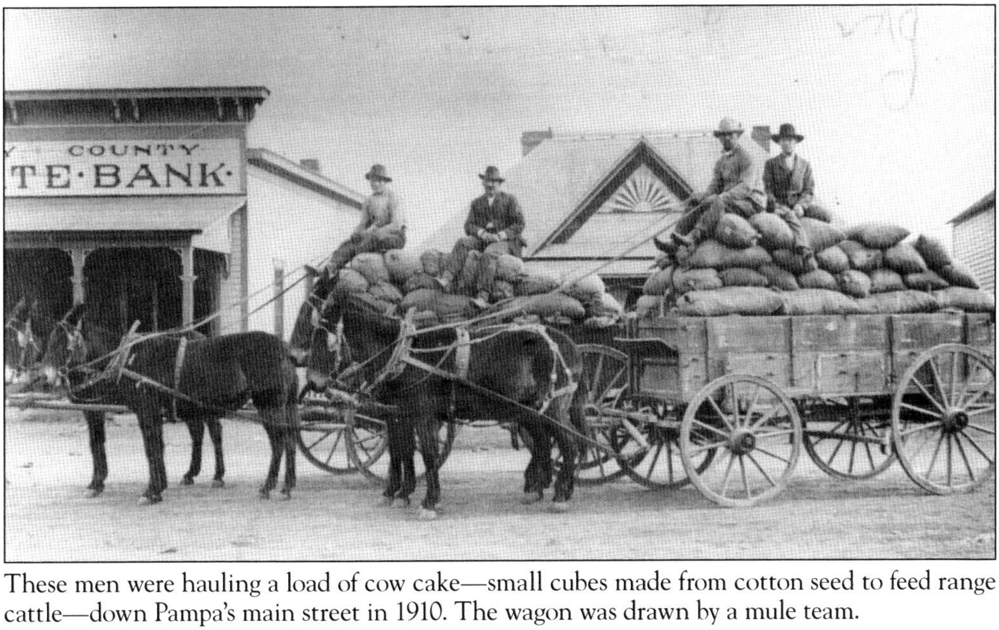

These men were hauling a load of cow cake—small cubes made from cotton seed to feed range cattle—down Pampa's main street in 1910. The wagon was drawn by a mule team.

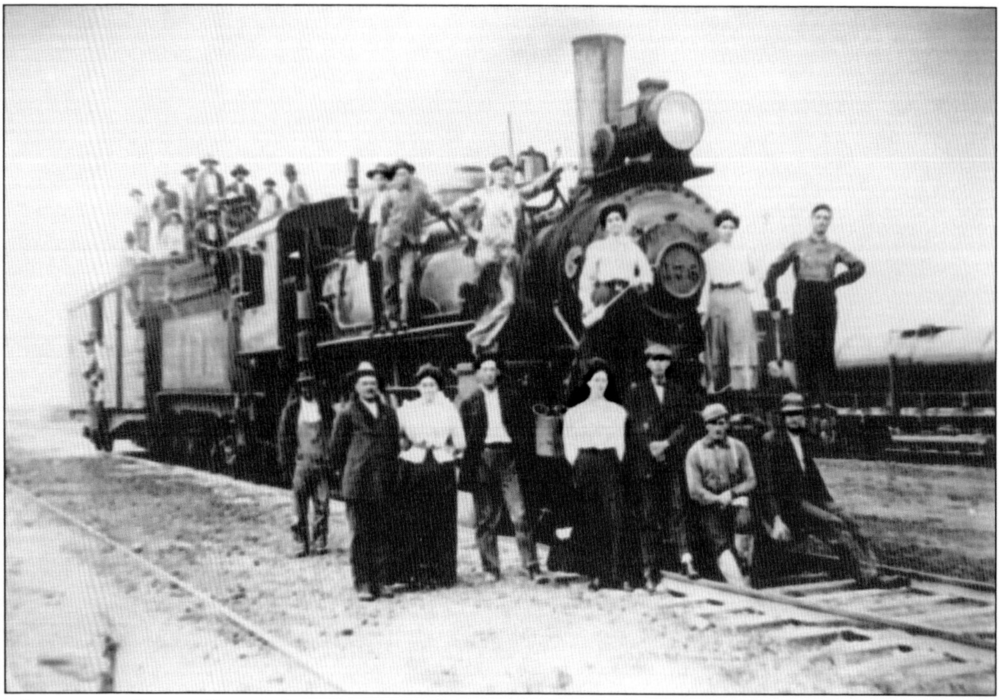

This was a Santa Fe wrecking crew in Pampa in 1908. It is unclear why the ladies are on the tracks.

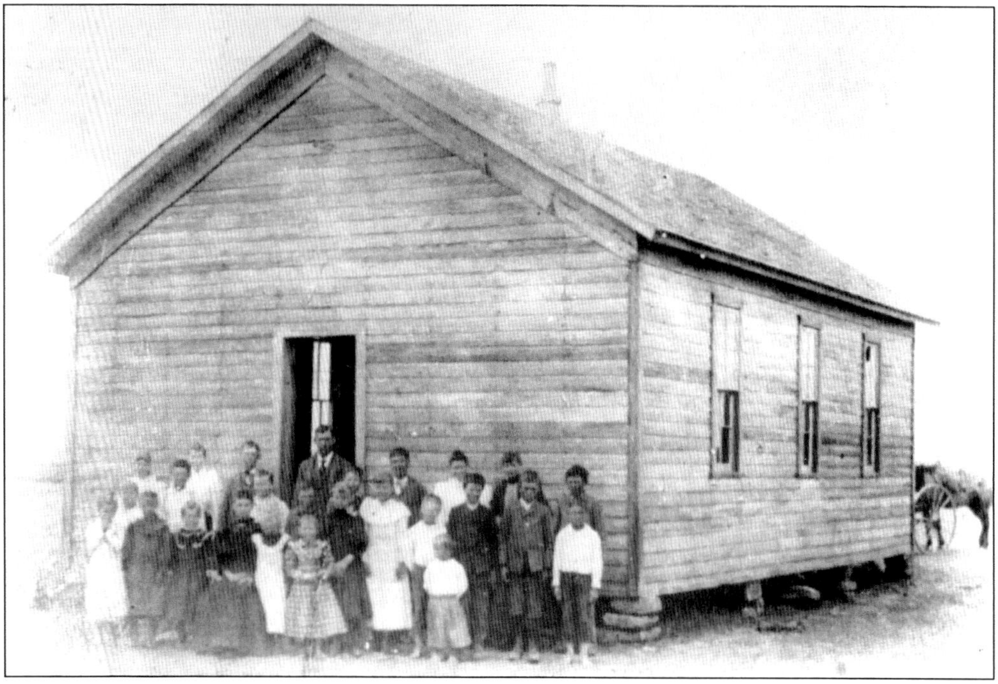

Some of the first church services in the Pampa area were held at the Highwindy school near Laketon. This photograph was taken in 1899.

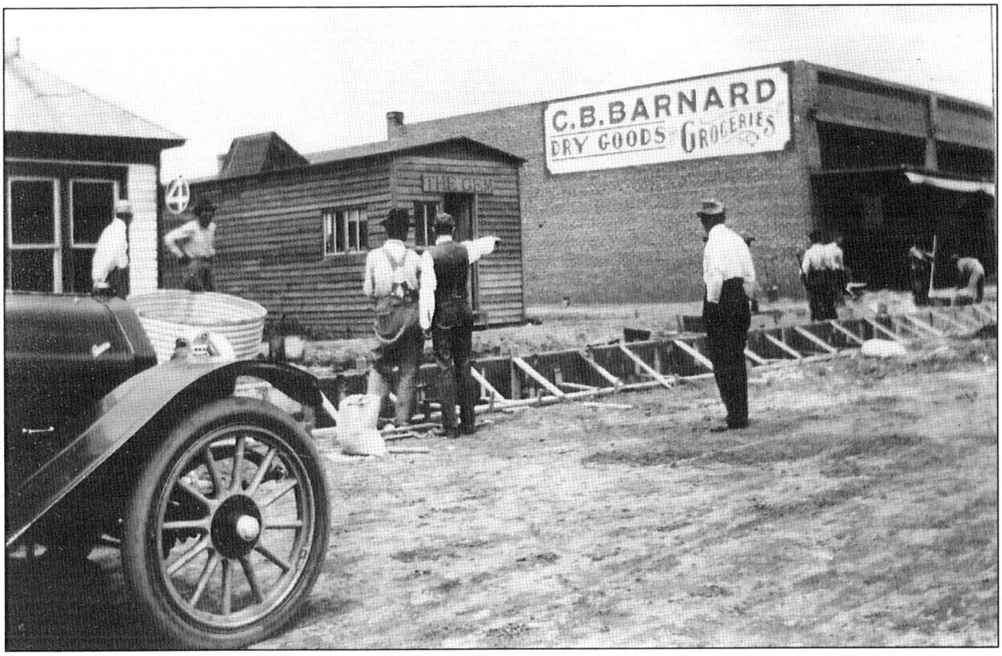

Pampa needed a sidewalk because of all the muddy streets. It looks like the men in this photograph are trying to figure out how to construct one.

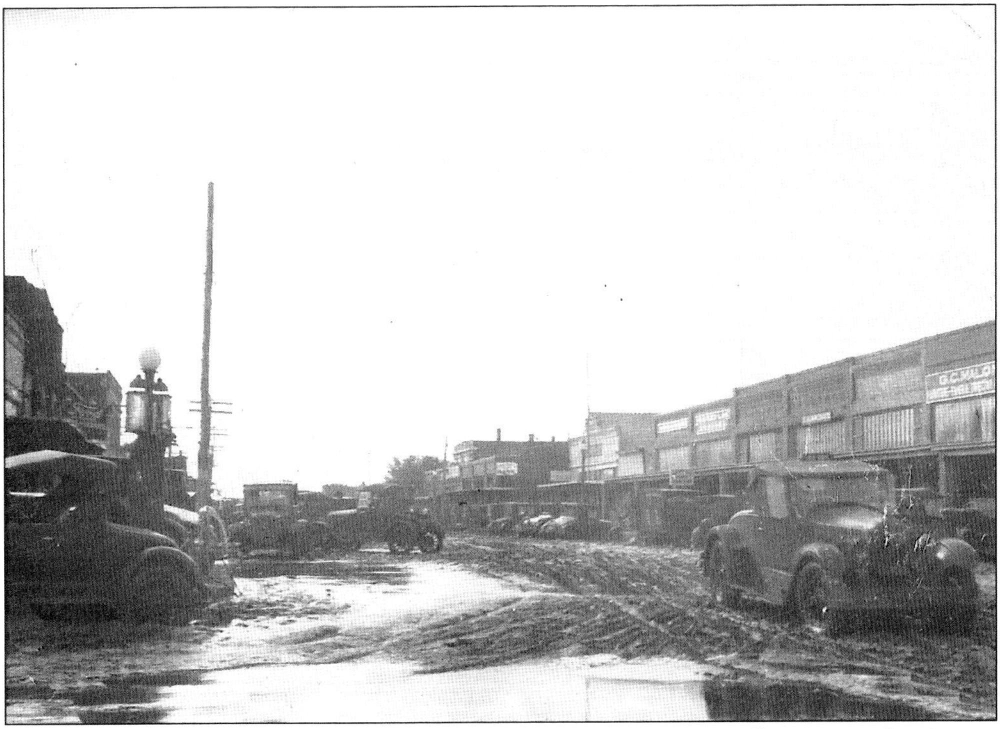

This scene, photographed sometime between 1905 and 1910, illustrates why Pampa needed sidewalks.

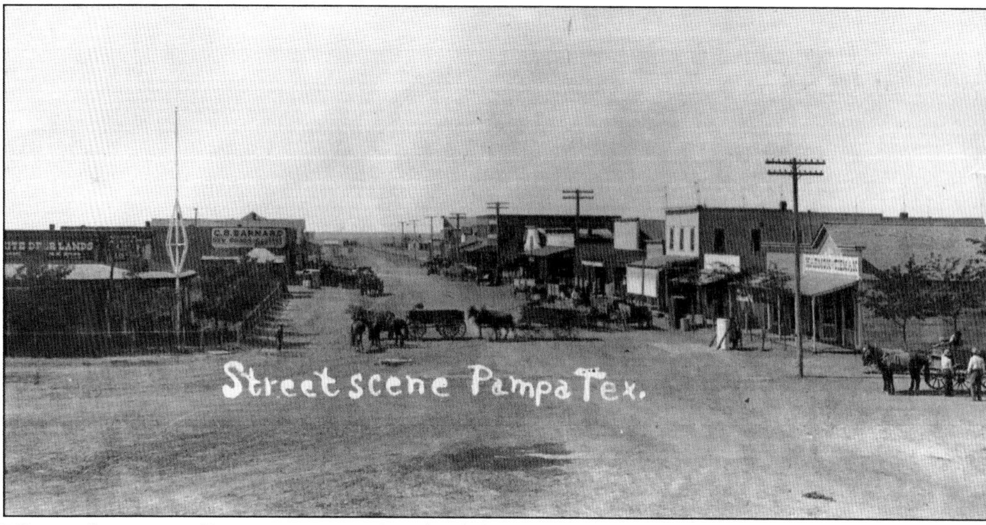

This is downtown Pampa in 1910. On the left, notice the White Deer Lands building in the white frame house. A strange flagpole can be seen in the front yard. Wagons seem to be ready for loading on the right side of the street.

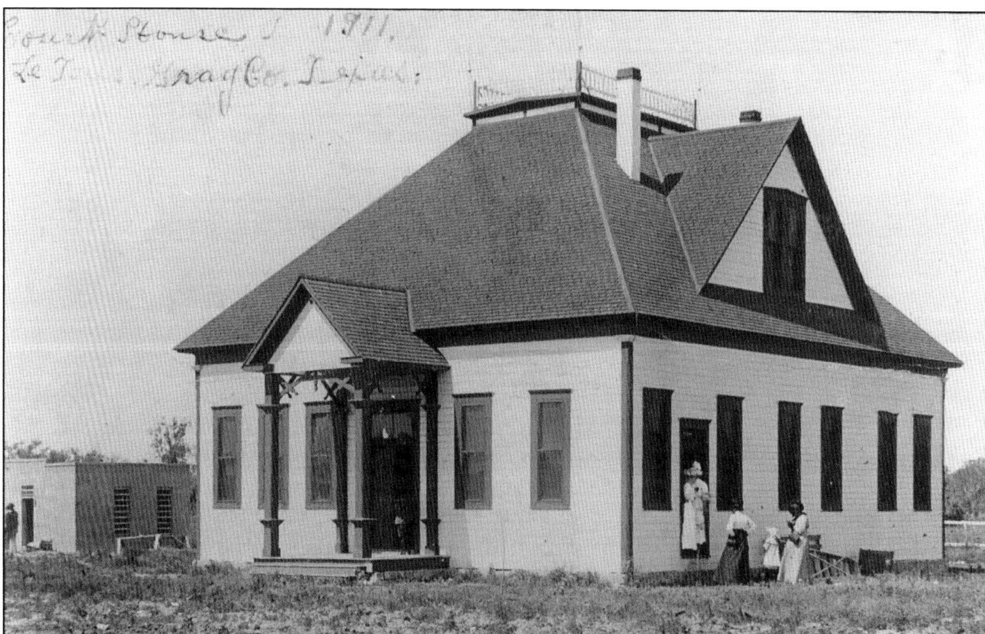

This prairie courthouse was built in Lefors in 1902, the year Gray County was organized. H. E. Wekessor of Miami was awarded the contract to build and furnish the courthouse for $2,208.50 with completion in 90 days. It was to have 22 windows and five rooms. The jail is on the left.

Judge Frank P. Greever was killed at the courthouse in 1915. A divorce and child custody case caused an angry defendant to wait for Greever and shoot him at noon on the courthouse grounds. The gunman's name was A. E. Hume, and he died of self-inflicted wounds.

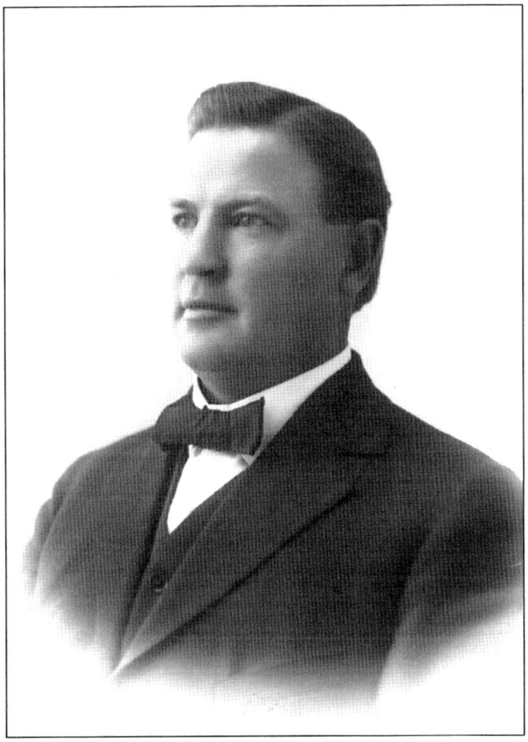

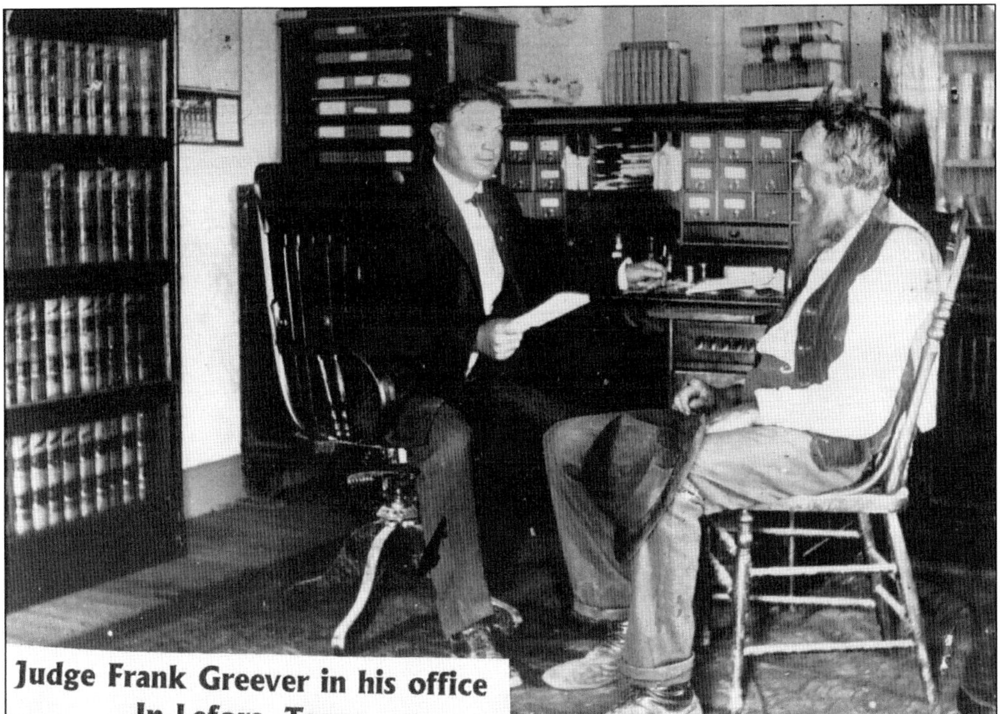

This is the office of the Honorable Frank P. Greever at the Lefors Courthouse before 1915. The man on the right is unidentified.

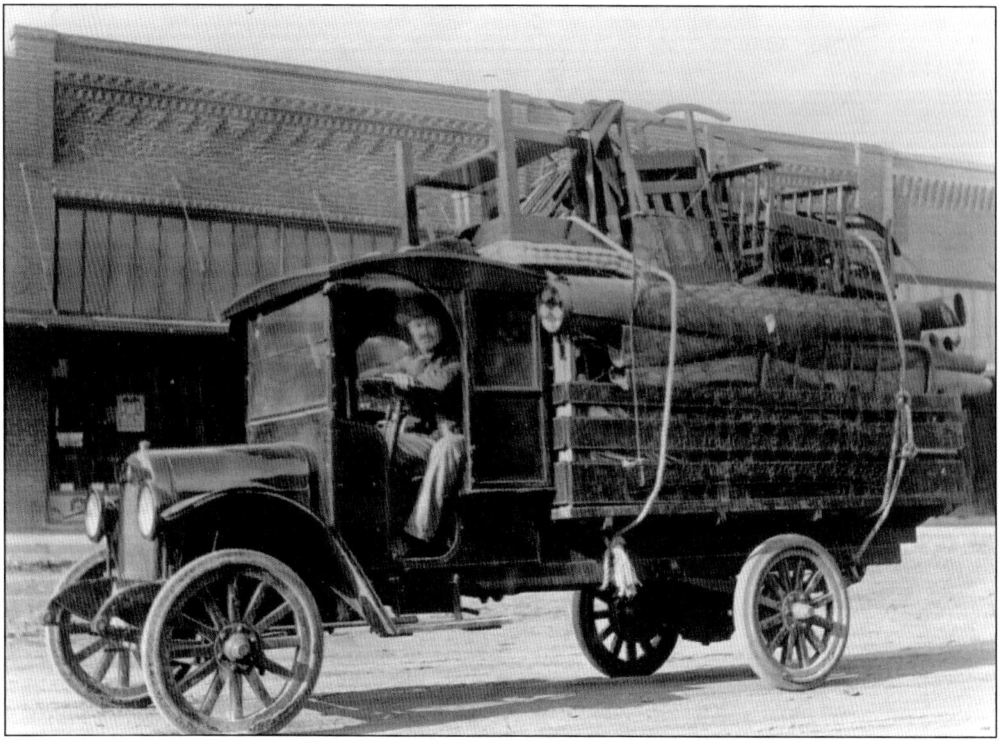

John Mack Patton owned a dray line, which meant that he would haul anything for a price. In this picture, it looks like he is moving rugs and chairs down Pampa's main street. He was in business in 1920.

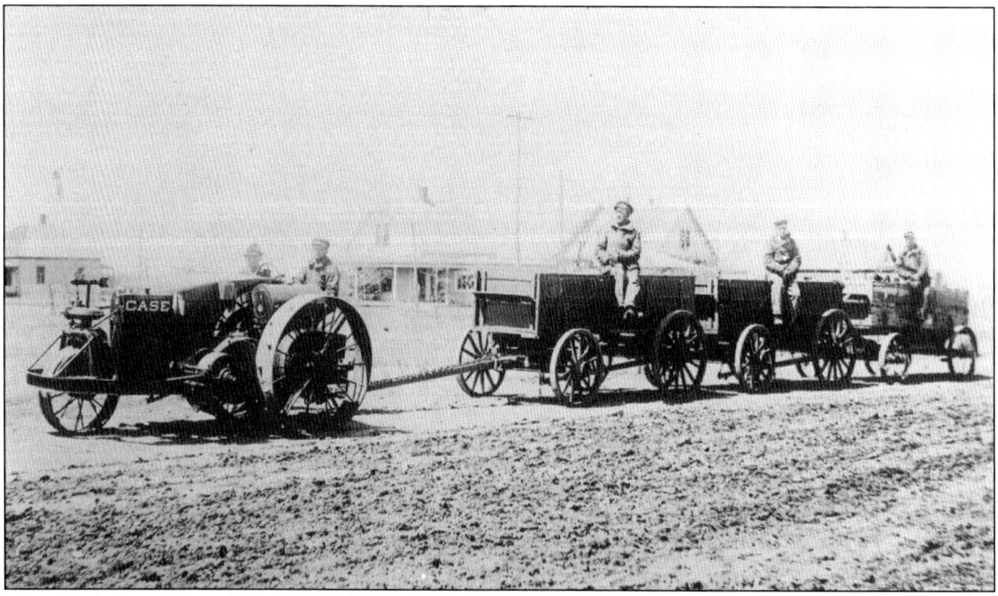

The O. A. Davis hands were hauling wheat to the elevator in Pampa in 1918. The Case tractor may have been fueled by kerosene.

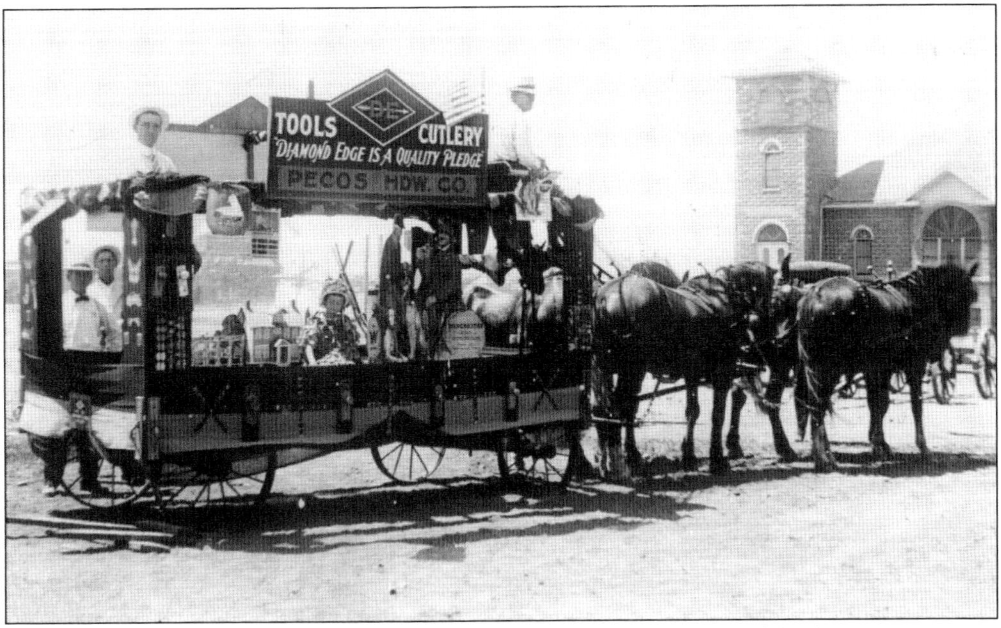

Traveling wagons came through Pampa in the mid-1920s. They played loud music to attract attention. Women gathered around to buy knives and hardware. In the background is the First Baptist Church, which was then on Kingsmill Street.

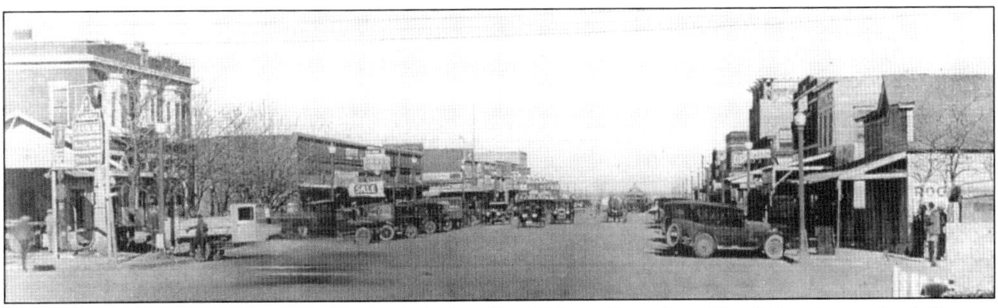

This is Pampa's main street in the mid-1920s. The White Deer Land building is on the left.

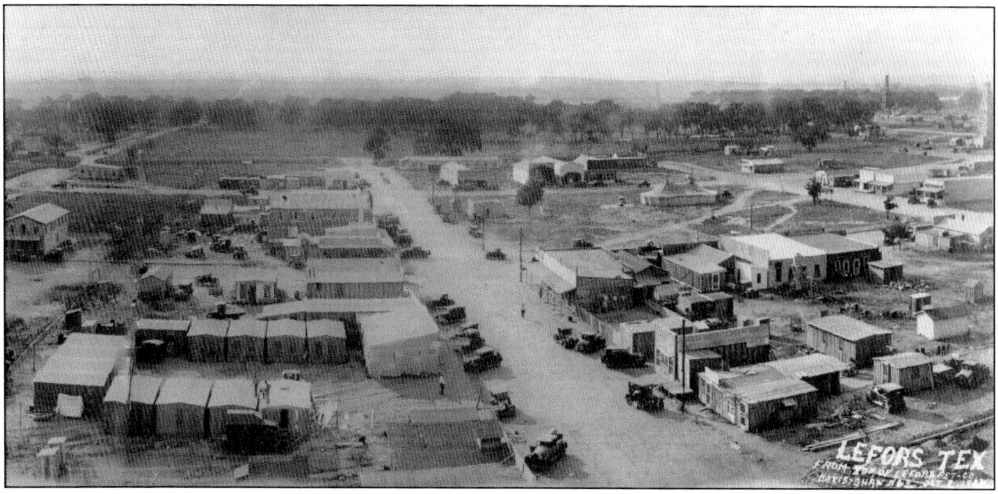

This is the county seat at Lefors just before they moved the records and the courthouse to Pampa. It also shows the town just as drilling for oil and gas had begun. Notice the derricks set up in the right back corner of the town.

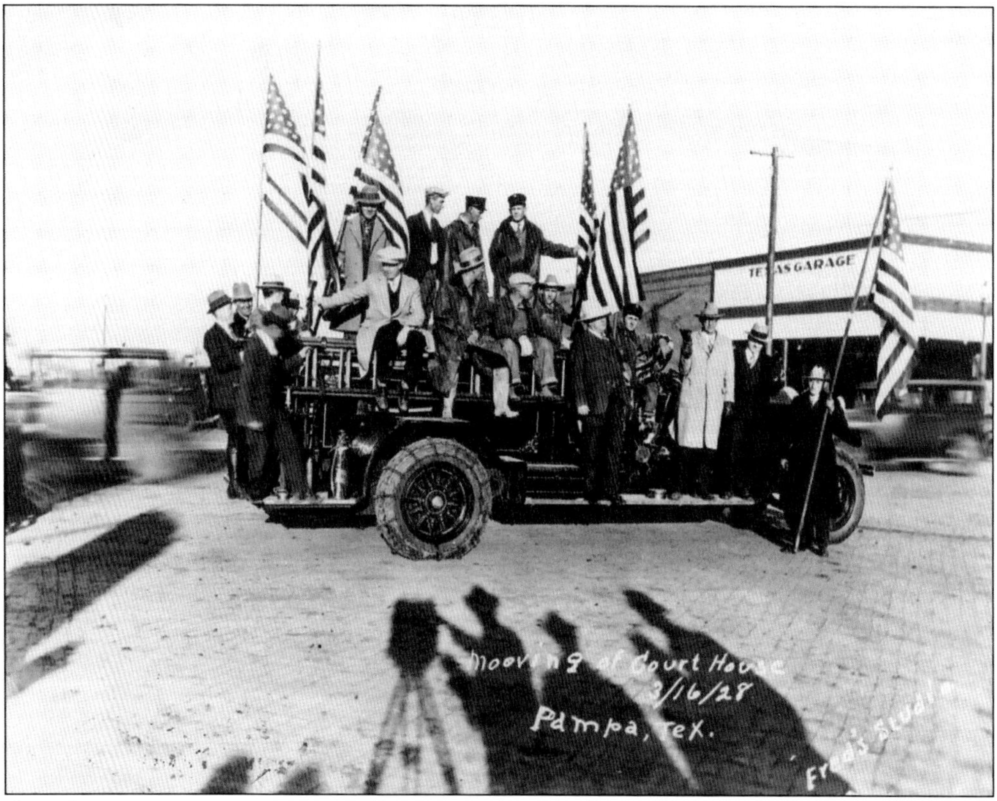

Gray County was moving its courthouse to Pampa as the result of a special election. The fire truck ceremoniously moved the records in 1928. Notice the newly bricked streets.

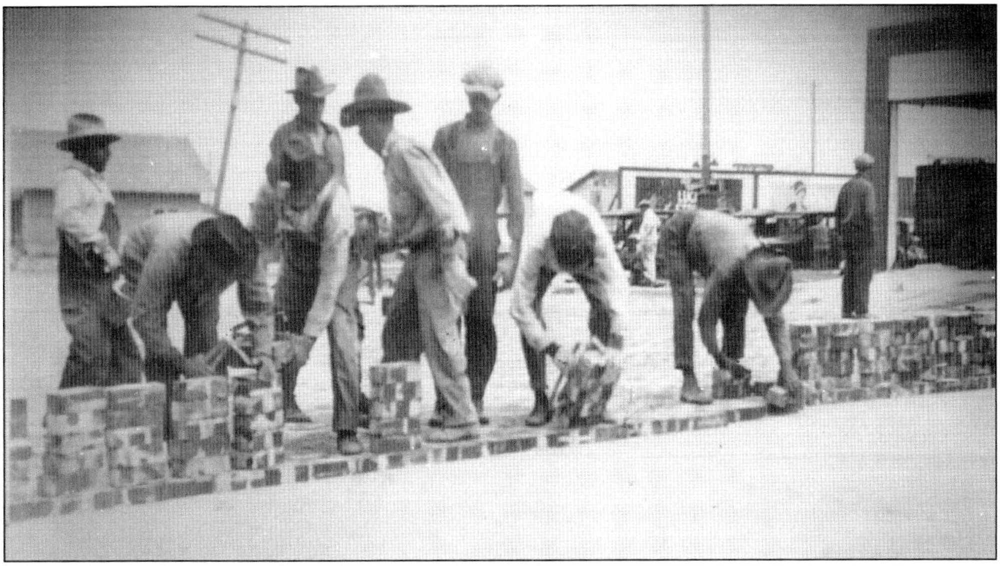

James Garfield Brown (fifth from the left, in profile), better known as "Indian Jim," came to Pampa in 1927 and bricked 11 streets. Brown was an Oneida Indian from New York, educated at Carlisle and Ontario Agricultural College in Canada. He set the world's record in 1925 in Olathe, Kansas, by laying 44,644 bricks in seven hours. It usually took more than three men carrying bricks to keep up with him.

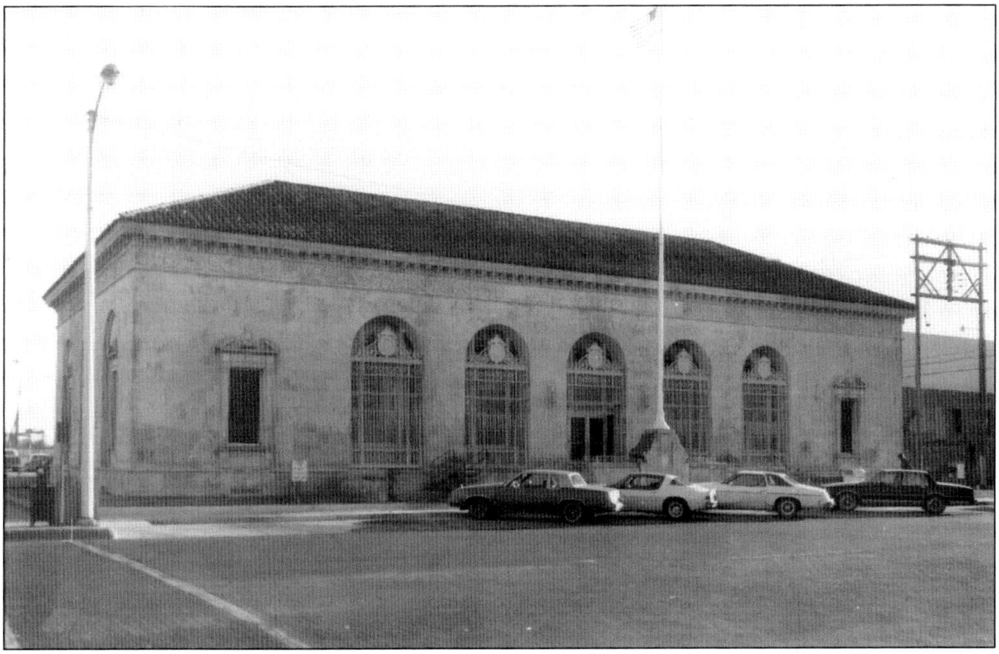

The Pampa post office is of Spanish colonial design. At the exterior roofline are carvings in limestone of a plow, wheat, and oil to depict the area's economy base. The structure was built in 1934 by talented people who came from the Works Progress Administration, part of Franklin D. Roosevelt's New Deal plan. The ceiling is hand-painted with murals on the east and west walls. Six to ten men and women worked on scaffolds for two months using 23-karat gold leaf and paint on the ceilings.

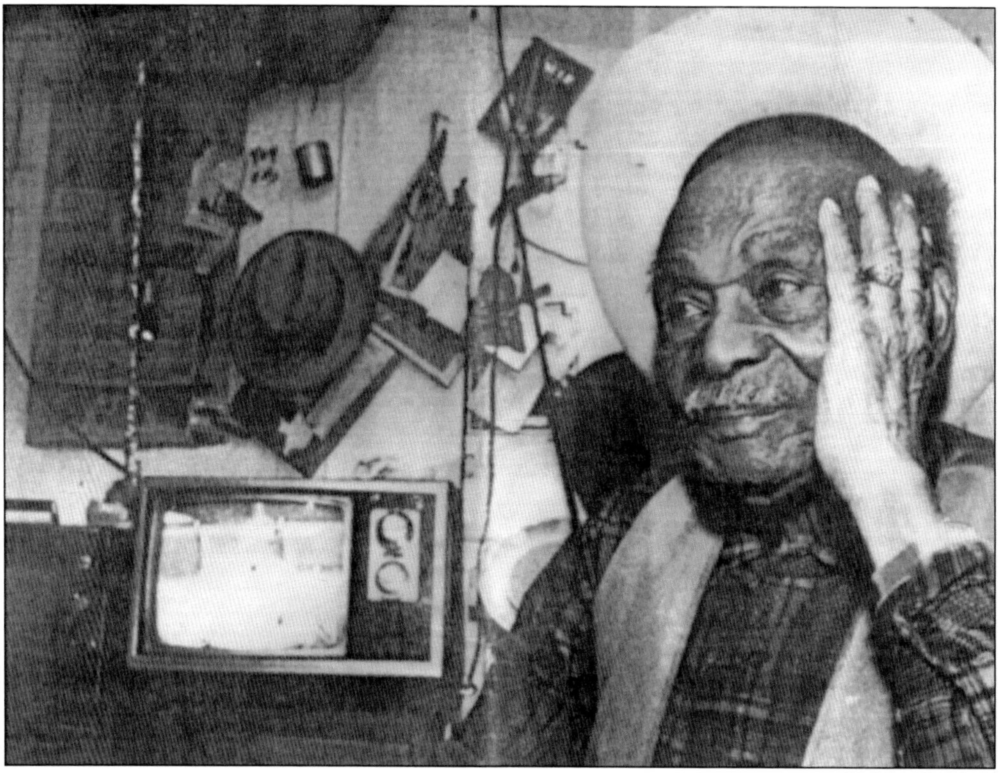

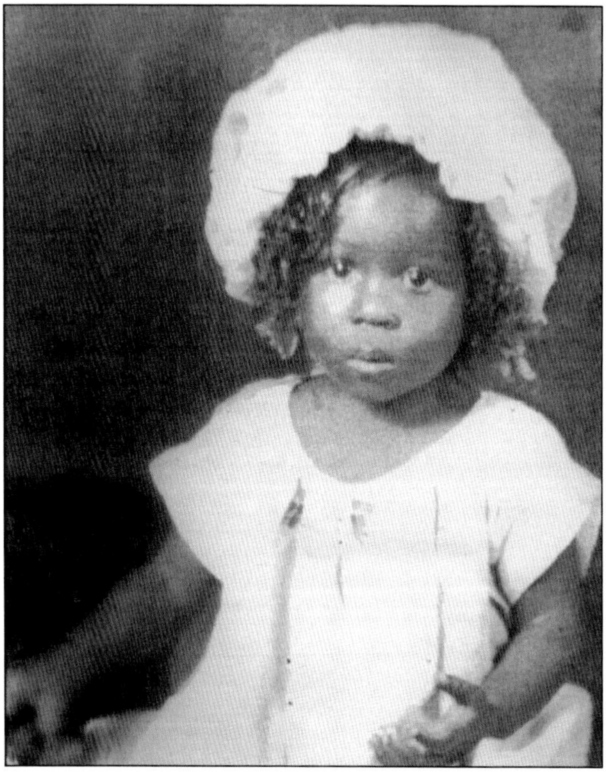

The first black man, whose mother was Native American, came to Pampa in 1926. He was born in July 1890, and his father was a freed slave. His name was Allen, but he was called "Butterbean" Thompson. His stepdaughter was the first black baby born in Pampa. Butterbean said that the children in town would bed to see him because they had never seen a black man before. He was very kind and humorous, and he died in 1991 at 100 years old.

At left is the first black child born in Pampa. Her name was Emma Lee Ponter, and she was raised by the O. F. Hunter family.

Pampa's first mayor, J. N. Duncan, was a merchant and early realtor. Duncan raised seven children, and the Duncan family was instrumental in developing Pampa.

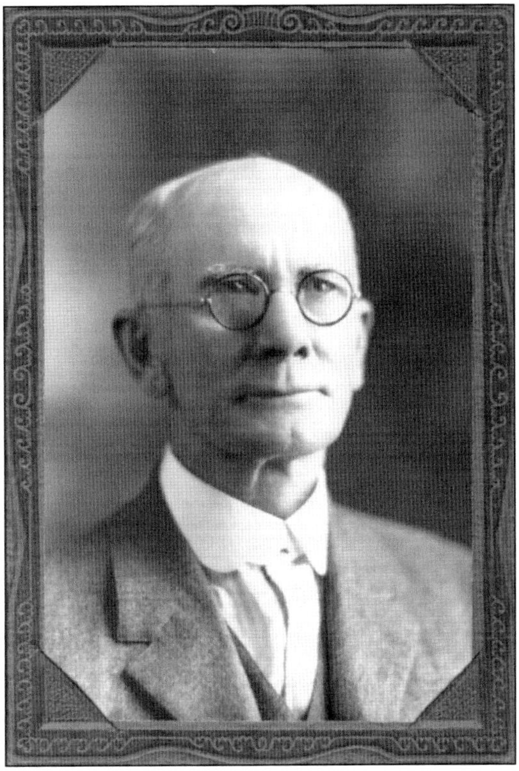

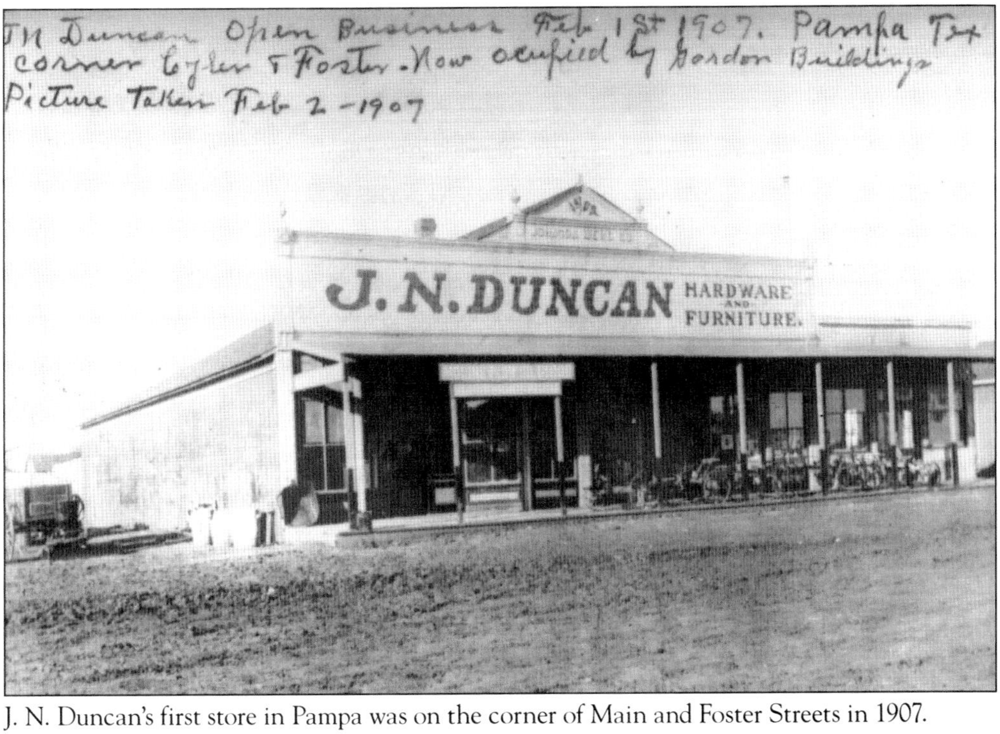

J. N. Duncan's first store in Pampa was on the corner of Main and Foster Streets in 1907.

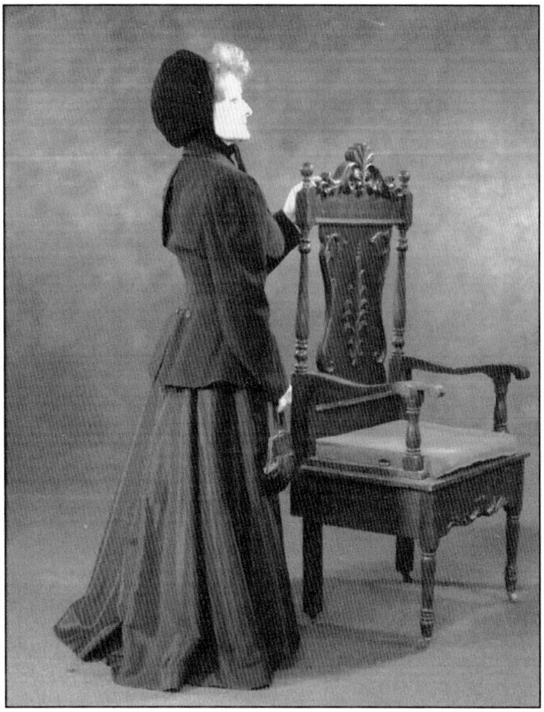

Angela Duncan Spearman, White Deer Land Museum Foundation board member, is shown wearing a dress belonging to her great-grandmother, Caroline Duncan, mother of J. N. Duncan. The jacket is styled after the Civil War–era soldiers' coats. Angela wore the dress at Pampa's 50th birthday and again in 1982. The dress is on display at the museum and is over 120 years old.

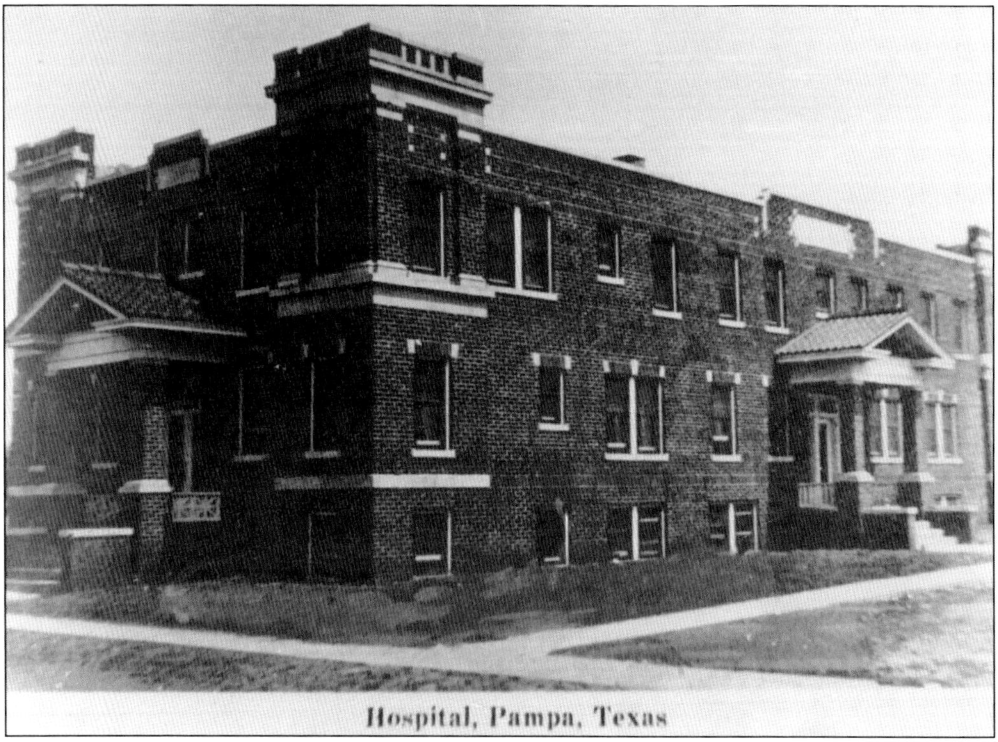

This hospital was opened in 1926 by doctors Archie Cole and W. B. Wilde. It operated as the Pampa Jarrett and later as the Pampa Hospital. This hospital was turned into apartments by 1951. The building caught fire in 1959, burning to the ground and killing five people.

Five

BLACK GOLD

Times were changing around the Pampa area. The 1920s were to mark important years for Gray County and Pampa. Charles N. Gould, a professor at the University of Oklahoma, was making surveys of underground water when he discovered oil and gas in the Panhandle Field.

In 1921, the Burnett No. 2 was located on the 6666 Ranch in Carson County, which joins Gray County. This land had been purchased from the White Deer Lands in 1903 at $2.65 per acre. But it was 1924 before the first well came into production about 5 miles south of Pampa on the No. 1 Worley-Reynolds.

This had also been part of the White Deer Lands. In two short years, the county was teeming with people, unemployment was nonexistent, and 110 separate corporations were showing a capital of $15 million. Pampa went from just over 900 to 30,000 people in 1930, according to the U.S. Census Bureau.

One of the most expensive leases was located 10 miles southeast of Pampa and was purchased by Phillips Petroleum Company for $1 million. A record producer was the Bowers No. 1, eight miles south of Pampa. This well produced more than two million barrels of crude oil by 1952. After rotary drilling was introduced to the Texas Panhandle, the average time to drill a 3,000-foot well was 20 days. Today it takes 4 to 5 days.

Oil-related businesses began to settle in this area, including Cabot (with 1,000 employees), Phillips, Halliburton, Magnolia, Danciger, carbon black plants, tool companies, and oil well servicing companies. The Panhandle Field was one of the largest and most productive deposits of oil and gas in the United States.

The oil boom and the Great Depression brought Woody Guthrie in a boxcar, brick streets, and the dust storms that nearly choked the whole area. It also brought a new type of criminal: a bank robber who wore a pinstriped suit and a clean, white shirt. Then there was the Marcel wave and the Charleston. Then came World War II, and Pampa built the Pampa Army Air Force Base.

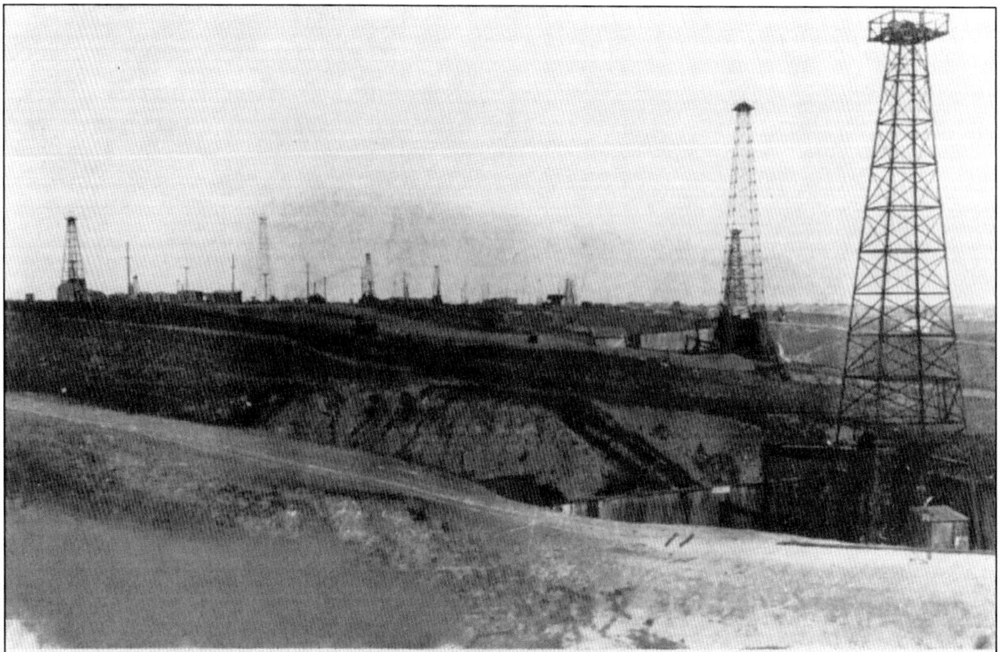

Oil Fields, Pampa, Texas.

Times had changed by the late 1920s and early 1930s. An oil boom had hit Pampa and the Depression was bearing down. This was the scene that dotted many fields in Pampa during the late 1920s and 1930s. There were oil fields north, east, south, and west of Pampa.

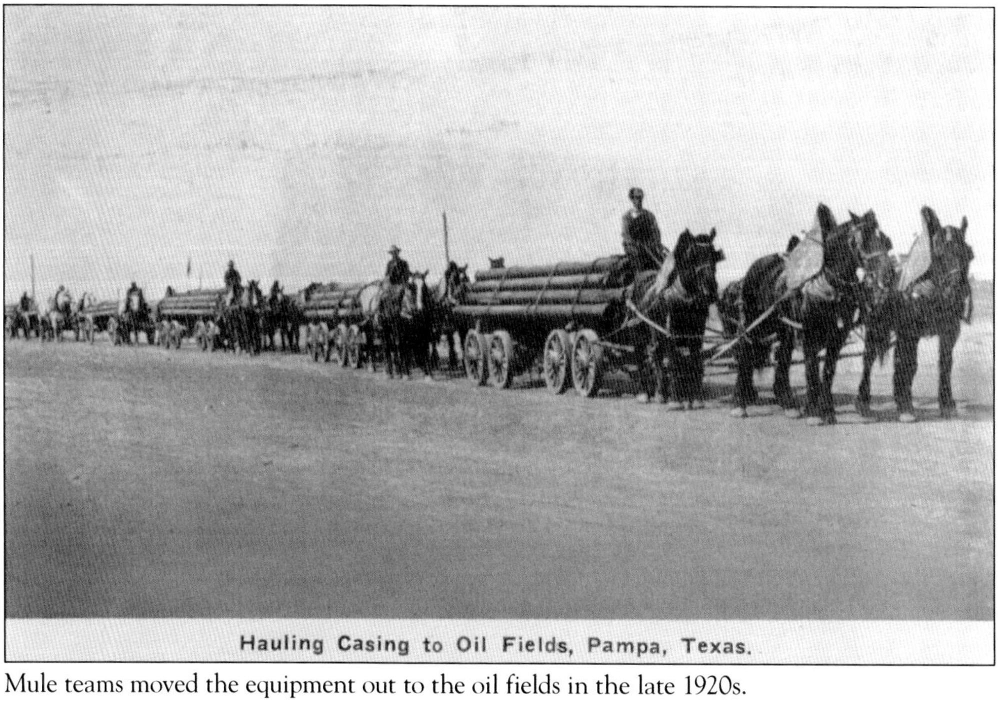

Hauling Casing to Oil Fields, Pampa, Texas.

Mule teams moved the equipment out to the oil fields in the late 1920s.

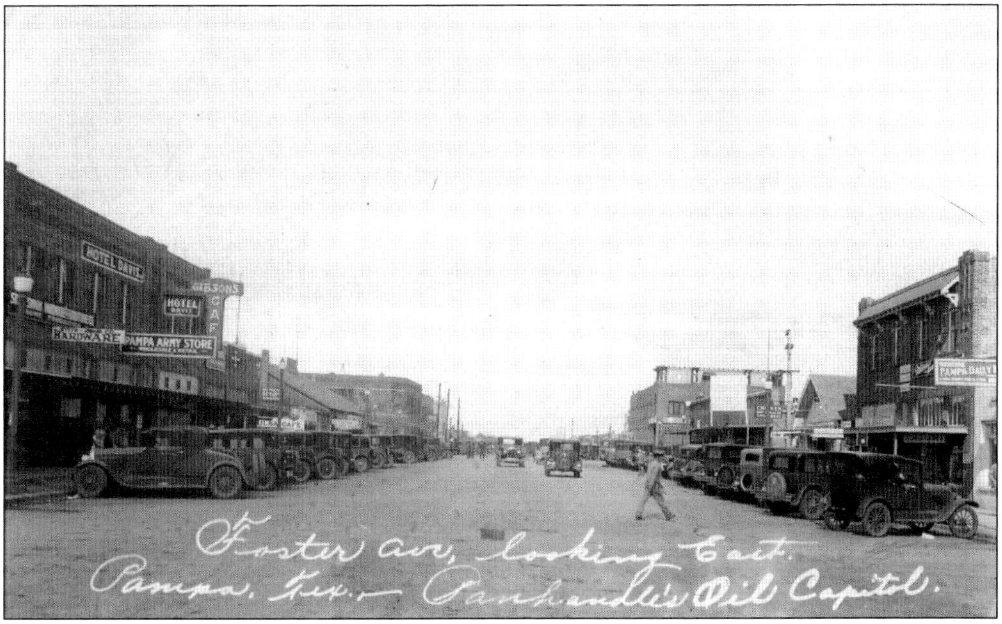

This street scene was taken before the streets were bricked. Foster Street in Pampa was pretty busy after the first wells were produced in 1924.

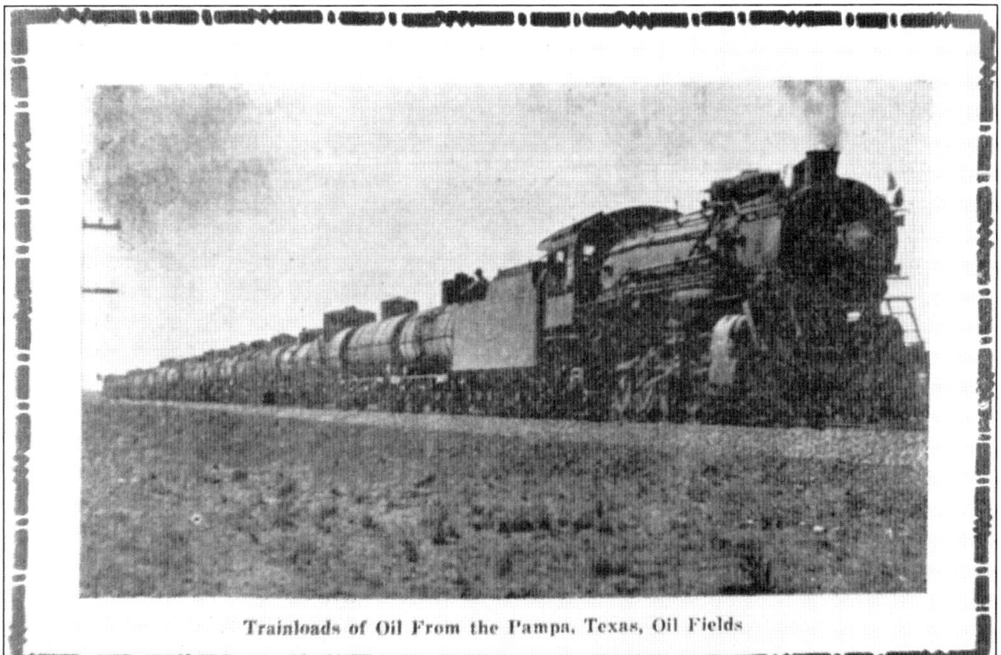

The producers had begun to haul oil from Pampa late in the 1920s. By 1929, the oil and gas production showed that the Panhandle Field was one of the nation's largest.

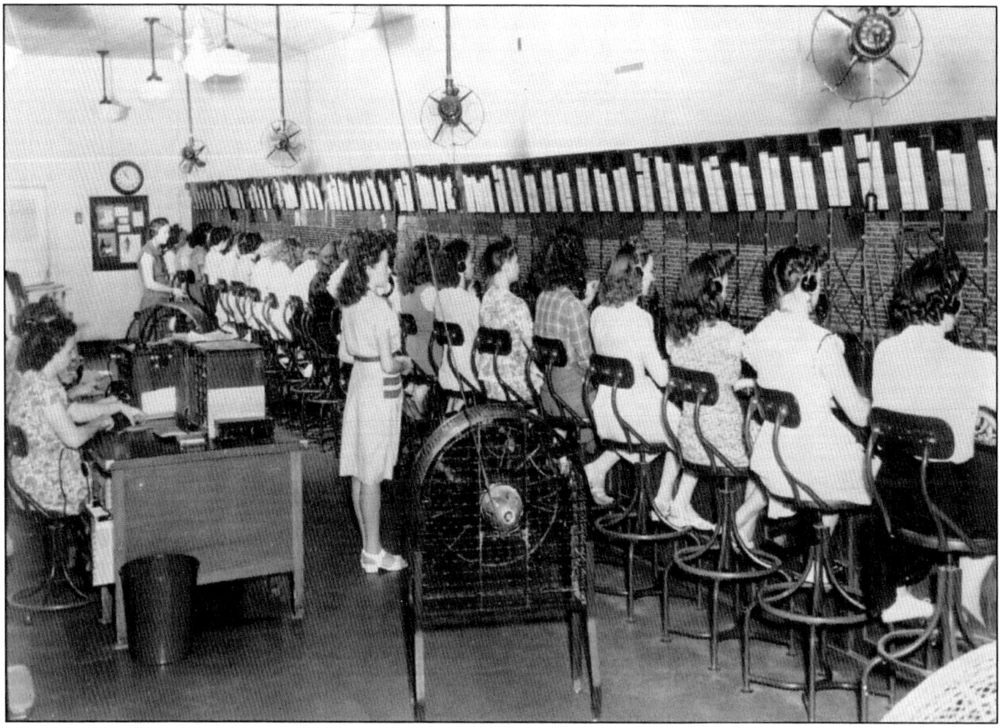

These operators were working on one switchboard system installed in 1900. By the 1920s and1930s, they had advanced to a larger system to accommodate the growth of the town. This system lasted through World War II.

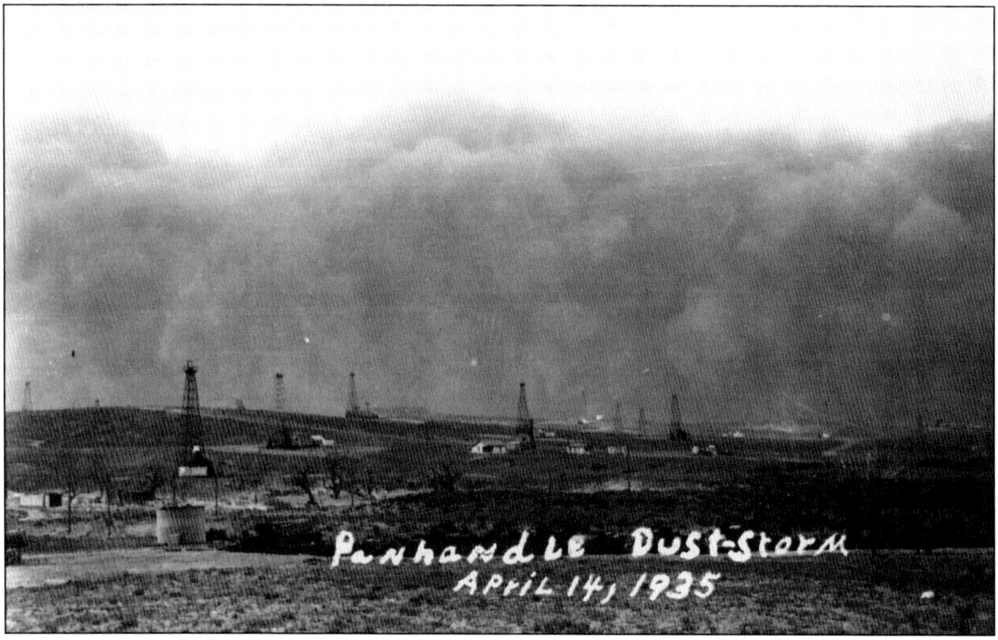

By the time the oil production was nearly at its peak, the Great Depression and the Dust Bowl had hit Texas. The most remembered dust storm in Pampa's history is recorded as Palm Sunday, April 14, 1935. You can see the darkness in the oil field.

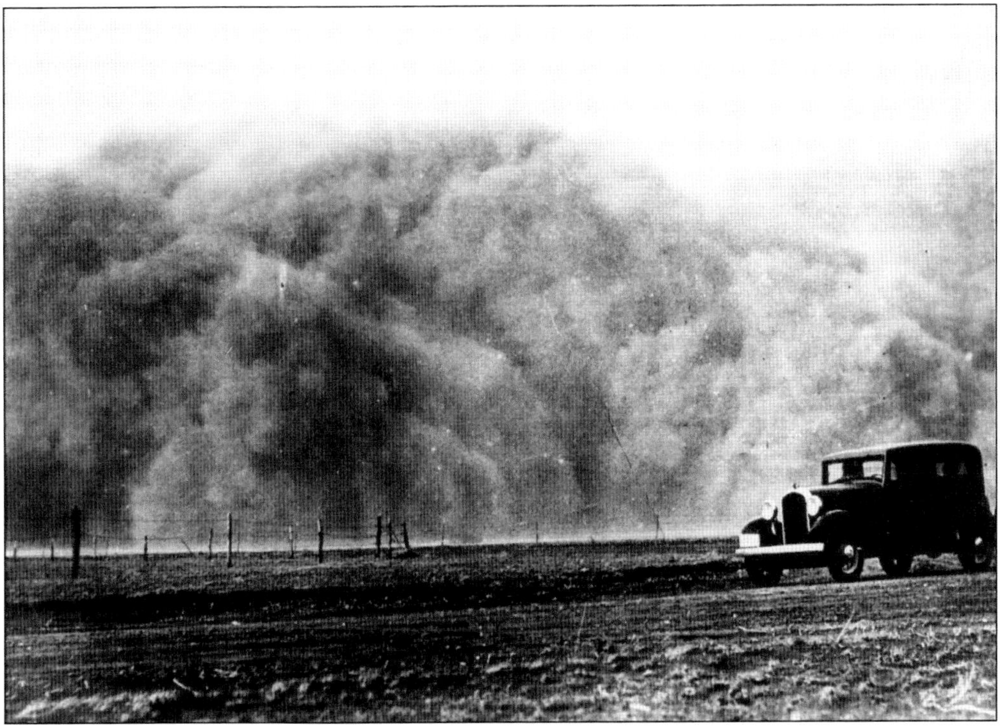

This location was somewhere west of Pampa in 1935. The car had come to a stop.

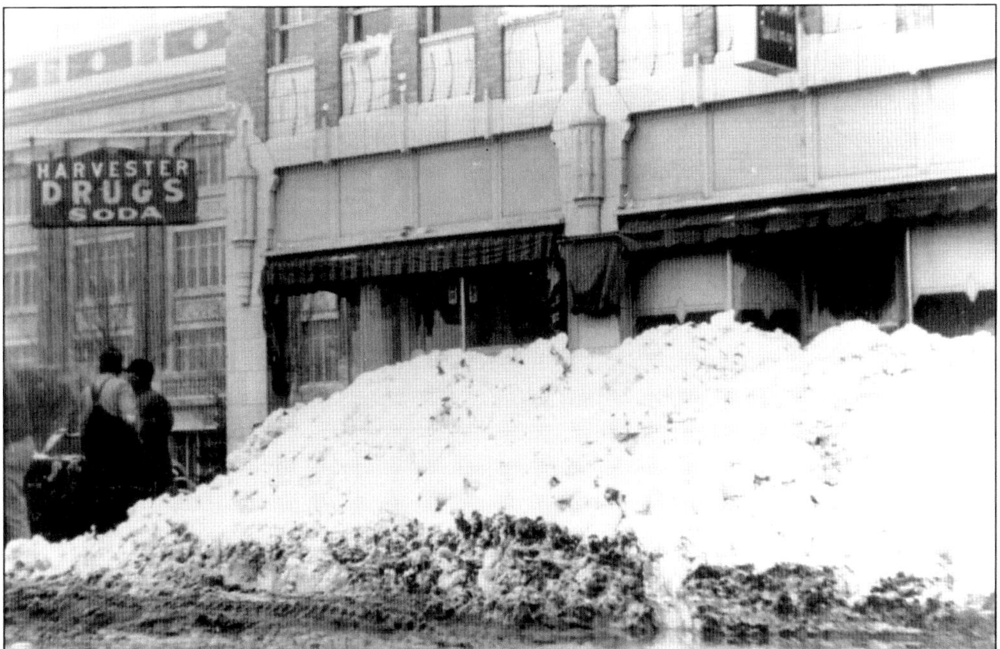

There were some hard winters, too. This snow scene shows Kingsmill Street in Pampa in 1938.

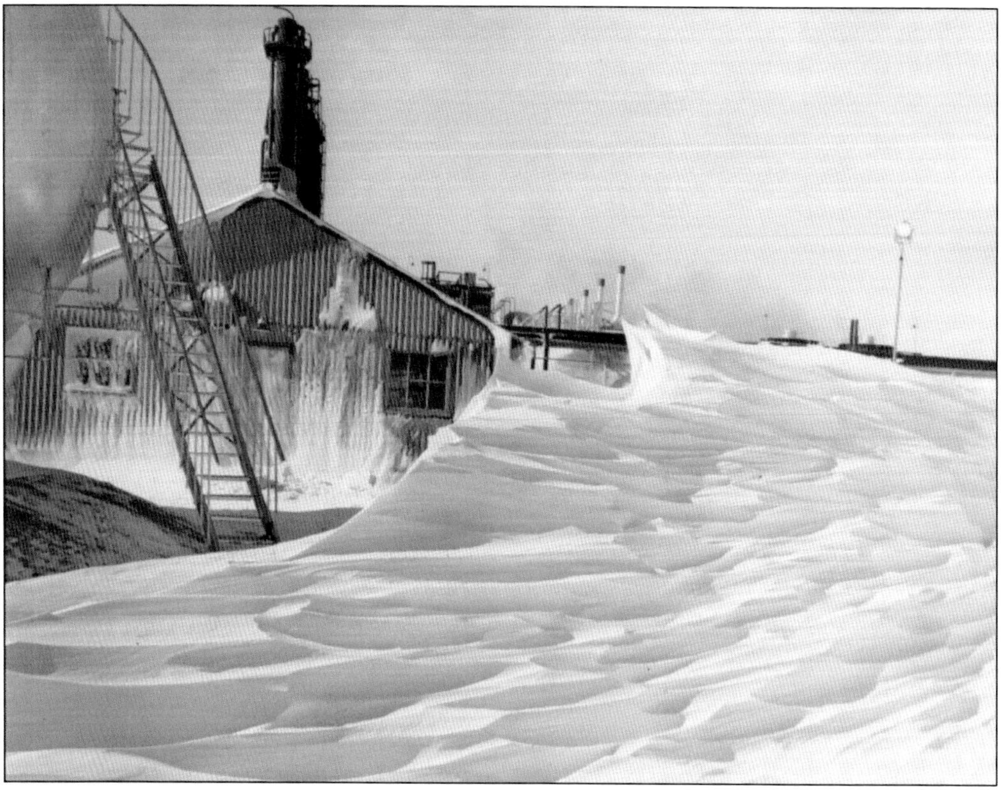

This beautiful snow was piled up at one of the gas plants west of Pampa in the late 1930s.

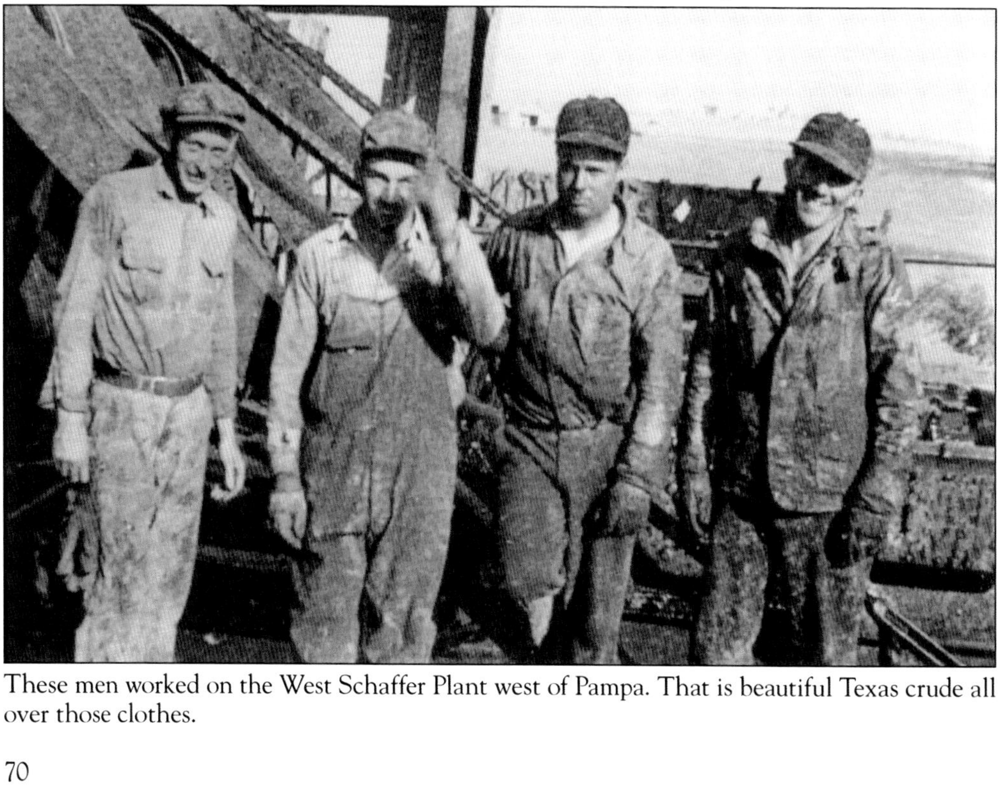

These men worked on the West Schaffer Plant west of Pampa. That is beautiful Texas crude all over those clothes.

This was the first well to produce at Pampa. It was the Combs-Worley lease and was drilled by the Wilcox Oil and Gas Company. It became a heavy oil producer in the area. Phebe Worley became a great benefactor to Pampa. She helped finance a hospital and an office building. The Combs-Worley Ranch is still in operation south of Pampa today.

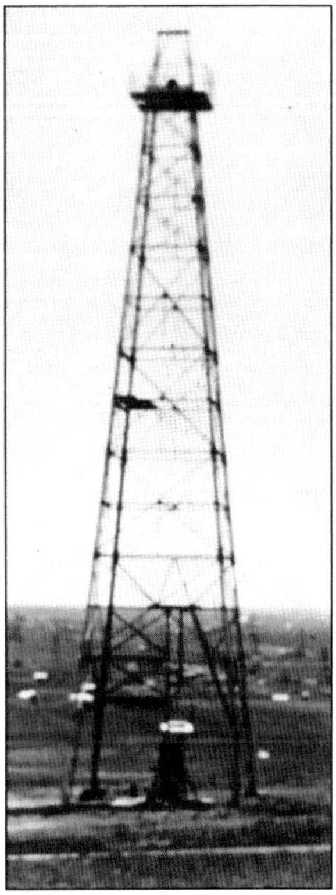

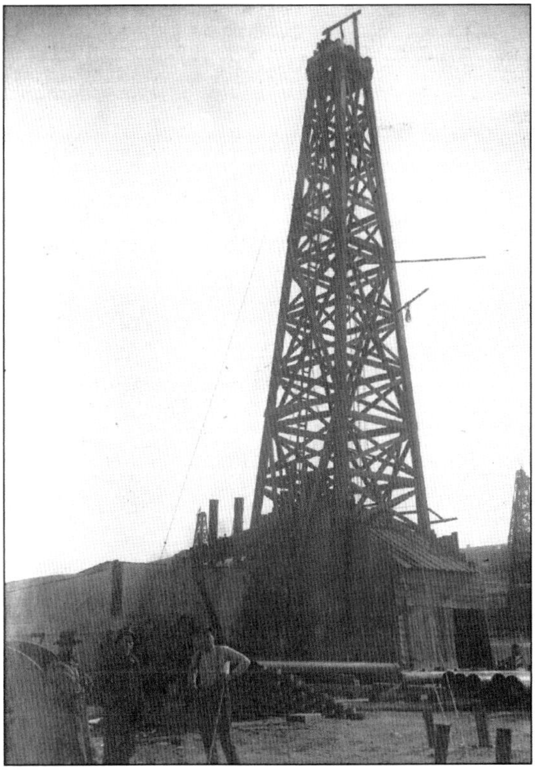

The old derricks, in the late 1920s, were made of wood with a cathouse below. They were very hard to set up, and materials for the wildcat well locations were transported by horse and mule teams. The crew consisted of a drilling superintendent, a construction boss, the driller (crew boss), and the roustabouts, who helped the driller in each shift.

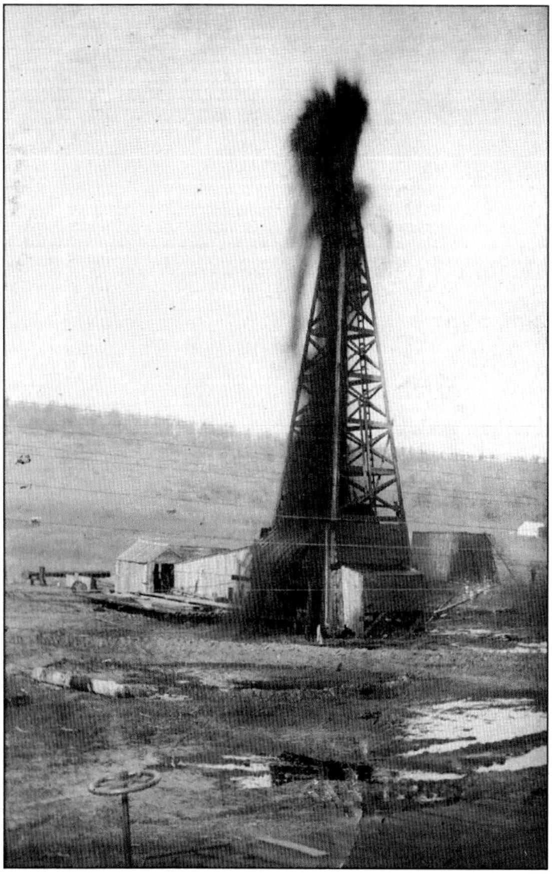

It looks like they just struck oil!

There were many oil-related services to help those people in the fields. For four decades, Pampa had many of these important businesses, such as WB Pump and Supply; Halliburton; Oil Well Servicing, Inc.; Beacon Supply; and the Sidwell Company.

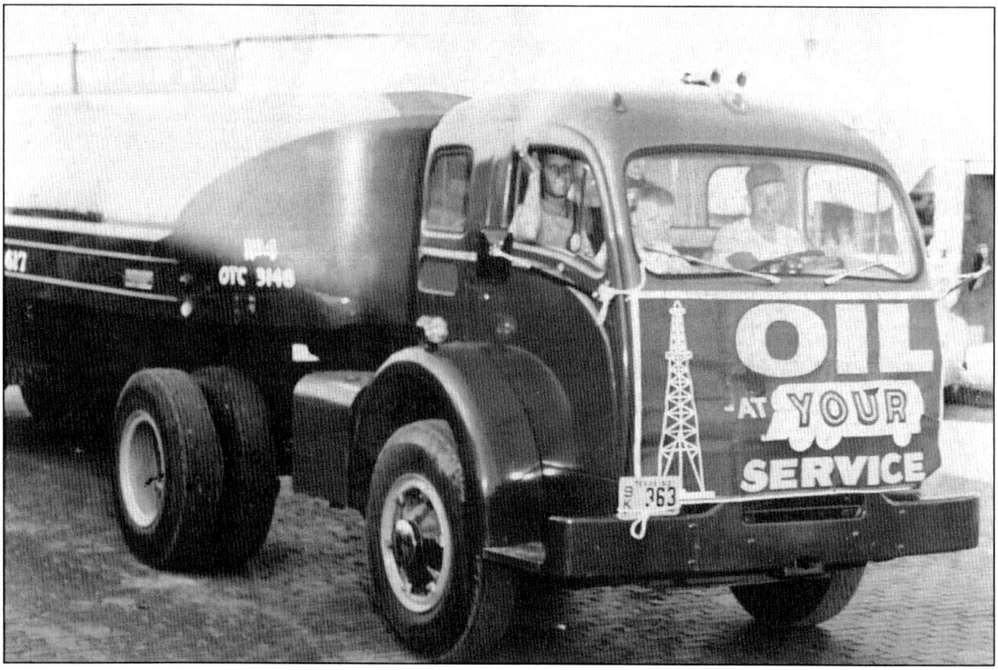

This rig was on fire, and because it was metal, it was melting.

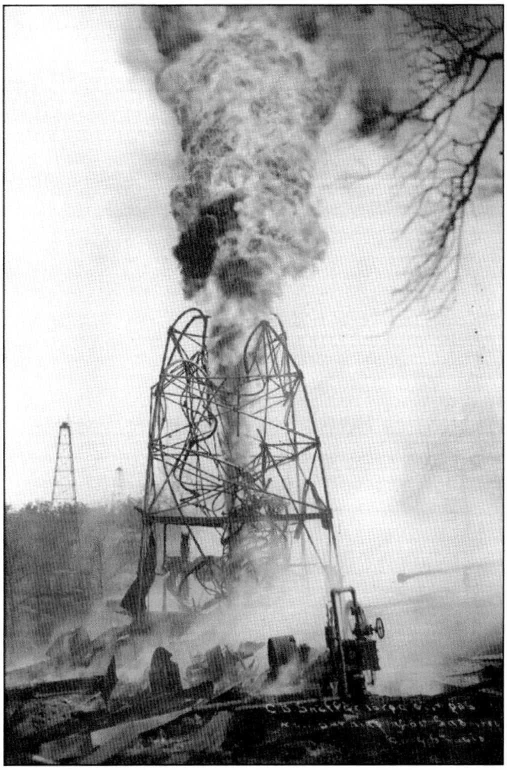

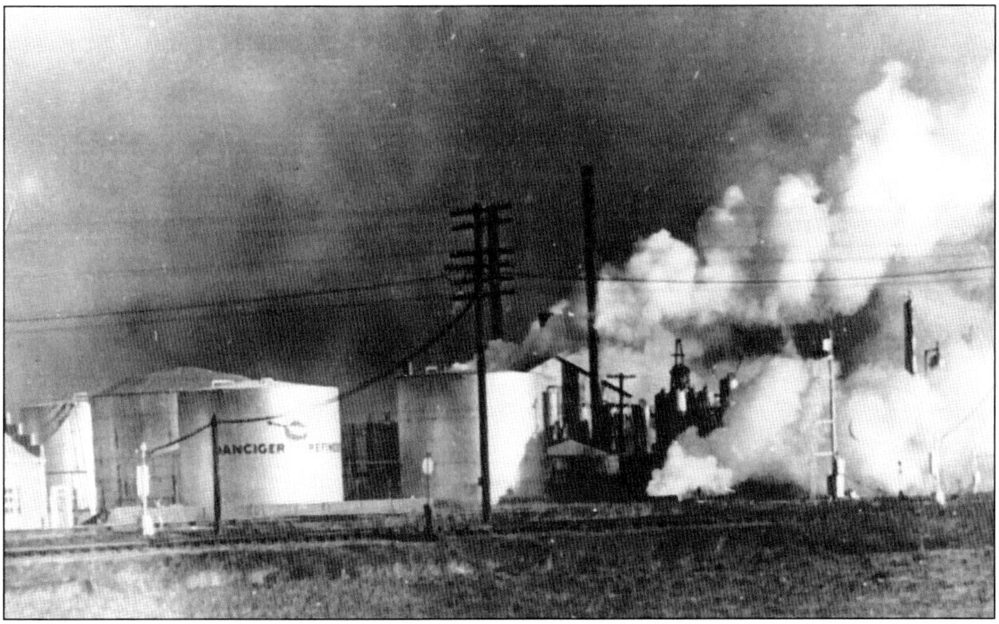

The Danciger Oil and Gas Refinery was east of Pampa. It employed 200 men and had a vast payroll. It could process 4,000 barrels of crude per day. The tanks at the refinery had a capacity of 340,000 barrels. During World War II, the refinery produced high-octane gasoline fuel for the B-25s at the Pampa Army Air Force Base as well as other military bases. The refinery closed down in 1946.

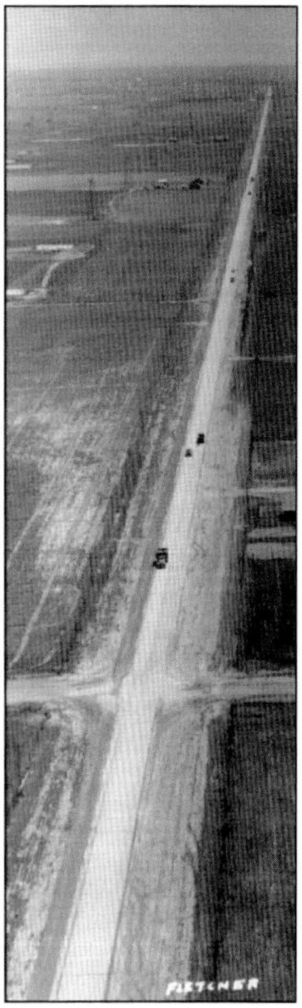

U.S. Highway 60 runs through Pampa and skirts much of the industry and the gasoline plants west of Pampa. This highway goes west into Amarillo and Albuquerque and east into Oklahoma City.

Cabot plants were built near Pampa in 1927 on U.S. Highway 60. The carbon black plant was purchased by Columbian Carbon. Columbian Carbon operated three carbon black plants in the Pampa area: the Coltexo, one on the Saunders lease, and the Kingsmill plant. These plants were significant to the Pampa economy for 60 years, but today no black emission plumes roll across Pampa. This is the mark of progress.

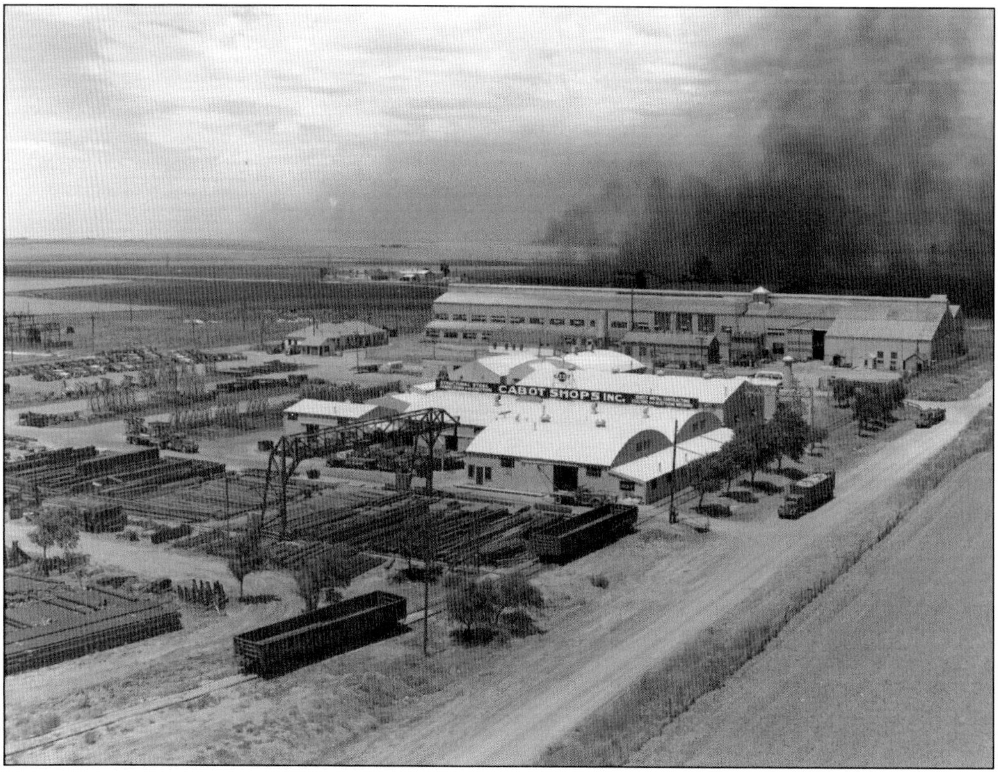

Another thing that came with the 1920s, besides the oil and gas discovery, was the wonderful Marcel wave. Ladies shortened their skirts, smoked cigarettes, cut off their hair, and permed it. This machine-made wave was the forerunner of today's cold waves, and it usually cost about $1 at a beauty shop.

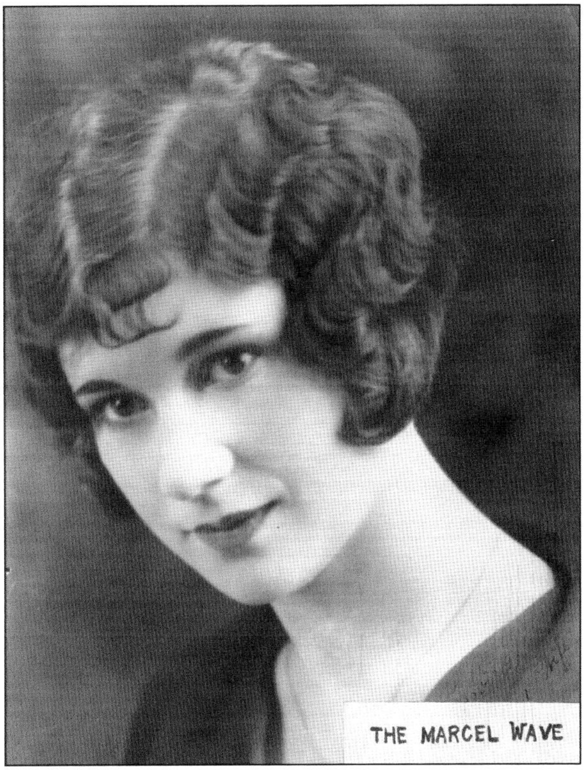

THE MARCEL WAVE

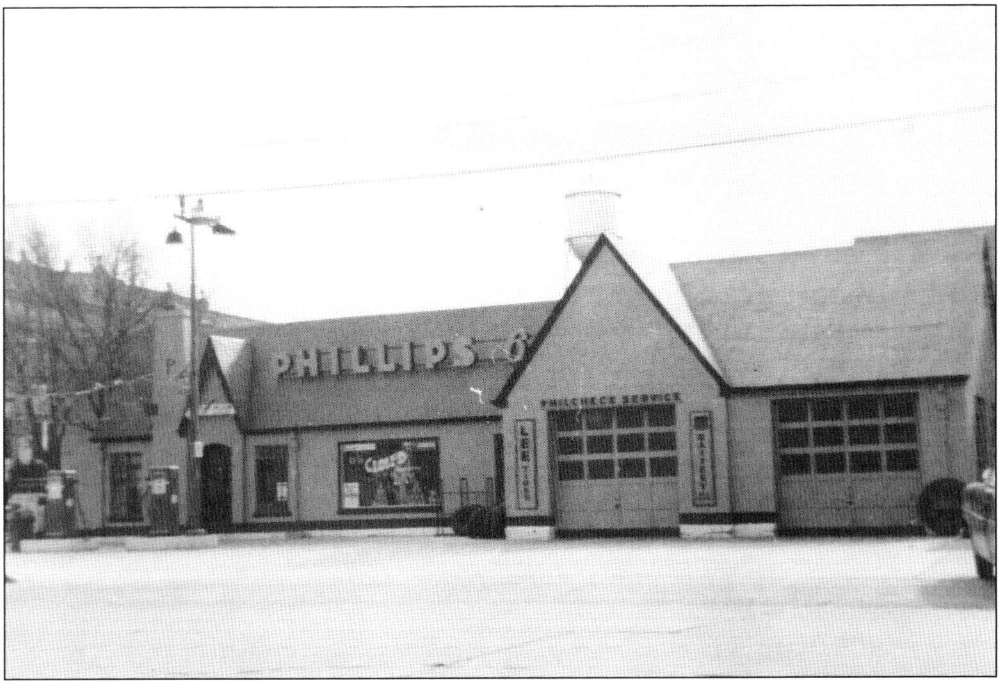

This was one of the Phillips 66 stations that appeared along the old Route 66. They were very plentiful on U.S. Highway 66, and many of them now have historical markers. This one in Pampa is now the law office of attorney Harold Comer at 301 W. Kingsmill Street.

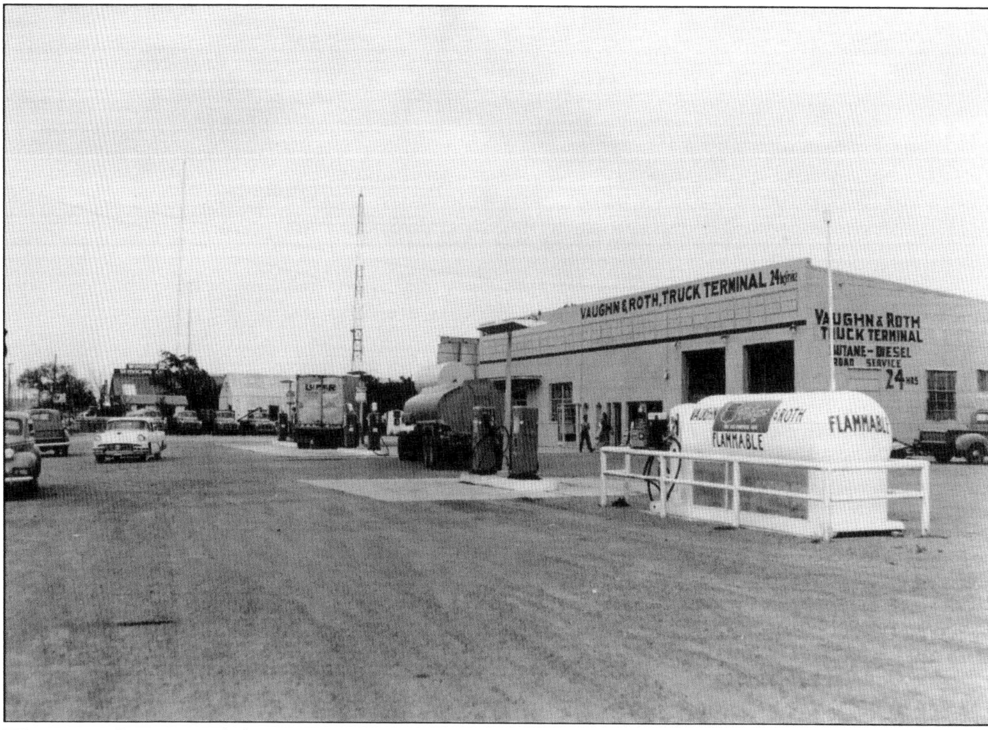

These truck terminals became a necessity when the oil fields were full of working men. They supplied tires, diesel, gasoline, and many truck parts.

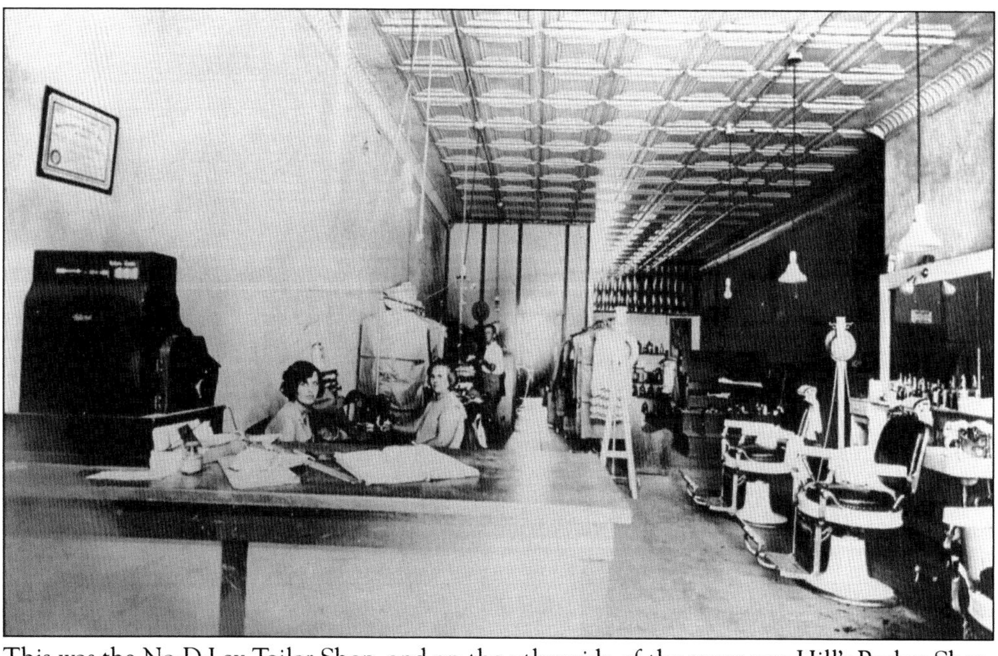

This was the No-D-Lay Tailor Shop, and on the other side of the room was Hill's Barber Shop. In 1929, this seemed to save on money.

Six

Ain't We Got Fun

Wherever people put down roots, they usually enjoy life and just have fun. As you can see by the street scenes in this book, life was not easy in this small Panhandle town, but locals found ways to celebrate everything. From dancing the waltz at retracted dances, playing ball, and racing horses, to the Fourth of July and Christmas, everybody loved the holidays and turned them into opportunities to spend time together.

By the 1930s, baseball was a favorite sport in the area. By 1939, a Class D league was formed, and in the next few years, they became the Pampa Oilers, a Class C West Texas-New Mexico League ball club. That ball team prospered for 16 seasons, breaking only for the war in 1942. Deck Woldt, an outstanding second baseman and shortstop, retired and still lives in Pampa. The club disbanded in 1957.

The Top O' Texas Rodeo became the largest amateur rodeo in the west. It started out as the "Top O' Texas Fiesta" and has earned its reputation as the Top O' Texas Rodeo for 64 years now. The parades have always been very unique and quite large. Floats and bands come from all over the state. Bob Wills and his brother Johnnie Lee Wills played at the rodeo dances for several years.

By the Depression years, Woody Guthrie had left Pampa and written, "So Long, It's Been Good To Know You." And the dust storms of the 1930s rolled in.

The Pampa High School Hall of Fame awardees are proof of the outstanding men and women who have been raised in Pampa. M. K. Brown Auditorium, a gift from Brown in 1972, is a beautiful building where citizens can enjoy a variety of entertainment throughout the year. Golf courses, swimming pools, the Youth Center, and some 35 parks combine to offer much more than the usual small town. Sports range from football to soccer to mud bogging. As for religion, there are some 55 churches in Pampa. Outstanding music programs in the schools and churches—along with community concerts, various art and dance programs, and even parades—add to the unusual quality of entertainment Pampans can enjoy.

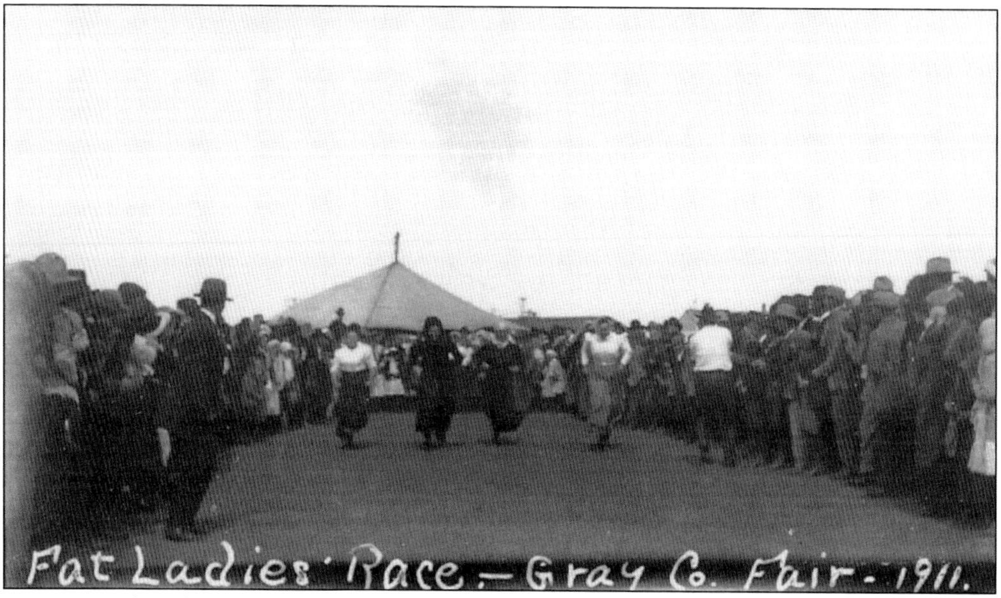

Someone's idea of fun was a "Fat Ladies Race." It appears that Pampa was hosting a fair in 1911. There were tents in the background where sweets and other goodies were being sold. Notice all the men watching this event.

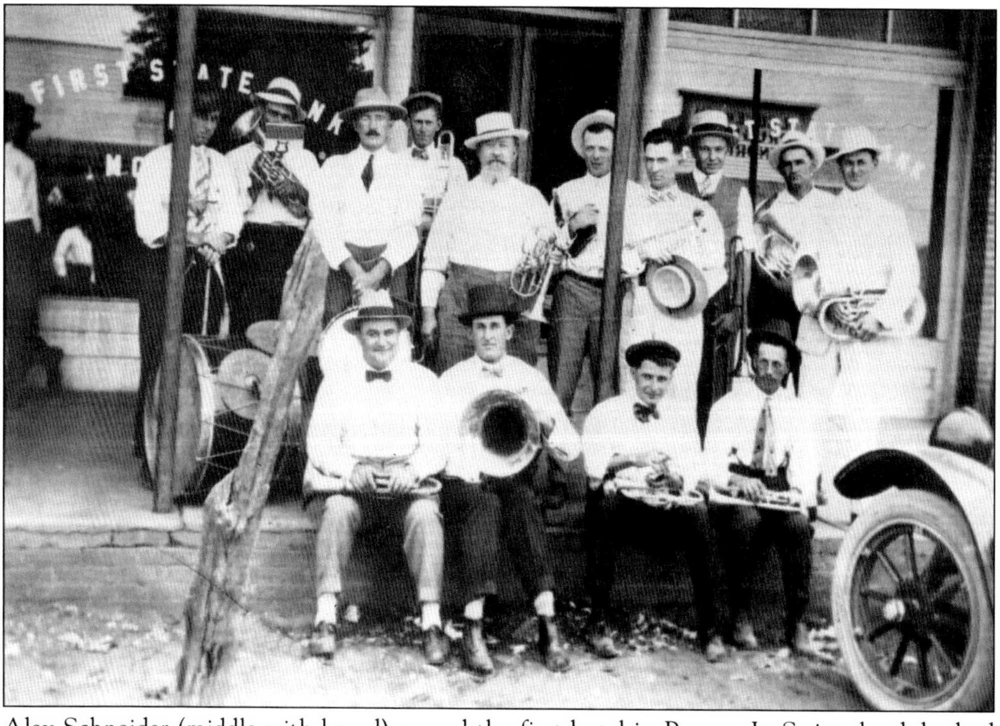

Alex Schneider (middle with beard) owned the first hotel in Pampa. In Switzerland, he had learned to play the trumpet, and his horn is in the White Deer Land Museum. The Schneider Band played for all the dances and concerts and on every street corner in town. In this picture in 1914, they were seated in front of the Mobeetie bank, advertising a chautauqua that was to be held in Pampa.

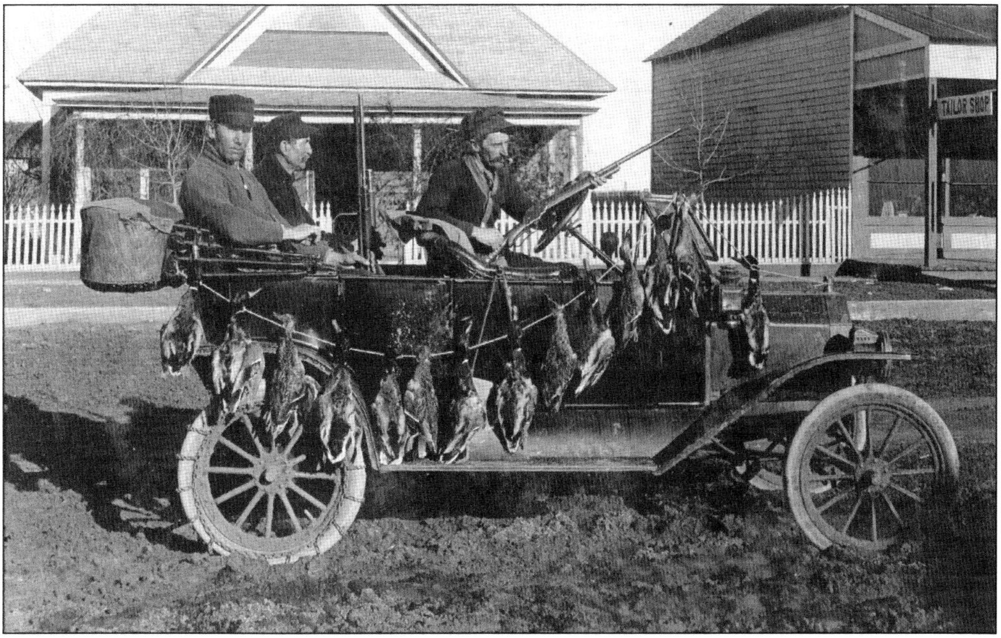

These gentlemen decided to go duck hunting in a 1907 Buick. They found 13 big ducks north of Pampa.

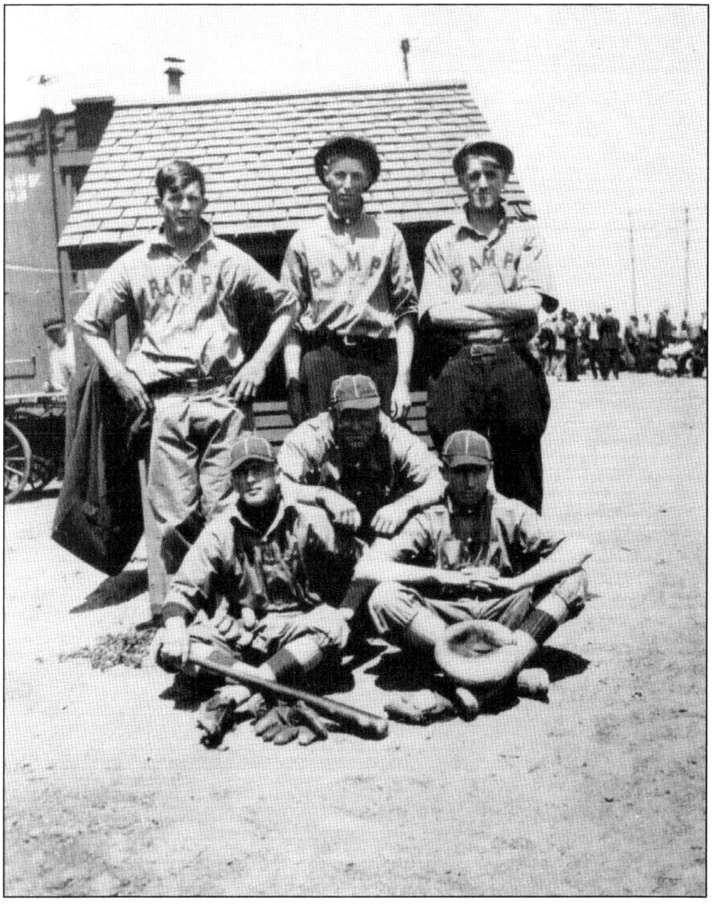

This was Pampa's first baseball team around 1915. Aren't they three short?

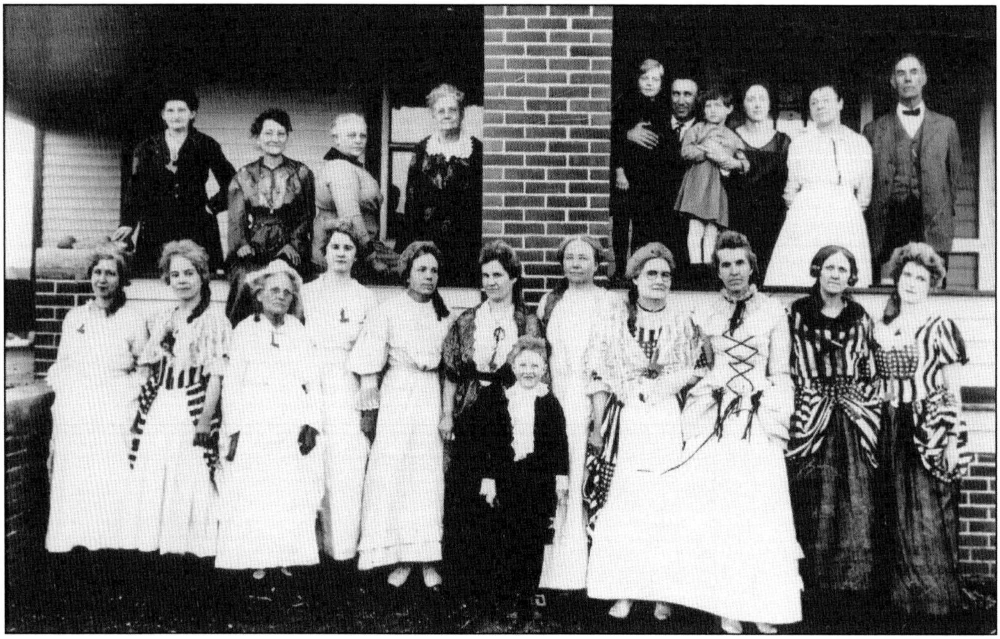

The guests at the Harold Lippold home were celebrating George Washington's birthday at a tea party on February 23, 1921, in Pampa. The ladies all dressed up like Martha Washington or wore patriotic costumes.

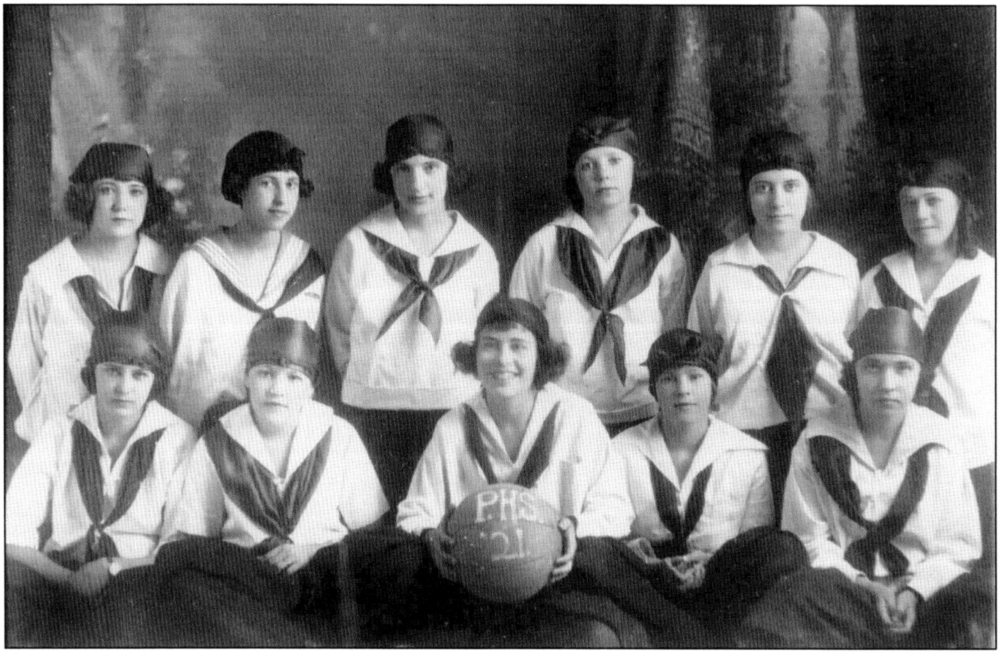

This is Pampa High School's first ladies basketball team. The girl holding the ball was Vera Cruz, stepdaughter of Pampa's first doctor, V. E. von Brunow. It looks like they all had the old Harvester spirit.

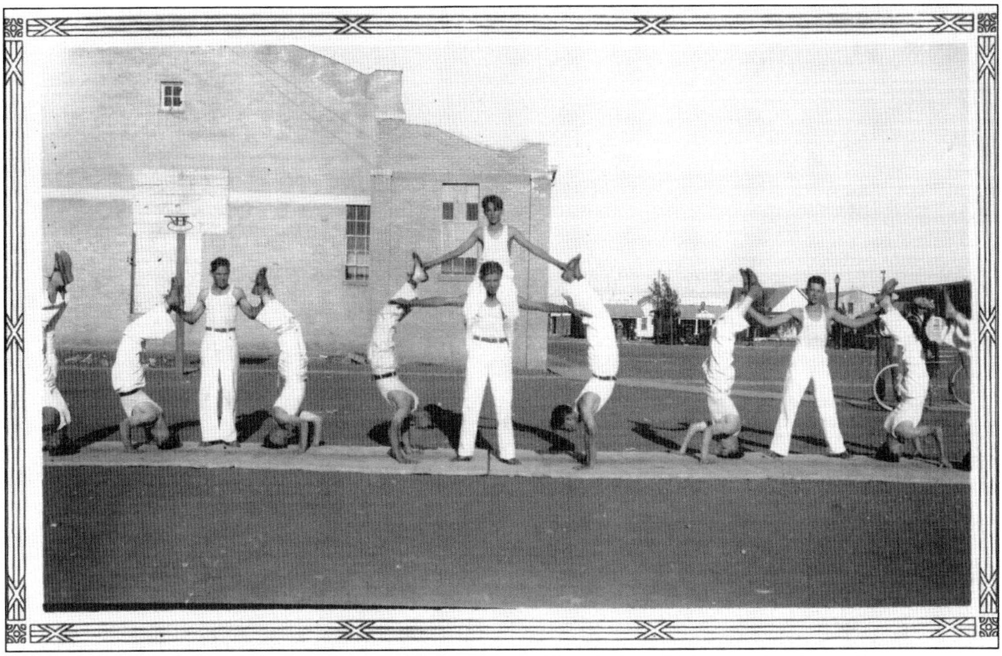

A boys' gymnastic class in 1930 shows off some tricks. That's the old high school gym behind them.

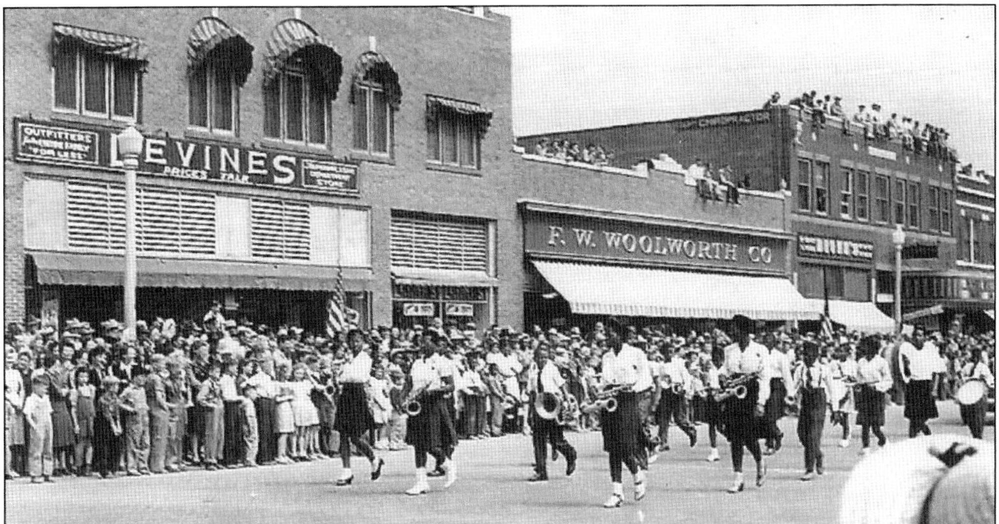

This was the band from the Hayden School in Pampa, built during the Depression. In 1950, it became Carver. Then in the 1960s, it was integrated with Pampa High School. This photograph was taken in the late 1940s at a parade on Pampa's main street.

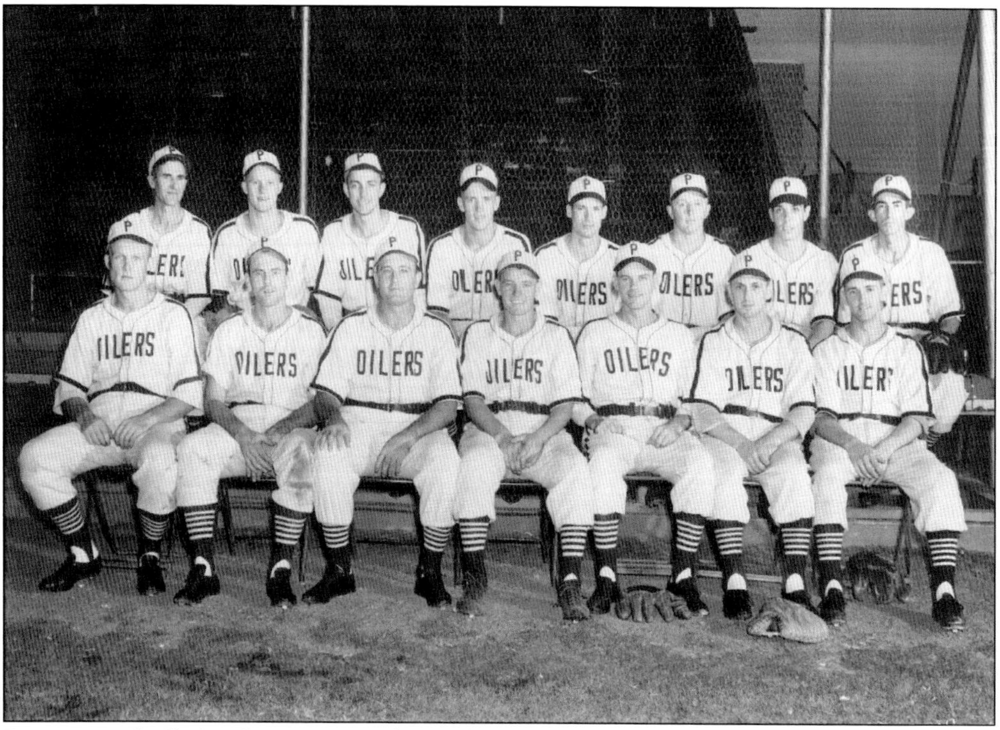

Pampa was thrilled to have a minor league ball team in the town. These were the champion Pampa Oilers. The West Texas-New Mexico League (WTNML) began as a class D league in 1937, and the Pampa Oilers were organized in 1940. The WTNML prospered for 16 seasons, breaking only for World War II in 1942. When play resumed, they moved up to Class C. With the onrush of television and live sports programming, the Oilers played their last game in 1957.

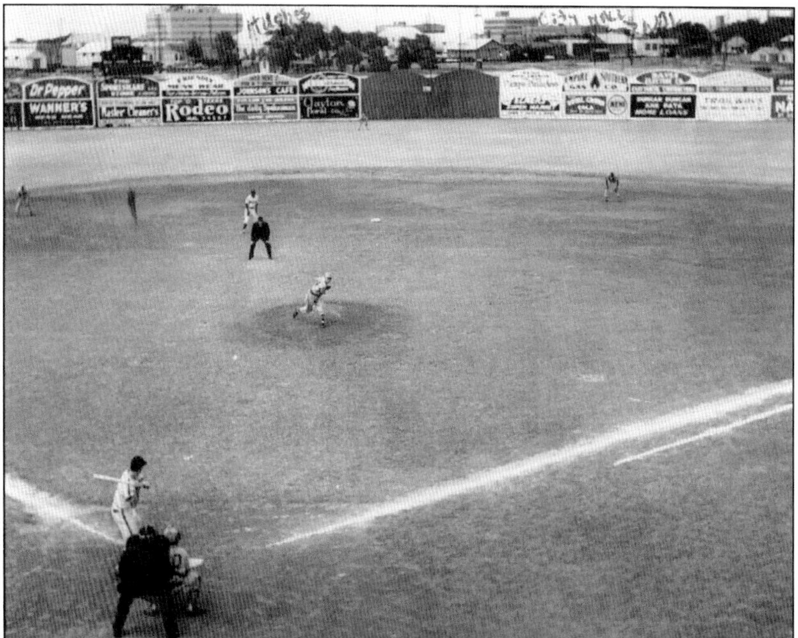

The Pampa Oilers' playing field was on Brown Street and was packed for every home game. After the last game, the bleachers were moved to the Top O' Texas Rodeo arena.

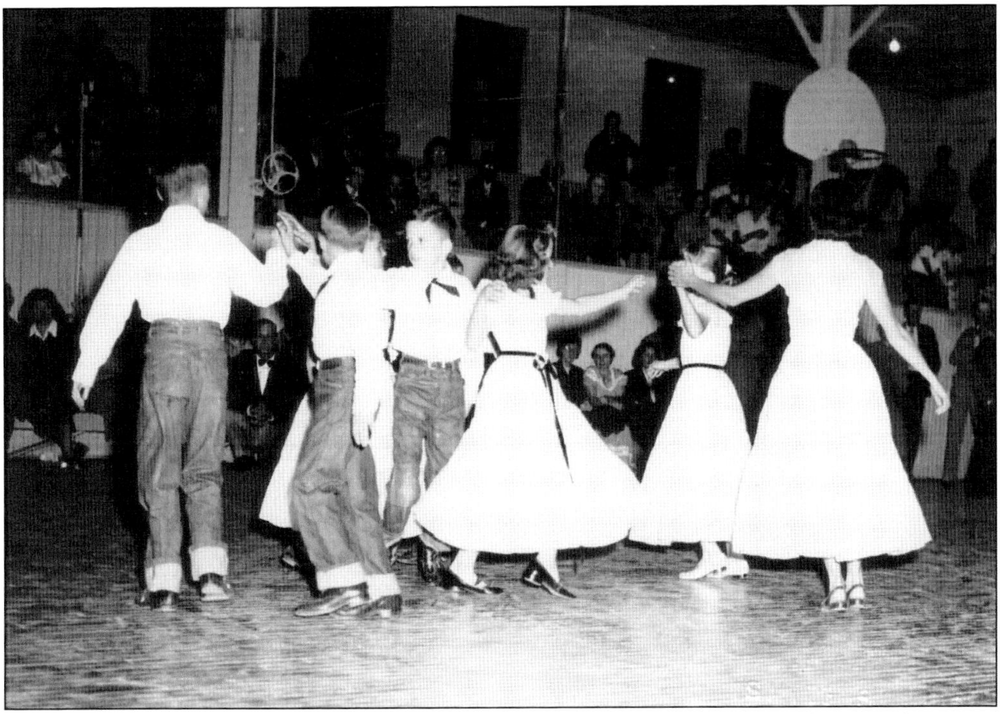

Gray County celebrated its 50th birthday in 1952, and its citizen were having fun. People square-danced and round-danced all night in the school gym.

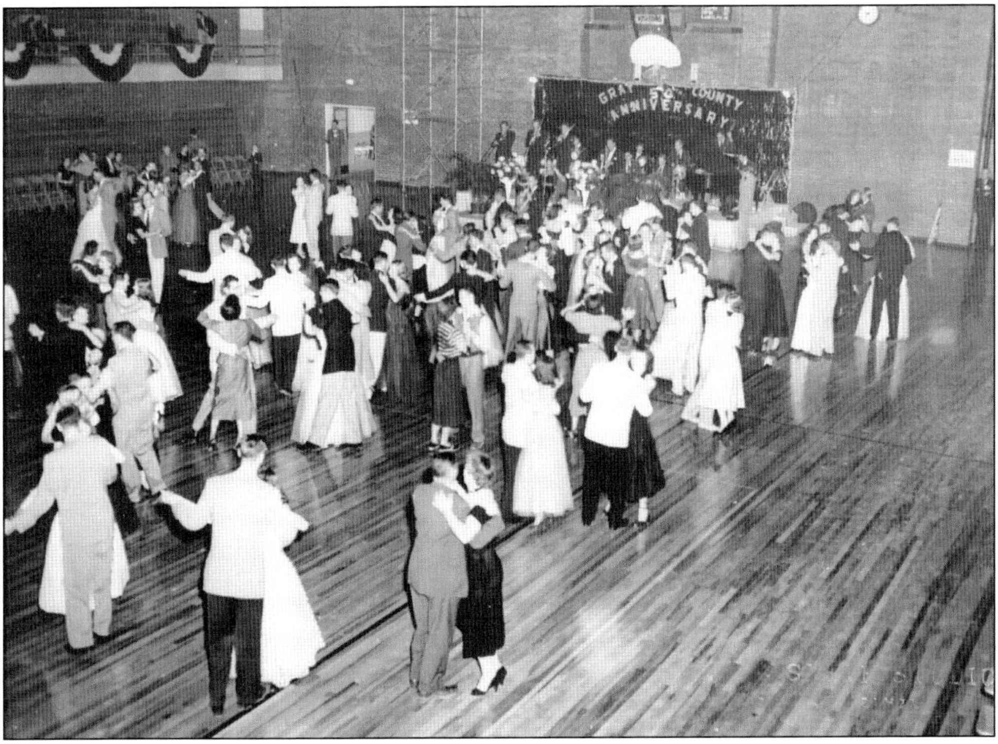

The crowd danced the night away to the Hal Mcintyre Orchestra.

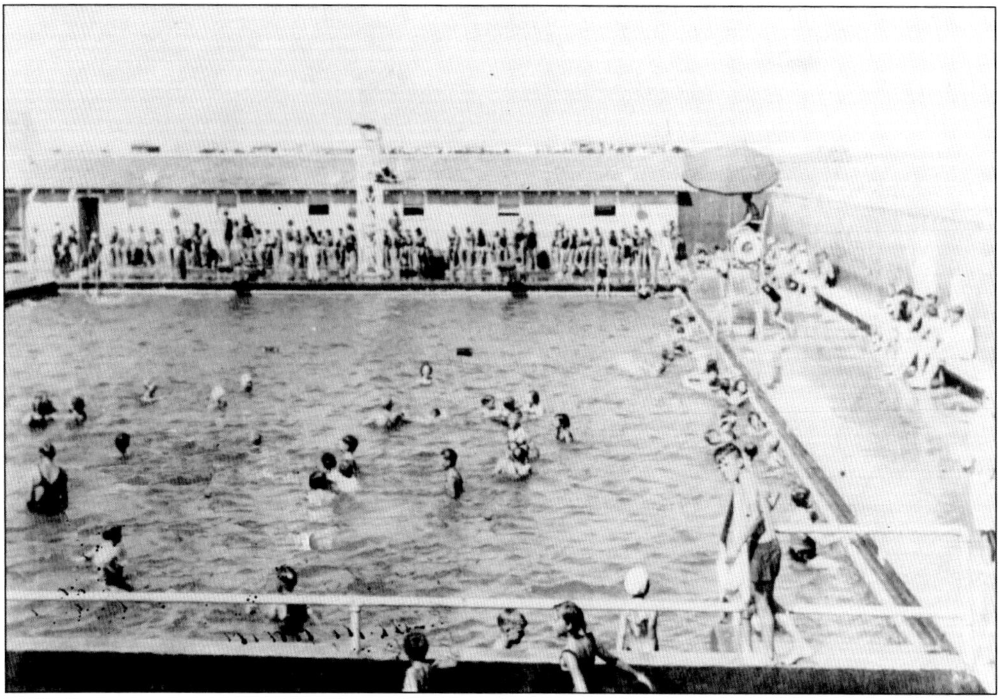

M. K. Brown, comanager of the White Deer Land Company, built a city swimming pool for Pampa kids in the 1930s. It has been remodeled and enlarged twice, but it is still in the same location. Pampa is now planning a new aquatic center for all ages.

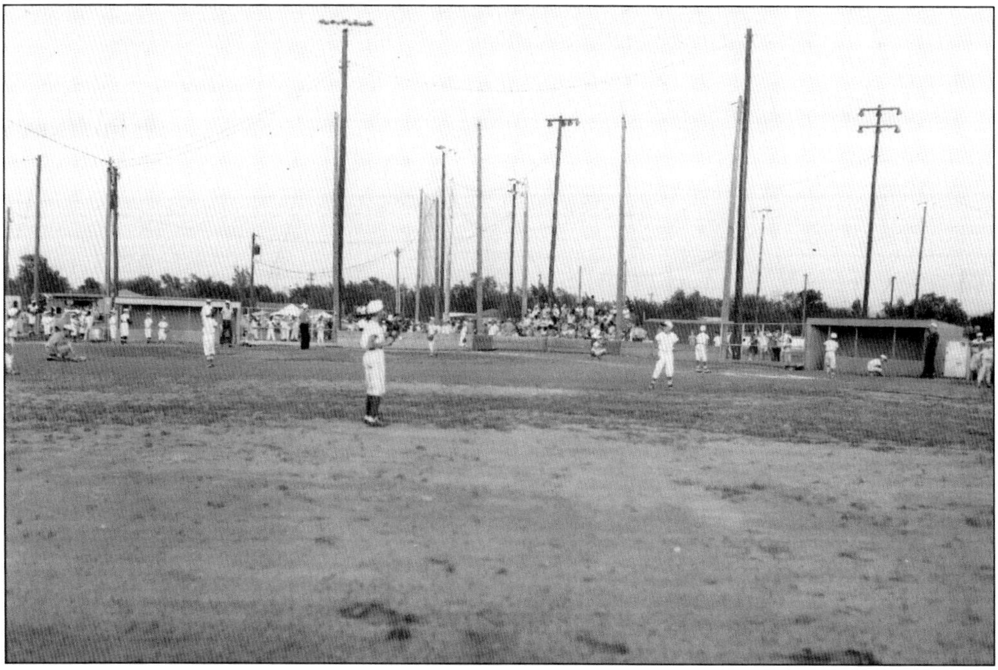

M. K. Brown is also the person who helped build the Pampa Optimist Club ballpark for kids. He had a great love for young people and awarded many grants for education. His foundation is still giving scholarships.

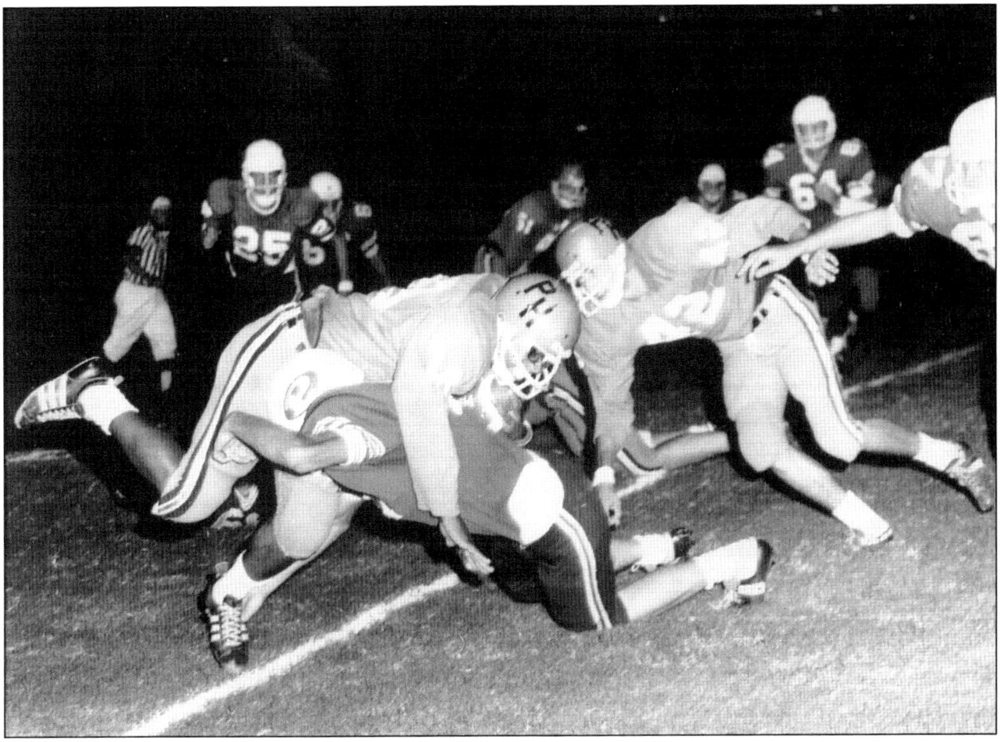

This is the fighting green and gold Harvester football team from Pampa High School. These kids have enjoyed the support of the whole community for many years. They have good coaches, great spirits, and they really enjoy the sport.

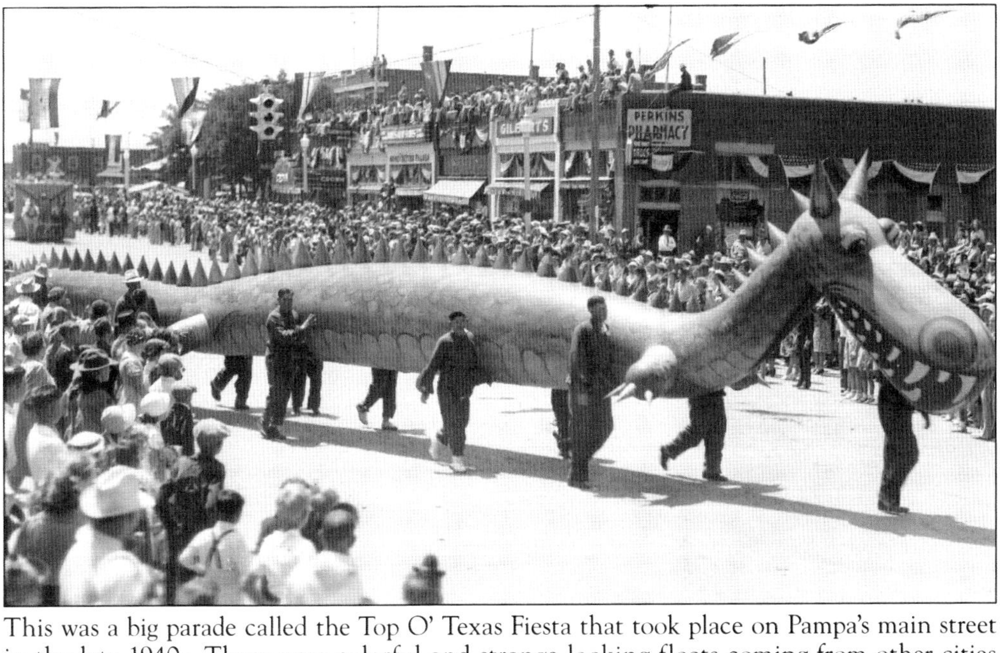

This was a big parade called the Top O' Texas Fiesta that took place on Pampa's main street in the late 1940s. There were colorful and strange looking floats coming from other cities to participate.

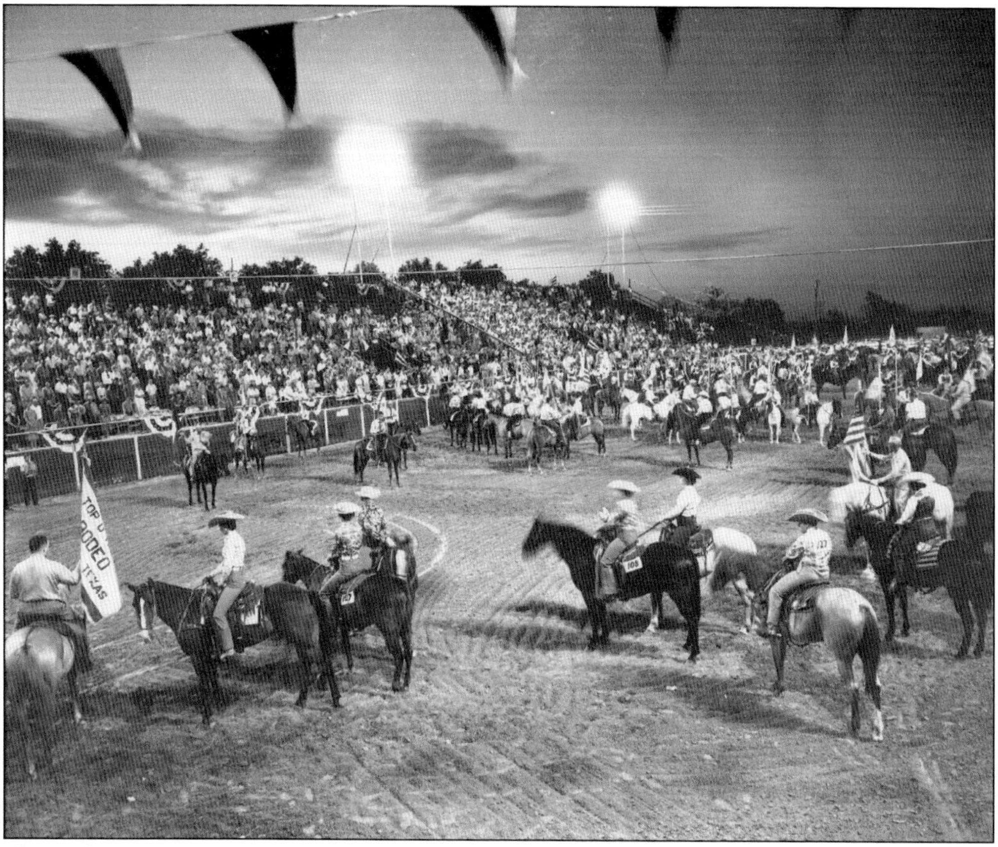

This is the opening ceremony of the famous Top O' Texas Rodeo and Kid Pony Show. It is called the grand entry, where every horse and performer is in the arena at the same time and the flags and national anthem are honored. Pampa had the largest amateur rodeo in the United States until it went professional in 1962. It has now gone back to its amateur status. Some of the best in their events have been in Pampa. World-class bull riders, bareback and saddle bronc riders, barrel racers, and calf ropers have been in the money at Pampa.

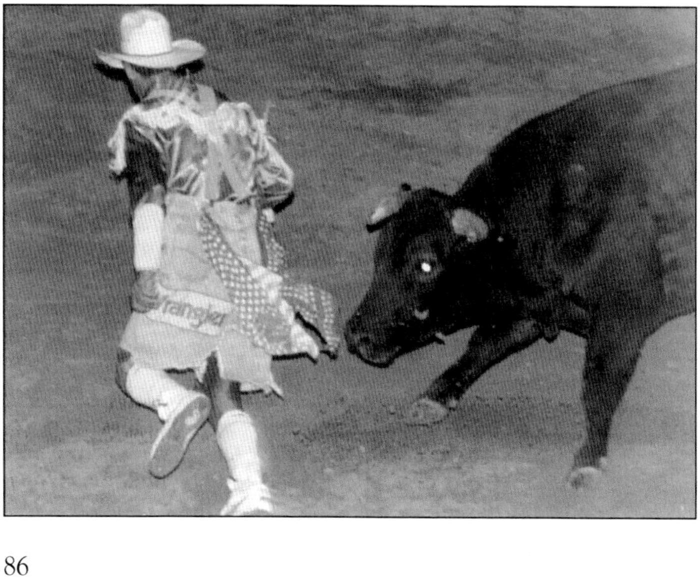

A good rodeo clown saves many cowboys a lot of grief.

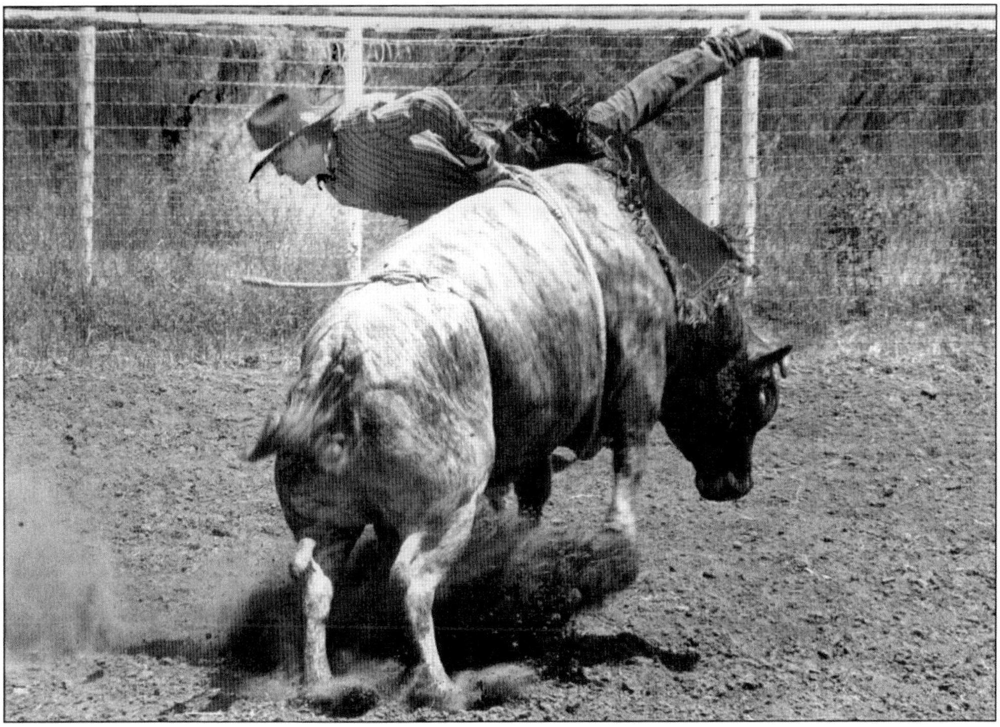

A bull rider braces himself for a nasty fall.

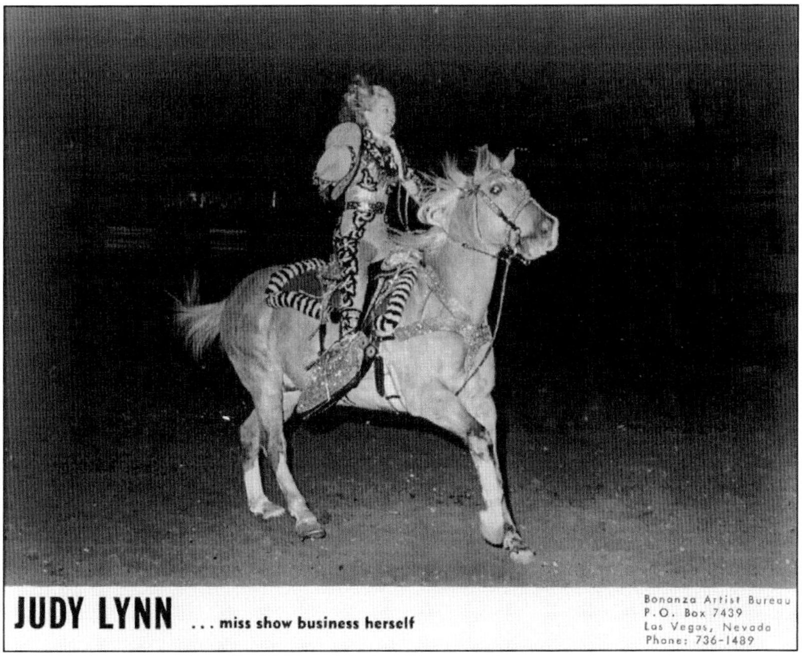

Judy Lynn was a singer and entertainer who came to Pampa for several rodeos. She was called "Miss Show Business Herself." She was a good horsewoman and sang a top-notch country song.

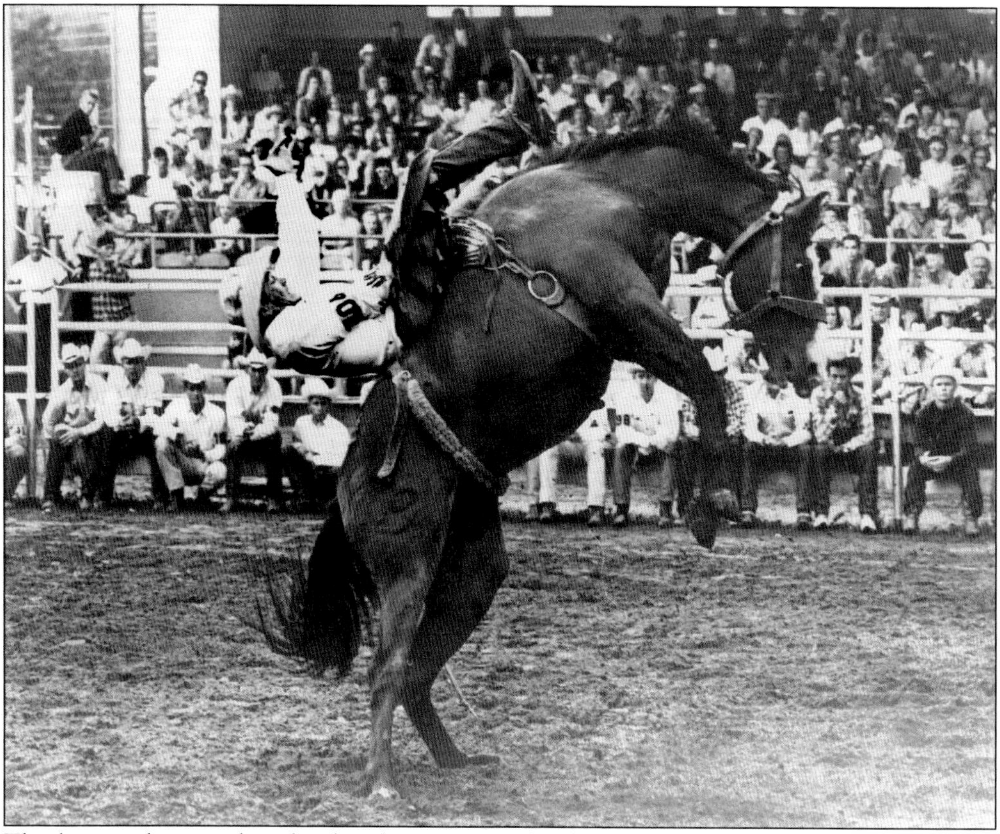

This bronc rider is working hard at the Pampa Rodeo, but it looks like it's too late.

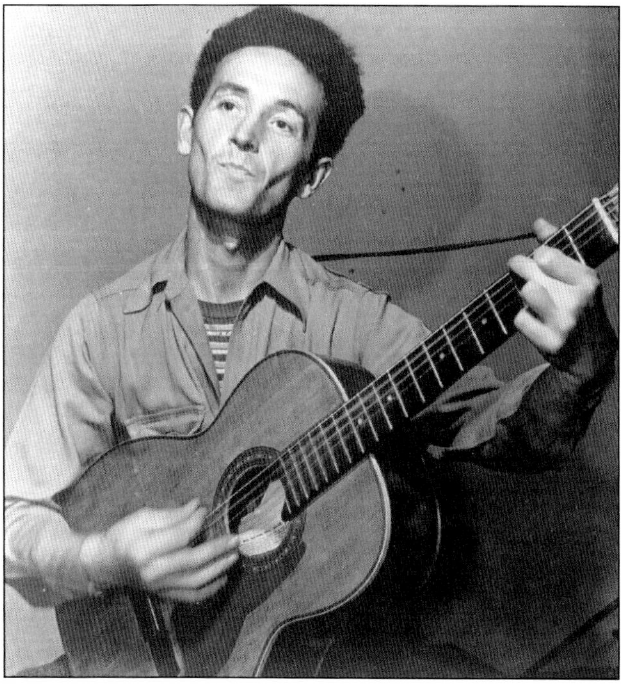

Woody Guthrie, folk singer, came to the area during the Depression days. He just drifted in because his father worked in Pampa. It was said that he came with a guitar and clothes in a paper sack. He was a kid who painted, read books, wrote songs, and rode the rails. He achieved national prominence in the 1930s writing songs about the dust bowl and the workingman. Guthrie died in New York in 1967.

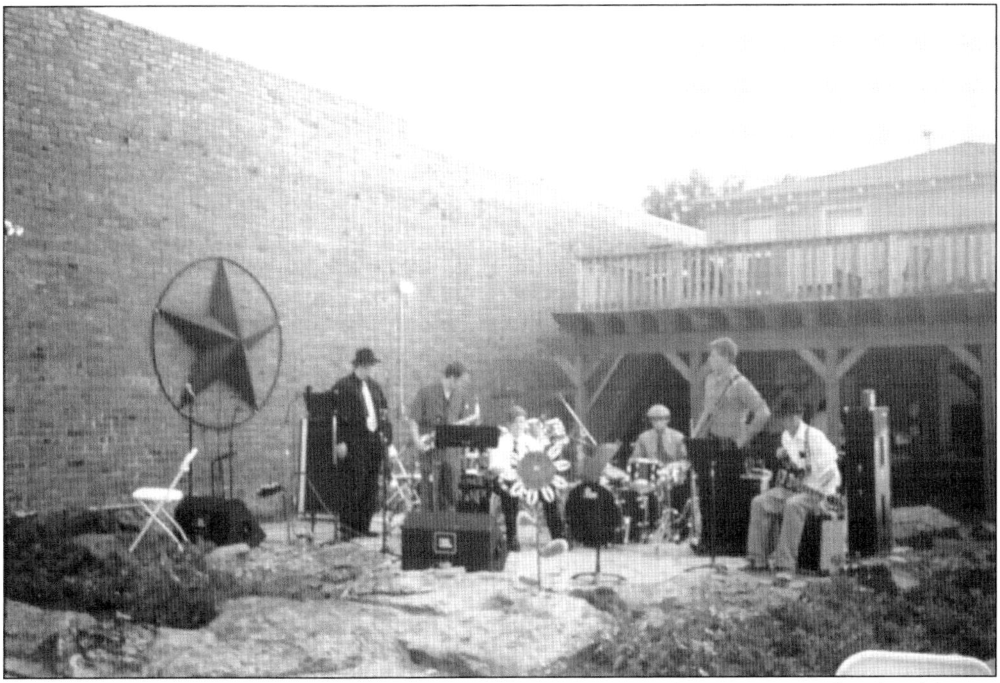

At the Woody Guthrie Folk Music Center every October, Woody's life is recognized with celebrities and jamming sessions. Some sessions are held in front of a beautiful inn in Pampa near the old Harris Drug Store where Woody worked as a teenager.

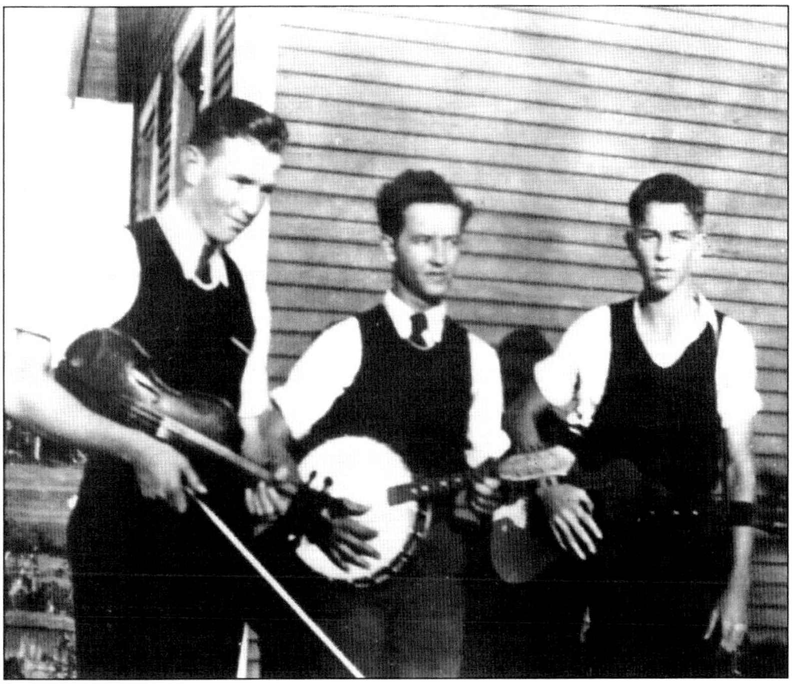

Woody Guthrie's first band in Pampa was comprised of Matt Jennings (left), Woody (center), and Cluster Baker. Jennings later became Woody's brother-in-law. This photograph was taken during the Depression, when times were really tough.

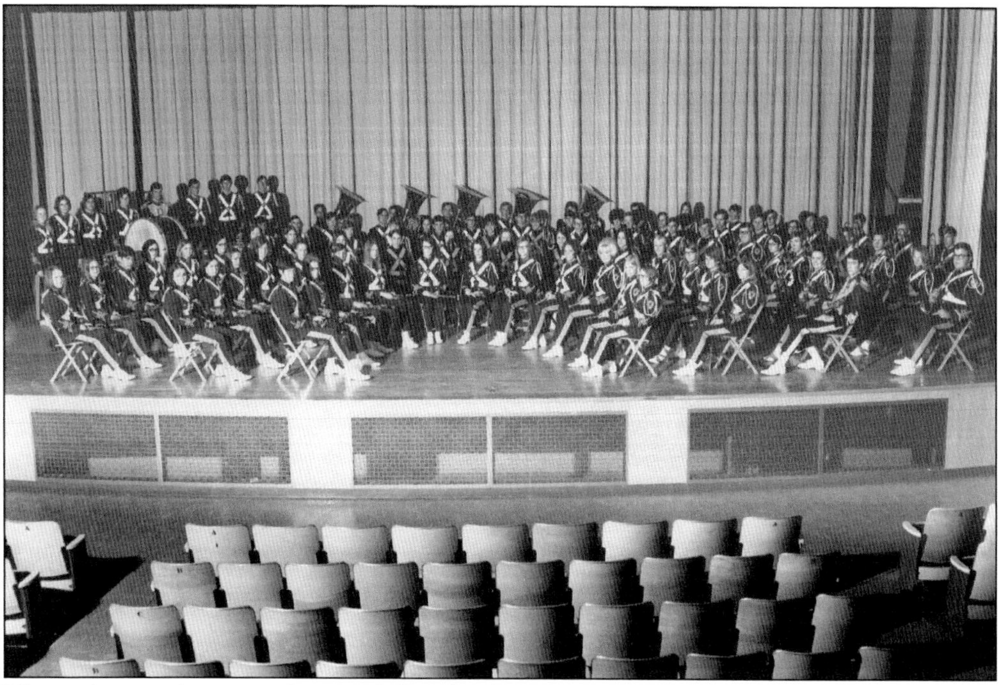

This is the award-winning Pampa High School Harvester band in concert. This band is called the "Pride of Pampa" and has won competitions in Ireland, Hawaii, and in the Tournament of Roses Parade in California. They looked pretty sharp in their tall, white cowboy boots, and they made Pampans really proud.

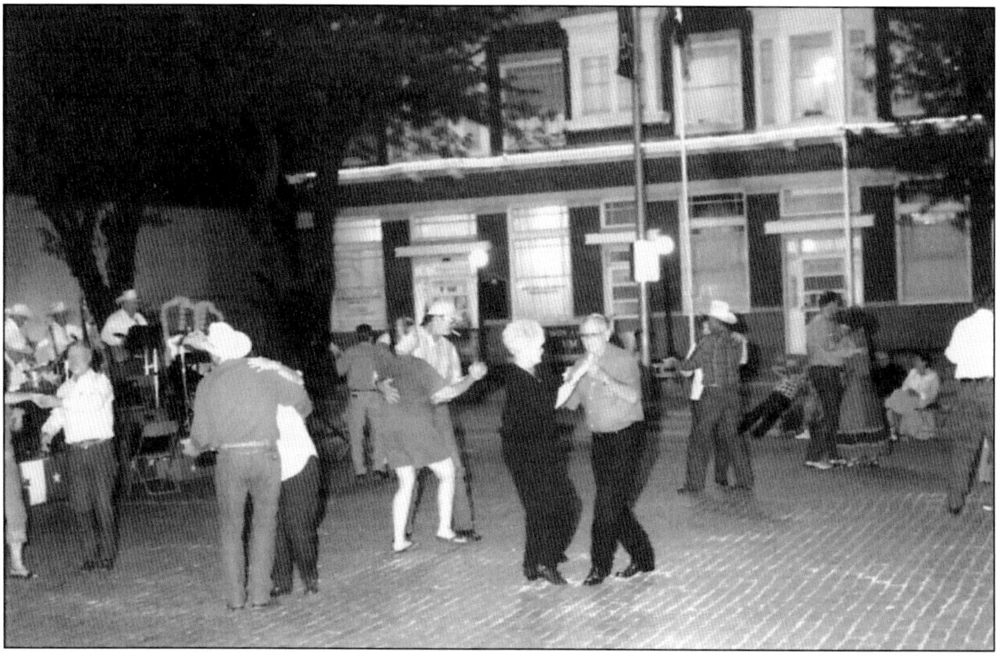

The White Deer Land Museum Foundation holds a street dance as a fund-raiser most years. This one was held in front of the museum on a beautiful night in August. Notice the brick street the dancers are using.

Virginia "Ginny" Simms was a big band singer in the 1940s. Her father opened the first restaurant in Pampa, called the Confectionary, in 1906 on the main street. He was proud of Ginny when she was singing with Kay Kaiser, Les Brown, and Tommy Dorsey. She made movies with Gary Grant and Edgar Bergen. Ginny married, had two children, and retired to Hawaii, where she died.

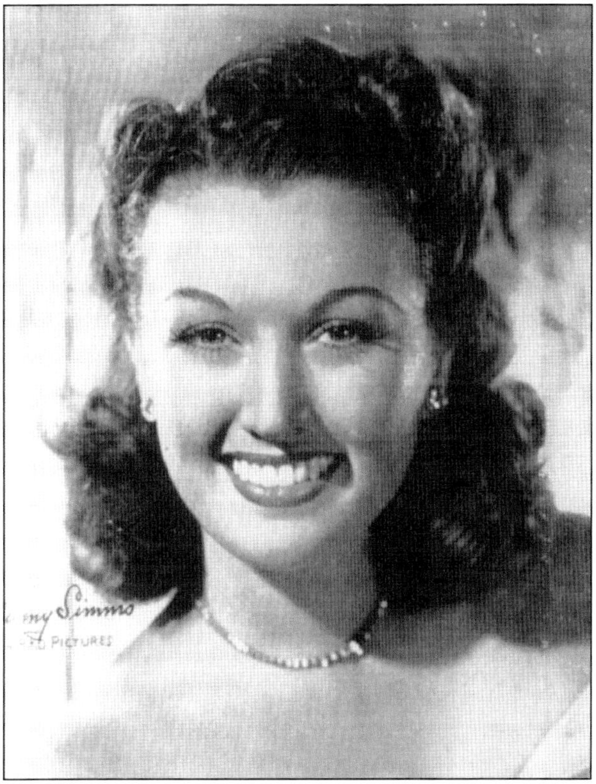

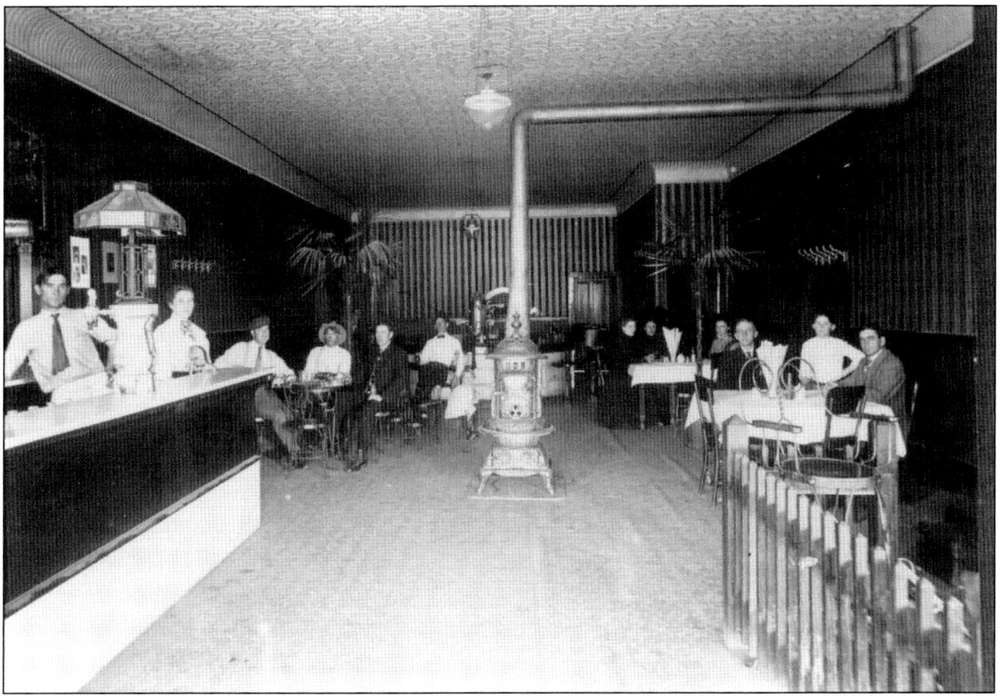

The Confectionary, owned by Ginny Simms' dad, Dormer Simms, was on the main street. It was said to have been a very elegant place to dine in 1910.

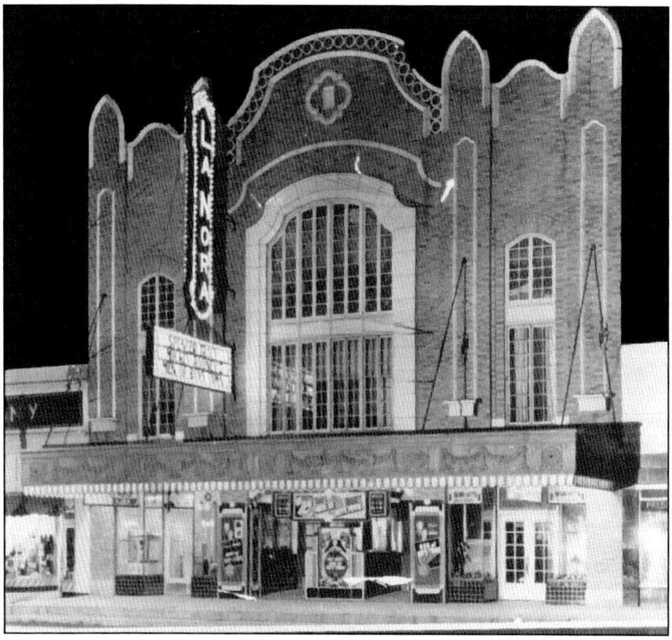

This LaNora Theatre burned to the ground in 1959, and Pampans have never forgotten it. It was said to have been the largest fire ever fought in the town. It was constructed in 1931, and the builder named the theater after his wife. It was such a beautiful theater, and citizens gathered there more than at any place. It had opera seats, velvet curtains, and a lovely cry room for babies, and a theater in Pampa has never been built since that matched its beauty. Pampa has had eight or nine movie houses, but none ever like this one.

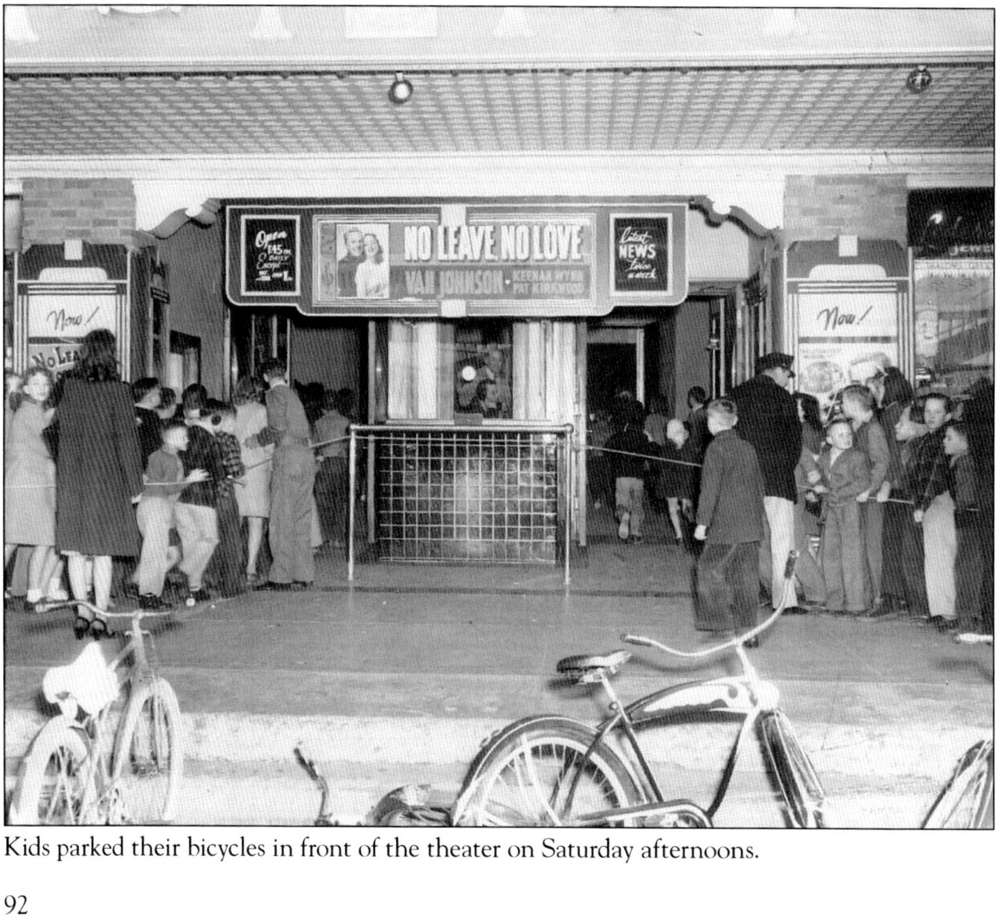

Kids parked their bicycles in front of the theater on Saturday afternoons.

Seven

TEXAS LAW ENFORCEMENT

Texas has always been famous for its law and lawmen. The state has constables, marshalls, and sheriffs, and Gray County has had 16 sheriffs since 1902. The first sheriff was J. T. Crawford, who served at the first courthouse in Lefors. Number 12 was R. H. "Rufe" Jordan, who sat at the same desk in the Gray County courthouse for 42 years. The Texas Department of Corrections (TDC) prison, located east of Pampa, is named the Jordan Unit. One of the area's finest Texas Rangers, Bill Baten, was stationed in Pampa for many years. The adjoining TDC Intermediate Sanction Facility is called the Baten Unit.

Two women, Mrs. C. E. (Violet) Pipes in 1934 and Mrs. Earl (Roberta) Talley in 1938, have served as sheriffs when their husbands died in office.

One colorful sheriff was Cal Rose, who was elected in 1939. An incident at the Southern Club occurred and Constable Otis Hendrix was killed. Sheriff Rose was called before the grand jury in Hendrix's death but, for lack of evidence, was not charged. Each sheriff lived in the courthouse apartment on the fourth floor, except the last three.

E. S. Graves, another former Gray County sheriff, was serving the last of his term in 1927 when the First National Bank of Pampa was robbed. On the morning of March 31, 1927, Blackie Thompson parked a seven-passenger Buick on the south side of the bank. Matthew Kimes and Whitely Walker entered a moment later. Ace Pendleton came in last. By the time they were ready to leave, 30 people had been held either at gunpoint or in the vault. It took 10–20 minutes, and the robbers left with $35,000. While heading west, they killed two officers at a roadblock.

Ace Pendleton was the only man brought back to Pampa. No one would testify against him because his friends were still at large. Blackie Thompson was killed later in a wheat field during a shoot-out with Amarillo officers, and Whitey Walker was shot down over the prison wall in Huntsville, Texas, escaping in 1934. Rufe Jordan, son of the officer guarding Pendleton and a future Gray County sheriff, was 15 years old when those men robbed the Pampa bank.

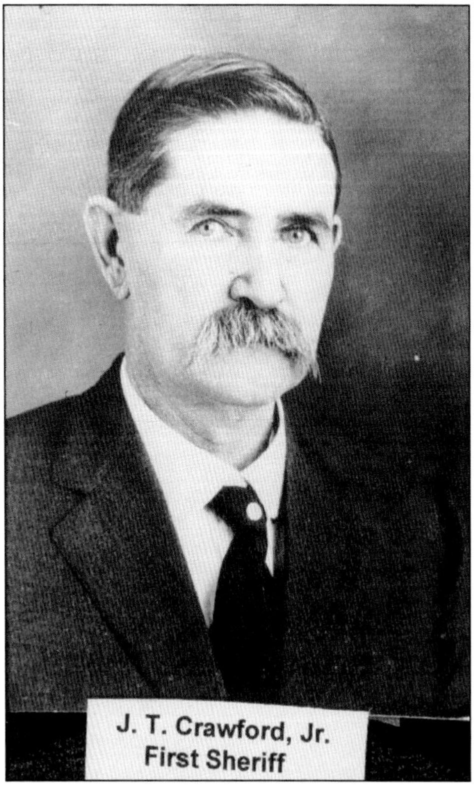

J. T. Crawford was the first sheriff elected in Gray County in 1902. His office was in the county seat in Lefors. He arrived in this territory in 1892.

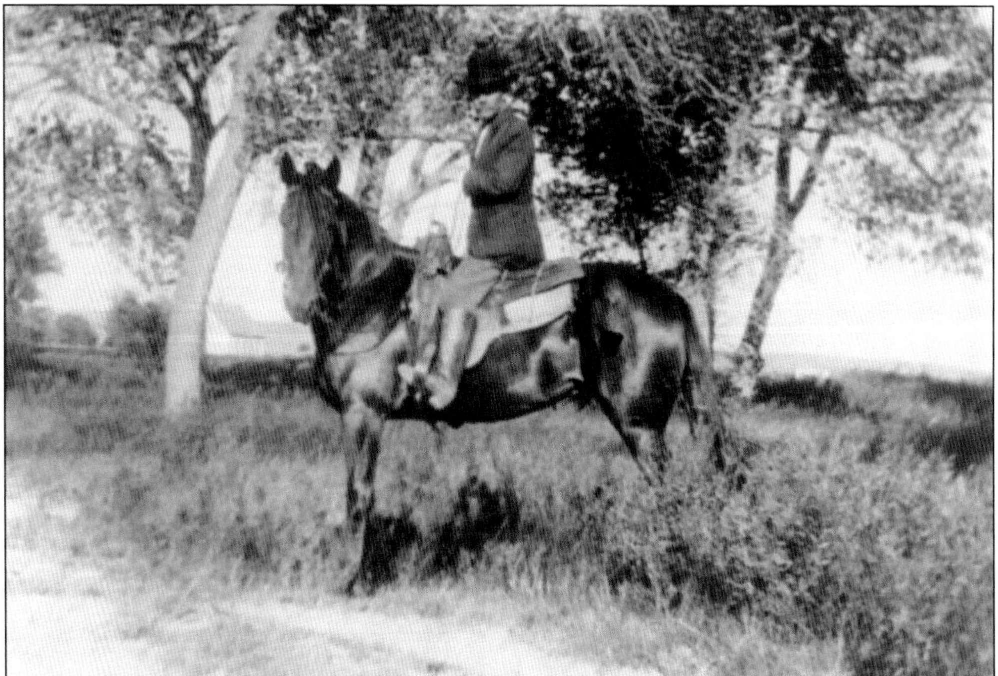

The fourth sheriff of this county was W. S. Copeland. He campaigned on his beloved horse, Ribbon, in 1914. E. S. Graves defeated him in 1920.

By 1915, the Pampa city fathers needed more law enforcement. They hired a man to come and freelance. He was called a "town tamer." His name was C. S. "Jake" Farrer. He killed a man on the main street. This photograph is the indictment for murder against Jake Ferrar. The outcome is unknown. He was either not billed or the jury found him not guilty. He left Pampa for Arizona.

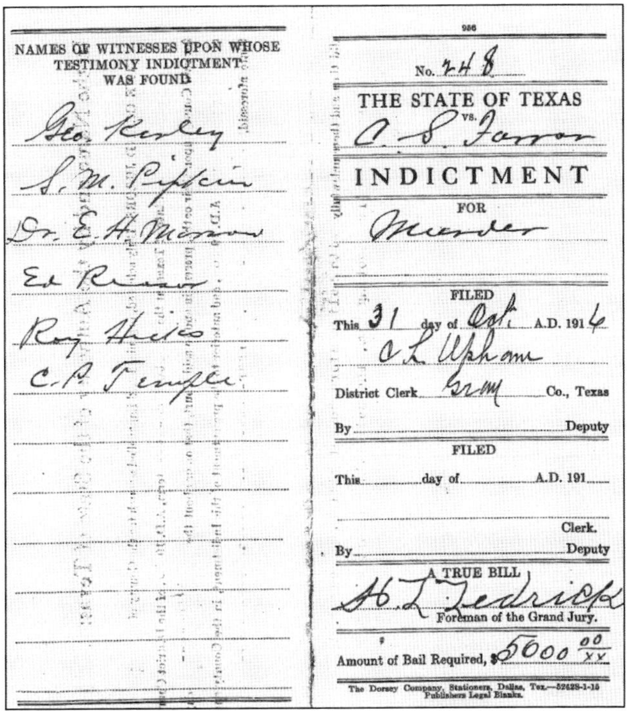

986

NAMES OF WITNESSES UPON WHOSE TESTIMONY INDICTMENT WAS FOUND

Geo. Kirley
S. M. Piffin
Dr. E. H. Moran
Ed Rima
Roy Hicks
C. P. Temple

No. 248

THE STATE OF TEXAS
vs.
C. S. Farrar

INDICTMENT
FOR
Murder

FILED
This 31 day of Oct. A.D. 1914
C. L. Upham
District Clerk Gray Co., Texas
By .... Deputy

FILED
This .... day of .... A.D. 191....
.... Clerk.
By .... Deputy

A TRUE BILL
H. L. Ledrick
Foreman of the Grand Jury.

Amount of Bail Required, $5000 00/xx

The Dorsey Company, Stationers, Dallas, Tex.—52428-1-15 Publishers Legal Blanks.

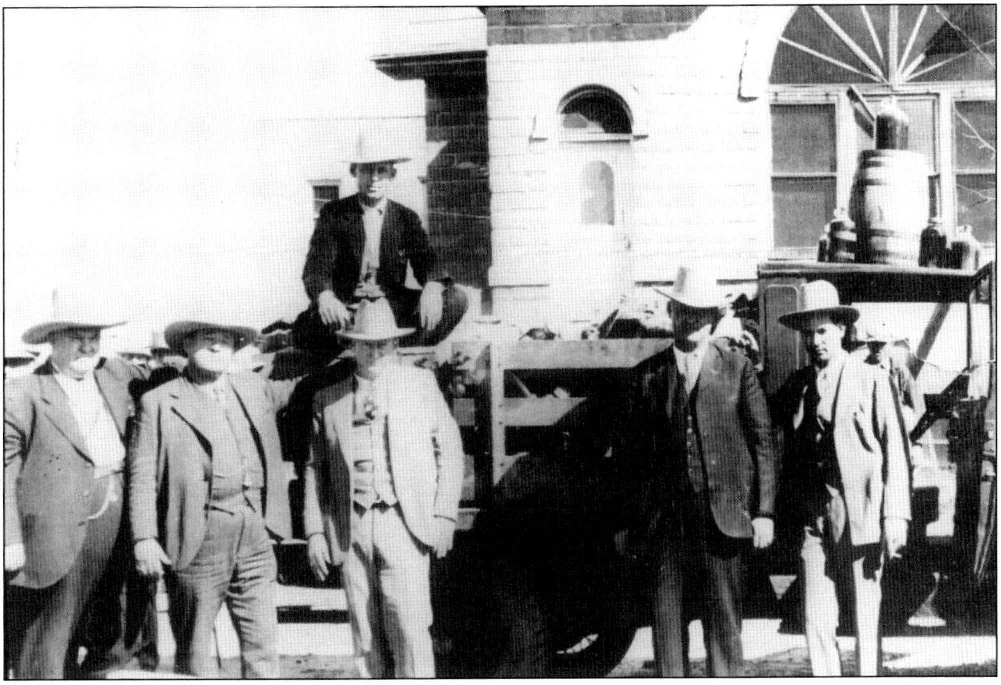

Sheriff E. S. Graves (second from left) had been elected in 1920. The first man on the left is Deputy Tiny Pipes, a former Texas Ranger. Sheriff Graves and deputies had confiscated booze and closed the stills. It was late 1927, and Gray County was dry. Pipes and Graves wore the classic Tom Mix–style hats. The old First Baptist Church, in the background, served as the courthouse until the new one was completed.

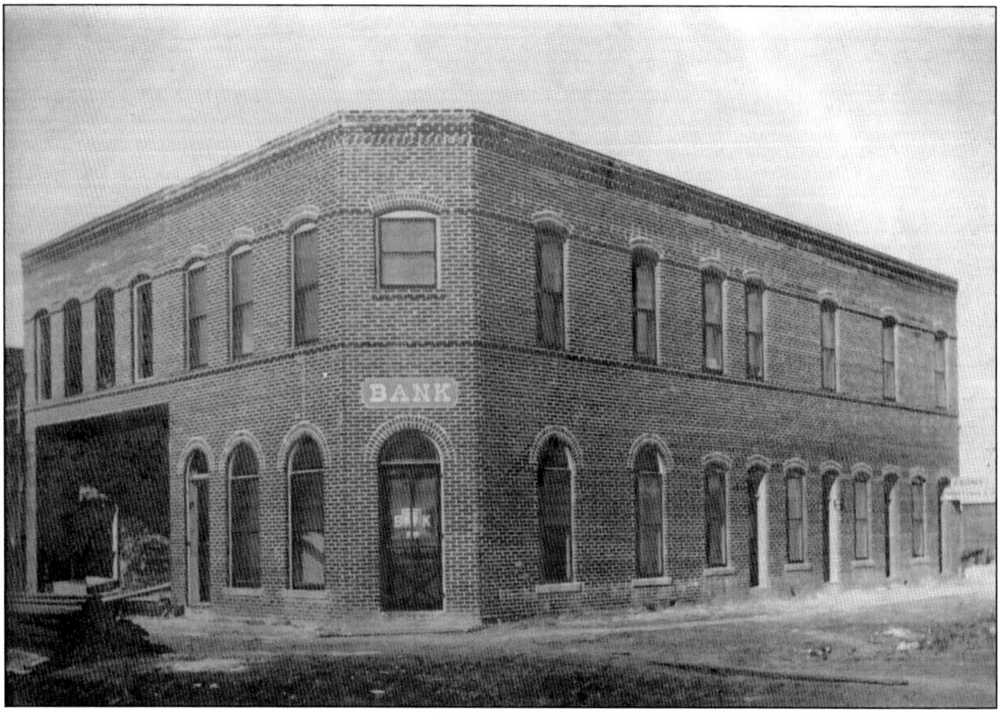

This was the First National Bank at 100 North Cuyler Street in Pampa. It was under construction in 1907. The building still stands here but has been remodeled and is now a Bank of America.

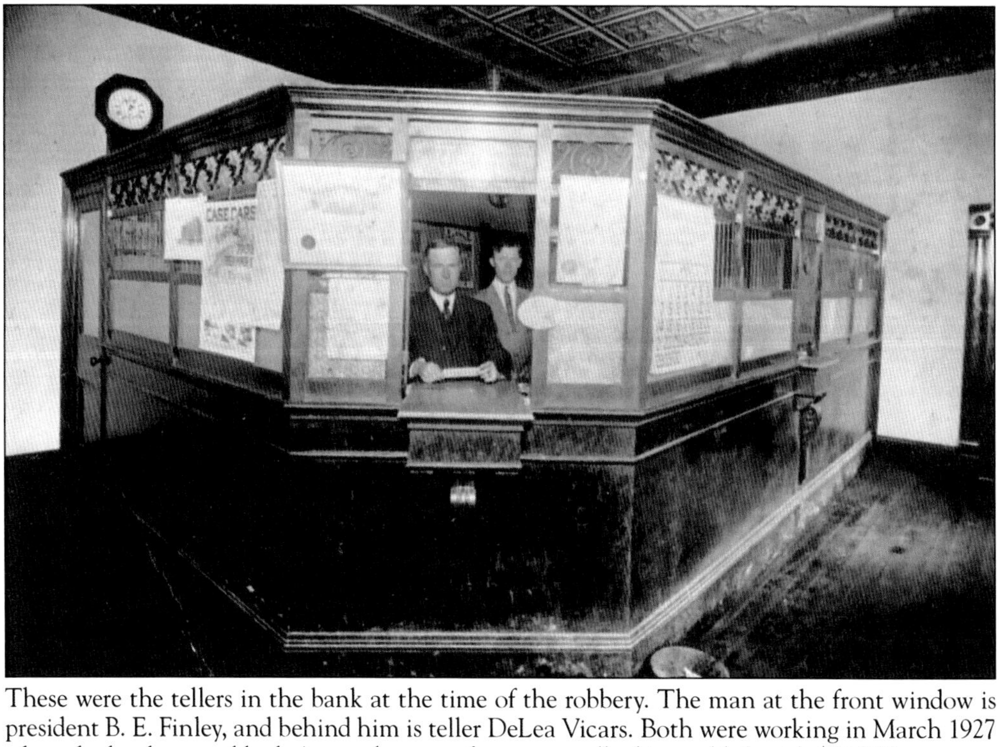

These were the tellers in the bank at the time of the robbery. The man at the front window is president B. E. Finley, and behind him is teller DeLea Vicars. Both were working in March 1927 when the bank was robbed. At nearly noon, four men walked in and left with $35,000.

This is a photograph of one of the Pampa bank robbers, Whitey Walker (21283) of the Cotton Top gang. He went to the penitentiary for another crime and was killed trying to escape. (Photograph courtesy of the Dallas Library.)

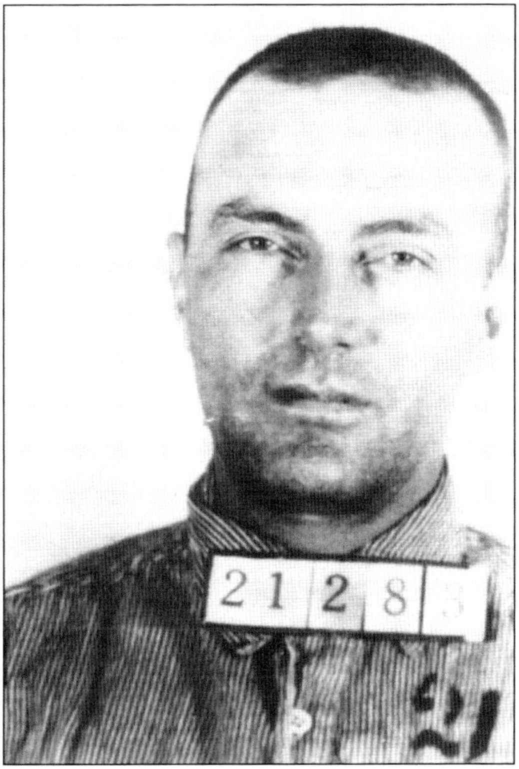

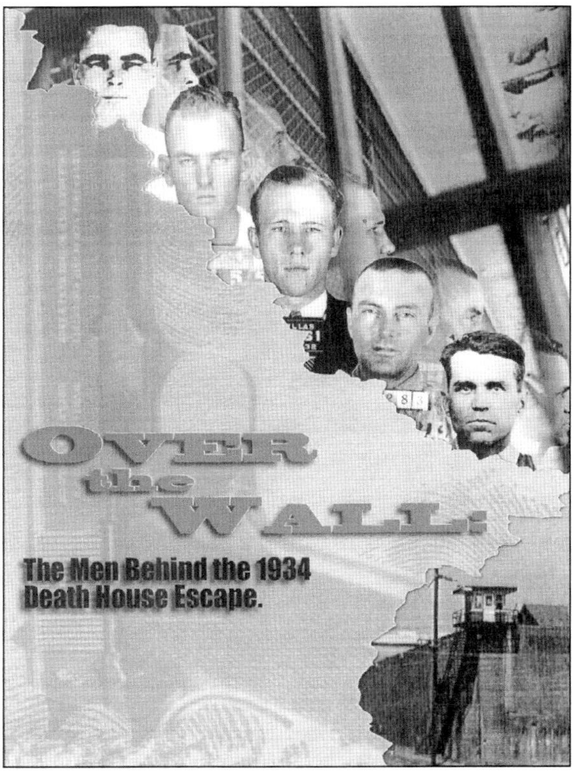

This shows the Walls unit at Huntsville, home of the state penitentiary. These men were incarcerated there for robberies and murder. From the top are Roy Johnson, Joe Palmer, Ray Hamilton, Whitey Walker, and Blackie Thompson. These men broke out in 1934, and Walker was killed at the wall. Hamilton and Palmer were caught and electrocuted.

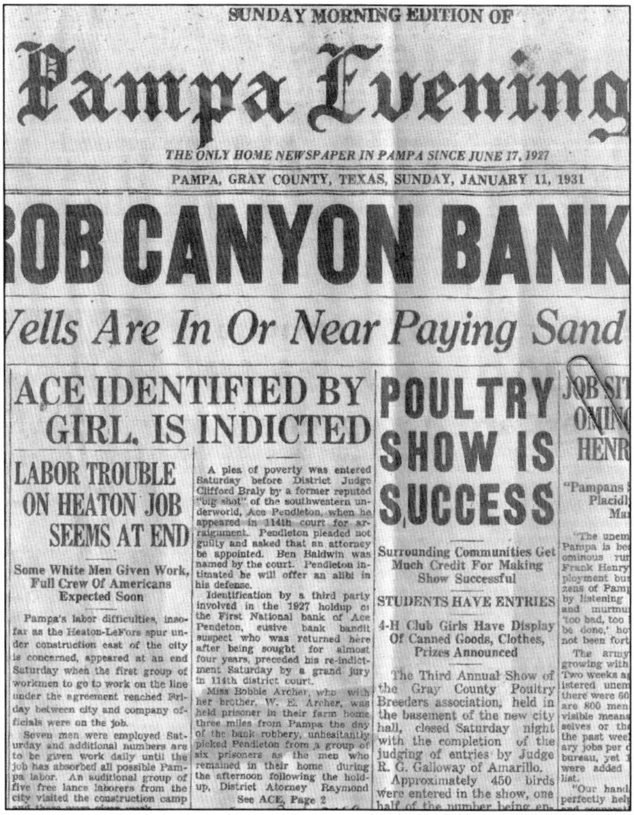

SUNDAY MORNING EDITION OF

Pampa Evening

THE ONLY HOME NEWSPAPER IN PAMPA SINCE JUNE 17, 1927

PAMPA, GRAY COUNTY, TEXAS, SUNDAY, JANUARY 11, 1931

OB CANYON BANK

Vells Are In Or Near Paying Sand

ACE IDENTIFIED BY GIRL, IS INDICTED

A plea of poverty was entered Saturday before District Judge Clifford Braly by a former reputed "big shot" of the southwestern underworld, Ace Pendleton, when he appeared in 114th court for arraignment. Pendleton pleaded not guilty and asked that an attorney be appointed. Ben Baldwin was named by the court. Pendleton intimated he will offer an alibi in his defense.

Identification by a third party involved in the 1927 holdup of the First National bank of Ace Pendeton, eusive bank bandit suspect who was returned here after being sought for almost four years, preceded his re-indictment Saturday by a grand jury in 114th district court.

Miss Bobbie Archer, who with her brother, W. E. Archer, was held prisoner in their farm home three miles from Pampa the day of the bank robbery, unhesitantly picked Pendleton from a group of six prisoners as the men who remained in their home during the afternoon following the holdup, District Atorney Raymond

See ACE, Page 2

LABOR TROUBLE ON HEATON JOB SEEMS AT END

Some White Men Given Work, Full Crew Of Americans Expected Soon

Pampa's labor difficulties, insofar as the Heaton-LeFors spur under construction east of the city is concerned, appeared at an end Saturday when the first group of workmen to go to work on the line under the agreement reached Friday between city and company officials were on the job.

Seven men were employed Saturday and additional numbers are to be given work daily until the job has absorbed all possible Pampa labor. An auditional group of five free lance laborers from the city visited the construction camp

POULTRY SHOW IS SUCCESS

Surrounding Communities Get Much Credit For Making Show Successful

STUDENTS HAVE ENTRIES

4-H Club Girls Have Display Of Canned Goods, Clothes, Prizes Announced

The Third Annual Show of the Gray County Poultry Breeders association, held in the basement of the new city hall, closed Saturday night with the completion of the judging of entries by Judge R. G. Galloway of Amarillo.

Approximately 450 birds were entered in the show, one

This newspaper tells the story of the identification of one of the bank robbers, Ace Pendleton. Bobbie Archer was the only person to ever identify him, but the grand jury still refused to indict him. He was eventually released and later died in Arizona.

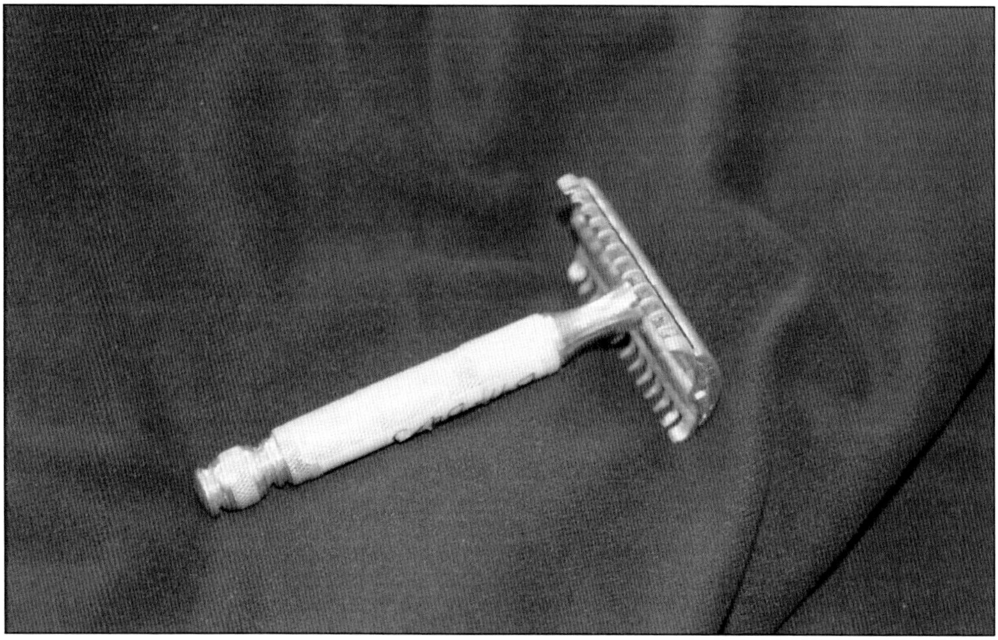

This is the razor given to Rufe Jordan (who was 15 years old) by bank robber Ace Pendleton in 1928. Jordan was a tubercular and his dad guarded him in isolation. Pendleton was found not guilty by the grand jury.

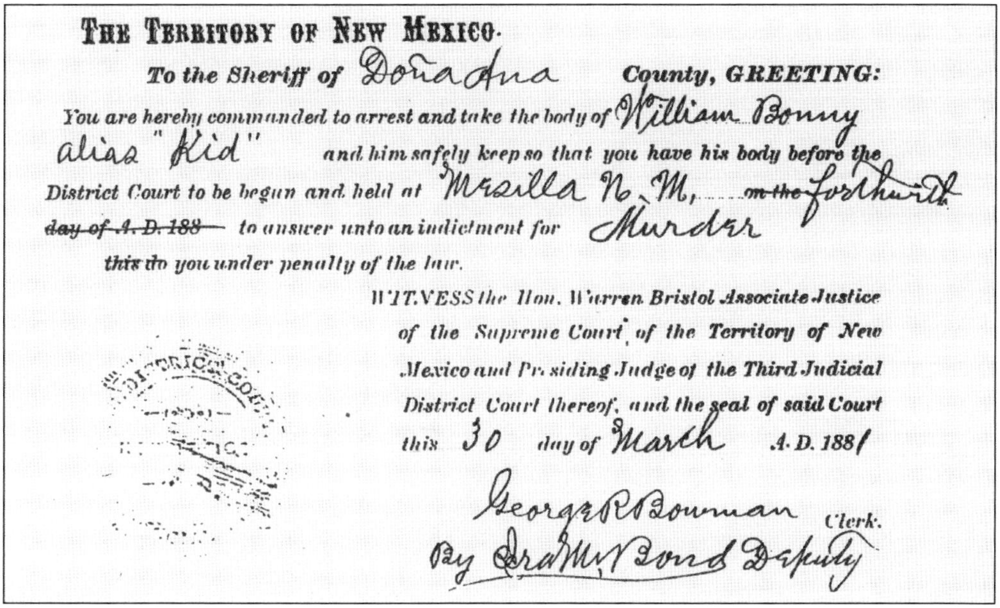

THE TERRITORY OF NEW MEXICO.

To the Sheriff of Doña Ana *County, GREETING:*

You are hereby commanded to arrest and take the body of William Bonny alias "Kid" *and him safely keep so that you have his body before the District Court to be begun and held at* Mesilla N. M., ~~on the~~ forthwith ~~day of A. D. 188~~ *to answer unto an indictment for* Murder

~~this~~ *do you under penalty of the law.*

WITNESS the Hon. Warren Bristol Associate Justice of the Supreme Court of the Territory of New Mexico and Presiding Judge of the Third Judicial District Court thereof, and the seal of said Court this 30 *day of* March *A. D. 188*1

George R Bowman *Clerk.*

By Ira M. Bond Deputy

This interesting document came into the hands of Sheriff Rufe Jordan. It is the arrest warrant for William "Billy the Kid" Bonny in New Mexico in 1881. Bonny also used the last name Antrim. Bill Bonny was brought in but escaped again, killing two guards. The next time he was found, he was shot and killed by Pat Garrett, sheriff of Lincoln County, New Mexico.

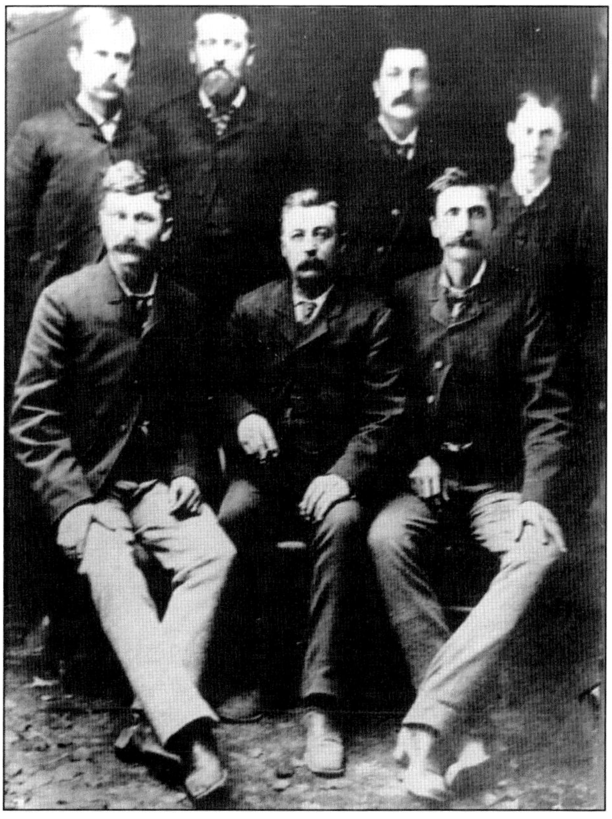

These are famous New Mexico lawmen of the early 1880s. Pat Garrett is seated on the far right, and the man standing second from the left is Frank James, brother of the infamous Jesse James.

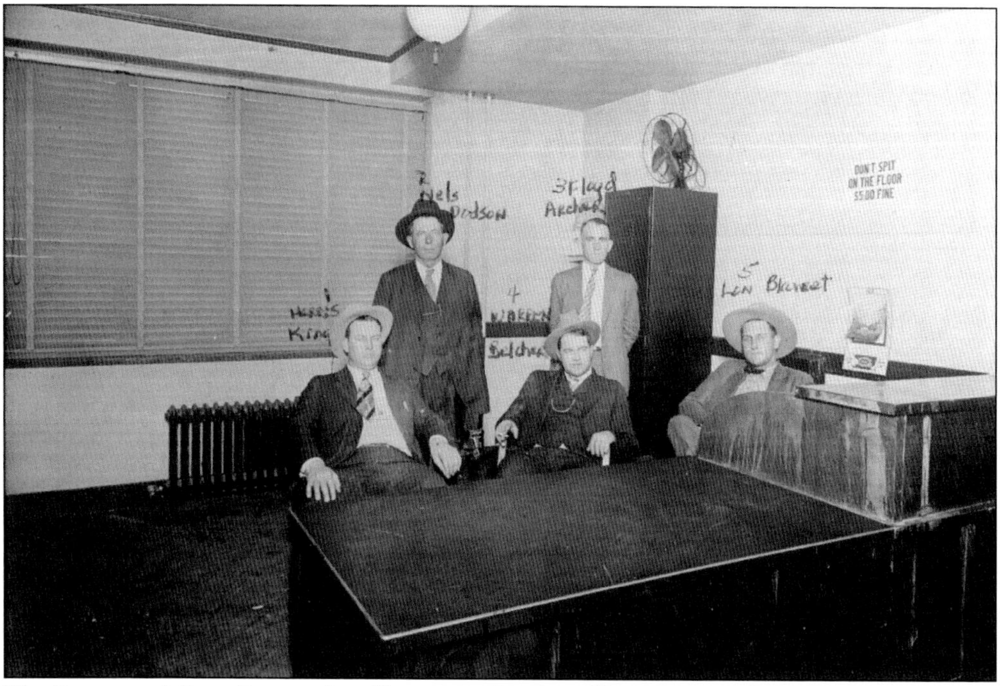

The Pampa and Gray County sheriff is pictured in his office in 1931. The man on the far right is Sheriff Lon Blancett. Blancett later lost his right arm in a rodeo event called bulldogging in 1932 or 1933. The courthouse was new, and that desk is now on display in the White Deer Land Museum.

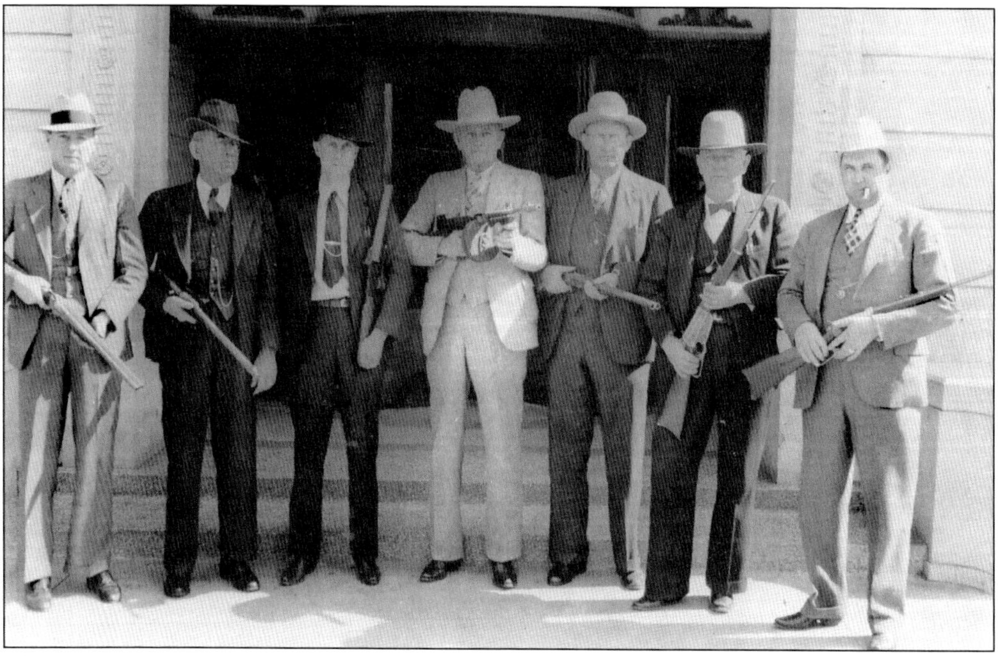

This is Sheriff Earl Talley (center) with the Tommy gun. This picture was taken in 1934, and Sheriff Talley died in 1935. Notice the Tom Mix hat again, which he always wore. The museum has one of his hats on display now.

Sheriff C. E. "Tiny" Pipes died in 1934, and his wife finished out his term for him. Fannie Pipes is pictured here with four of her deputies. She ran for the office when her term was up, but she was defeated.

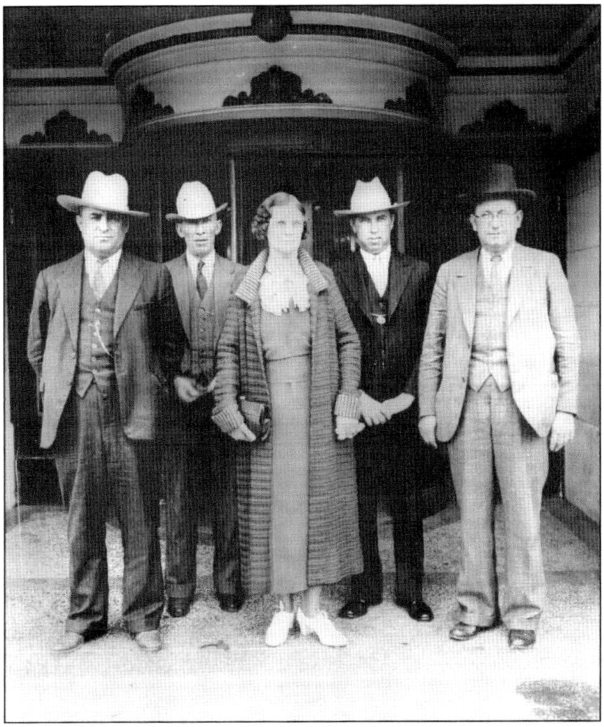

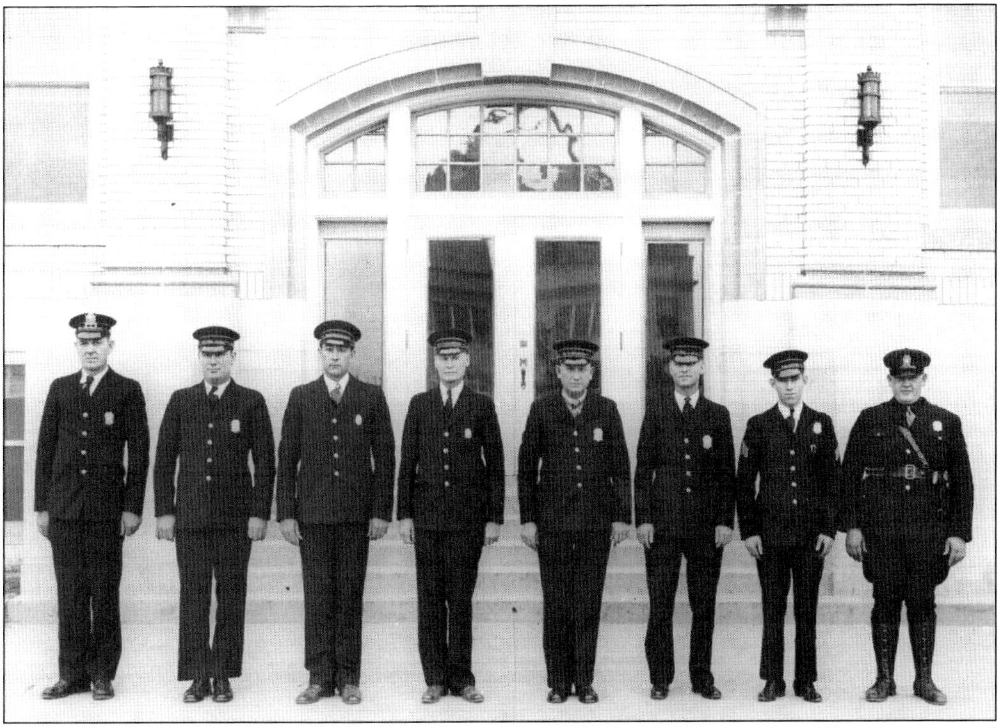

These were Pampa's boys in blue. The police department had eight men in 1930. They are pictured in front of the new city hall. The Pampa Police Department has grown since, employing 26 uniformed officers in 2009.

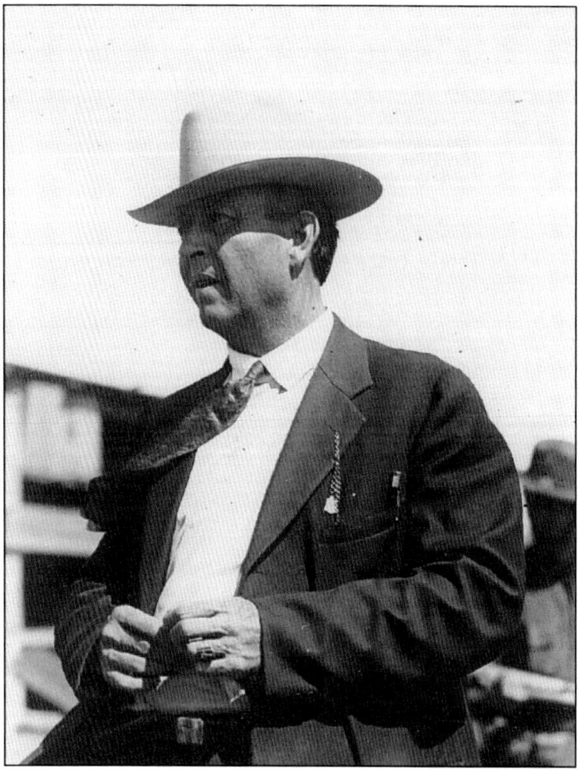

This is Frank Hamer, the Texas Ranger who came to clean up the boomtowns. He was recommended for a position in the Texas Rangers in 1906 and became an expert shot. He came to Borger in 1927. Later he tracked Bonnie Parker and Clyde Barrows for three months before killing them in May 1934. He was portrayed in the movie *Bonnie and Clyde* in 1967. (Photograph courtesy of the Texas Ranger Hall of Fame and Museum.)

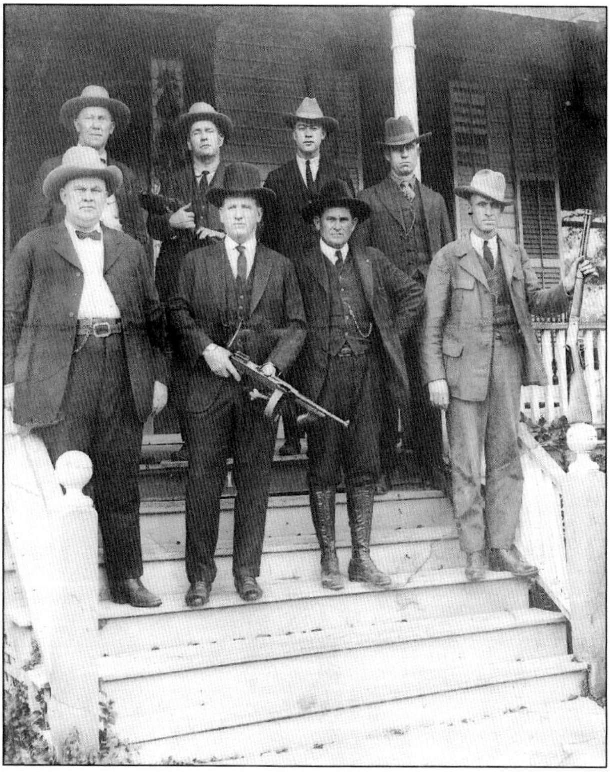

In 1930, this group, called the Cotton Bowl Rangers, was appointed by the Texas governor. In the first row, at left, is Tiny Pipes of Pampa. In the second row, far right, is Frank Hamer, who killed Bonny and Clyde. Hamer cleaned up the boomtown of Borger and the Pampa area. First row, far right, is the famous lawman M. T. "Lonewolf" Gonzaullas. (Photograph courtesy of the Reverend Charles Pipes.)

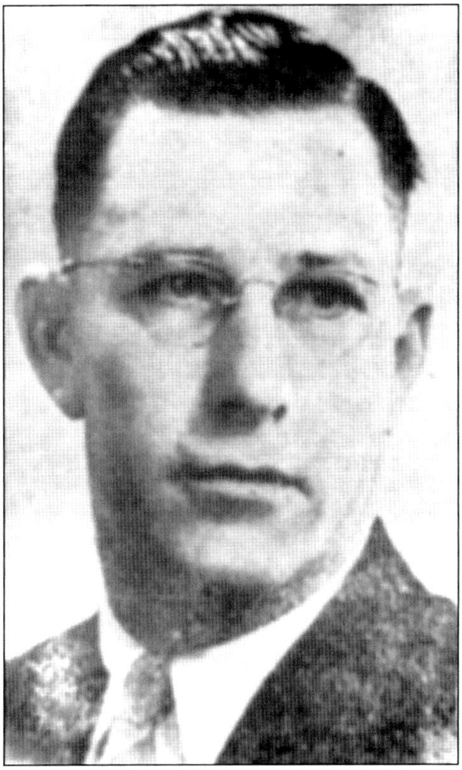

This is Sheriff Cal Rose, Gray County's 11th elected sheriff. People remember the sheriff, elected in 1939, to be of questionable character. It is said that he disliked Constable Otis Hendrix, so on the night of January 30, 1939, Rose went to the Southern Club to check the liquor license, and he called Hendrix to meet him there. A fight ensued, started by the bartender, Rose said, and a stray bullet killed Hendrix. Officers returned the fire and the bartender J. D. White was also killed. Four customers were wounded. Rose was no billed by a Gray County grand jury. Hendrix was 44 years old and was survived by five children. The newspaper below was one of many that carried the story the next day.

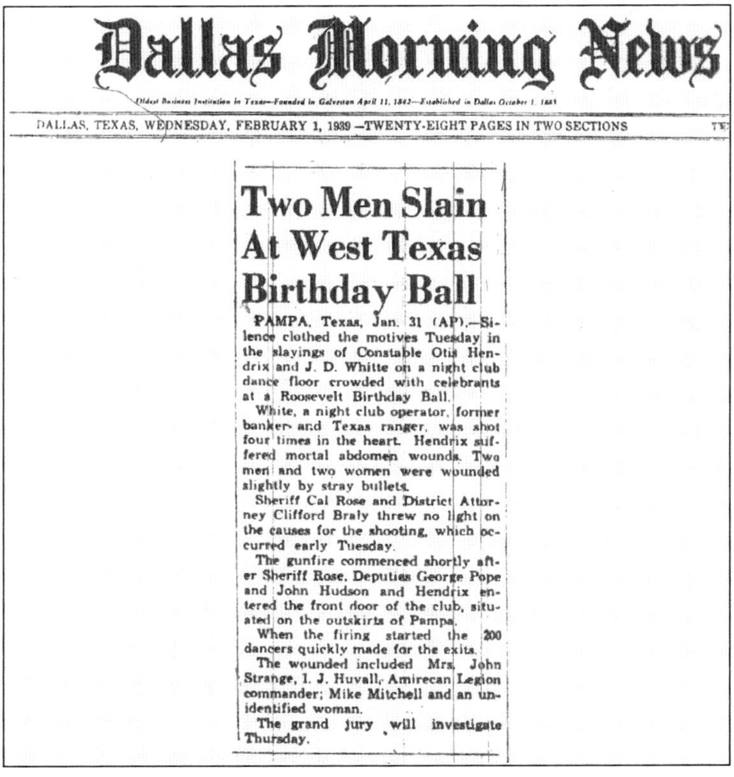

Dallas Morning News

Oldest Business Institution in Texas—Founded in Galveston April 11, 1842—Established in Dallas October 1, 1885

DALLAS, TEXAS, WEDNESDAY, FEBRUARY 1, 1939 —TWENTY-EIGHT PAGES IN TWO SECTIONS

Two Men Slain At West Texas Birthday Ball

PAMPA, Texas, Jan. 31 (AP).—Silence clothed the motives Tuesday in the slayings of Constable Otis Hendrix and J. D. Whitte on a night club dance floor crowded with celebrants at a Roosevelt Birthday Ball.

White, a night club operator, former banker and Texas ranger, was shot four times in the heart. Hendrix suffered mortal abdomen wounds. Two men and two women were wounded slightly by stray bullets.

Sheriff Cal Rose and District Attorney Clifford Braly threw no light on the causes for the shooting, which occurred early Tuesday.

The gunfire commenced shortly after Sheriff Rose, Deputies George Pope and John Hudson and Hendrix entered the front door of the club, situated on the outskirts of Pampa.

When the firing started the 200 dancers quickly made for the exits.

The wounded included Mrs. John Strange, I. J. Huvall, Amirecan Legion commander; Mike Mitchell and an unidentified woman.

The grand jury will investigate Thursday.

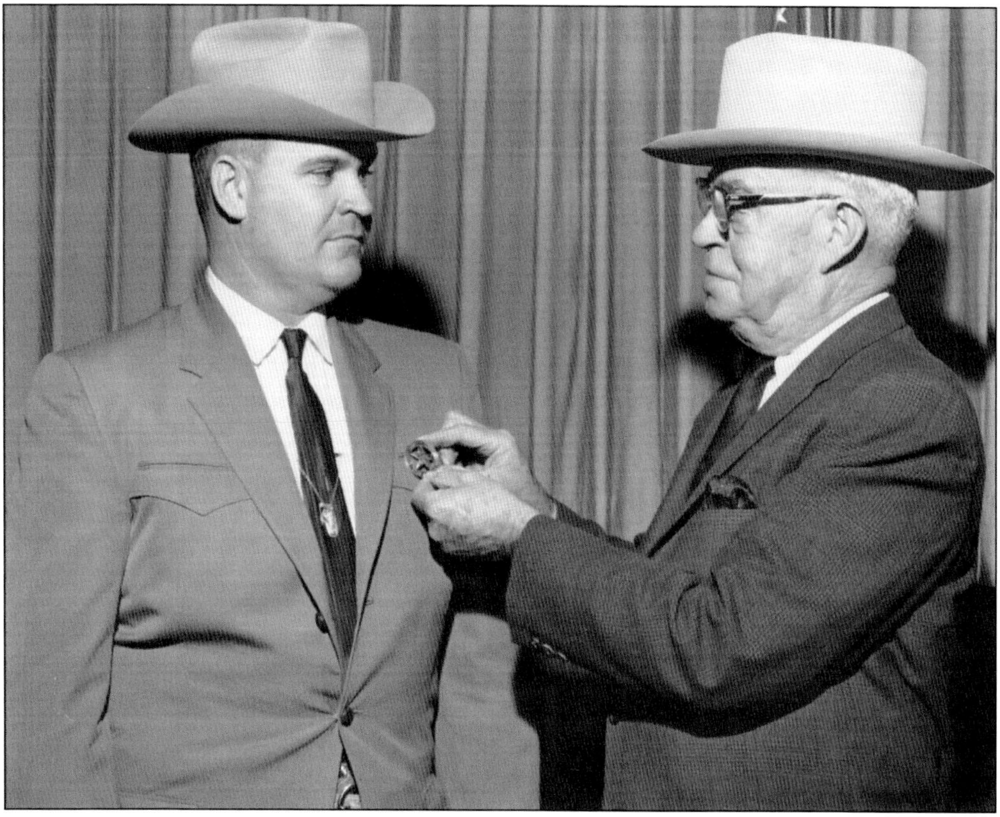

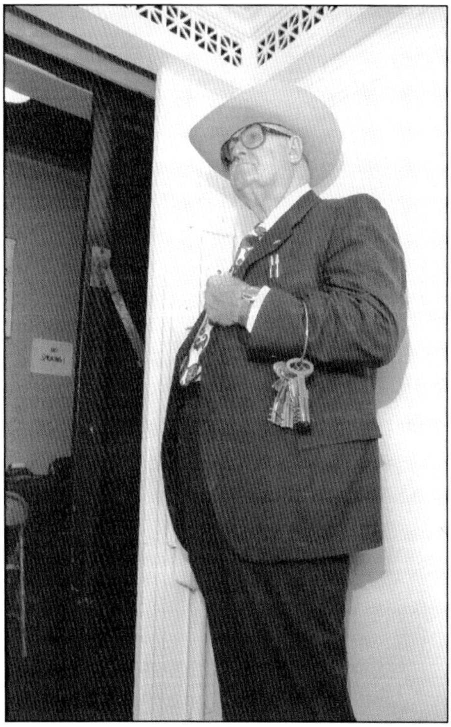

This is W. P. "Bill" Baten (left), Texas Ranger Company C, and Homer Garrison, Texas Department of Public Safety, swearing Baten into the Ranger service in 1962. Previously, Bill had a long record of law enforcement in Hall County. The Baten Unit in Pampa, which is an Intermediate Sanction Facility (ISF), joined the Jordan Unit, a minimum-security prison, and both belong to the Texas Department of Criminal Justice. He was honored by the Texas Senate for his years of service in 1985.

R. H. "Rufe" Jordan was the most elected peace officer in Texas, according to Texas records in 2008. He served 38 elected years as sheriff and four years as chief deputy. He is shown at left entering the courthouse elevator to go to the jail. Rufe and Viola Jordan lived in the apartment on the fourth floor of the courthouse until 1988. (Photograph by Michael Hartsock.)

This article was about Rufe Jordan, the man for whom the prison was named. He served Gray County for 38 years as sheriff and as chief deputy sheriff four years before that.

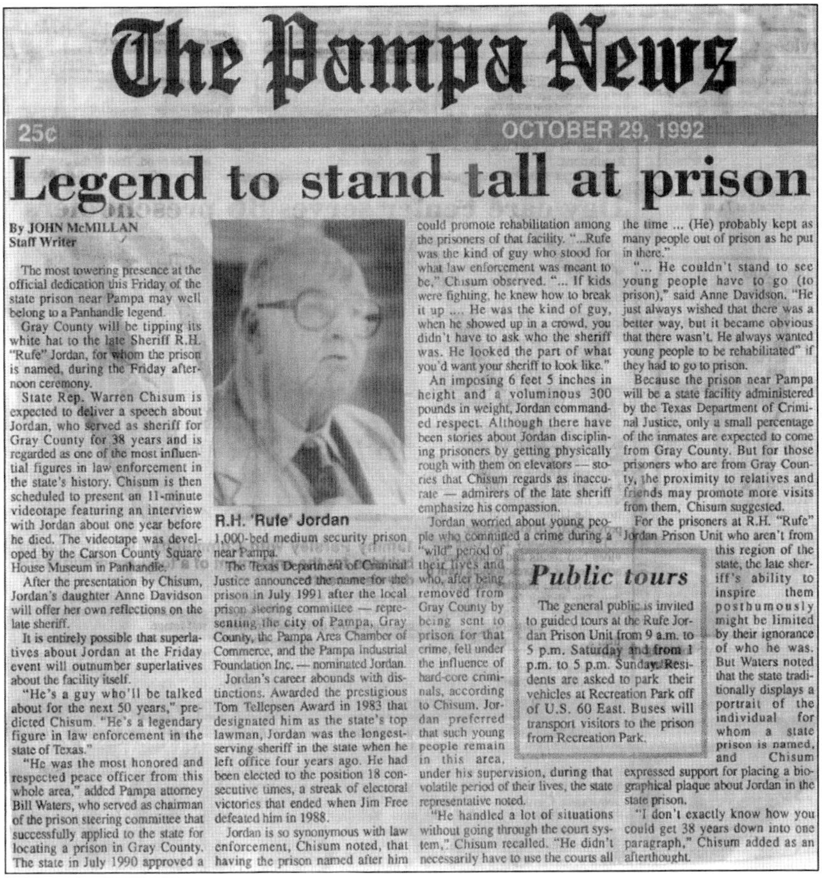

The Pampa News

25¢ OCTOBER 29, 1992

Legend to stand tall at prison

By JOHN McMILLAN
Staff Writer

The most towering presence at the official dedication this Friday of the state prison near Pampa may well belong to a Panhandle legend.

Gray County will be tipping its white hat to the late Sheriff R.H. "Rufe" Jordan, for whom the prison is named, during the Friday afternoon ceremony.

State Rep. Warren Chisum is expected to deliver a speech about Jordan, who served as sheriff for Gray County for 38 years and is regarded as one of the most influential figures in law enforcement in the state's history. Chisum is then scheduled to present an 11-minute videotape featuring an interview with Jordan about one year before he died. The videotape was developed by the Carson County Square House Museum in Panhandle.

After the presentation by Chisum, Jordan's daughter Anne Davidson will offer her own reflections on the late sheriff.

It is entirely possible that superlatives about Jordan at the Friday event will outnumber superlatives about the facility itself.

"He's a guy who'll be talked about for the next 50 years," predicted Chisum. "He's a legendary figure in law enforcement in the state of Texas."

"He was the most honored and respected peace officer from this whole area," added Pampa attorney Bill Waters, who served as chairman of the prison steering committee that successfully applied to the state for locating a prison in Gray County. The state in July 1990 approved a 1,000-bed medium security prison near Pampa.

R.H. 'Rufe' Jordan

The Texas Department of Criminal Justice announced the name for the prison in July 1991 after the local prison steering committee — representing the city of Pampa, Gray County, the Pampa Area Chamber of Commerce, and the Pampa Industrial Foundation Inc. — nominated Jordan.

Jordan's career abounds with distinctions. Awarded the prestigious Tom Tellepsen Award in 1983 that designated him as the state's top lawman, Jordan was the longest-serving sheriff in the state when he left office four years ago. He had been elected to the position 18 consecutive times, a streak of electoral victories that ended when Jim Free defeated him in 1988.

Jordan is so synonymous with law enforcement, Chisum noted, that having the prison named after him could promote rehabilitation among the prisoners of that facility. "...Rufe was the kind of guy who stood for what law enforcement was meant to be," Chisum observed. "... If kids were fighting, he knew how to break it up .... He was the kind of guy, when he showed up in a crowd, you didn't have to ask who the sheriff was. He looked the part of what you'd want your sheriff to look like."

An imposing 6 feet 5 inches in height and a voluminous 300 pounds in weight, Jordan commanded respect. Although there have been stories about Jordan disciplining prisoners by getting physically rough with them on elevators — stories that Chisum regards as inaccurate — admirers of the late sheriff emphasize his compassion.

Jordan worried about young people who committed a crime during a "wild" period of their lives and who, after being removed from Gray County by being sent to prison for that crime, fell under the influence of hard-core criminals, according to Chisum. Jordan preferred that such young people remain in this area, under his supervision, during that volatile period of their lives, the state representative noted.

"He handled a lot of situations without going through the court system," Chisum recalled. "He didn't necessarily have to use the courts all the time ... (He) probably kept as many people out of prison as he put in there."

"... He couldn't stand to see young people have to go (to prison)," said Anne Davidson. "He just always wished that there was a better way, but it became obvious that there wasn't. He always wanted young people to be rehabilitated" if they had to go to prison.

Because the prison near Pampa will be a state facility administered by the Texas Department of Criminal Justice, only a small percentage of the inmates are expected to come from Gray County. But for those prisoners who are from Gray County, the proximity to relatives and friends may promote more visits from them, Chisum suggested.

For the prisoners at R.H. "Rufe" Jordan Prison Unit who aren't from this region of the state, the late sheriff's ability to inspire them posthumously might be limited by their ignorance of who he was. But Waters noted that the state traditionally displays a portrait of the individual for whom a state prison is named, and Chisum expressed support for placing a biographical plaque about Jordan in the state prison.

"I don't exactly know how you could get 38 years down into one paragraph," Chisum added as an afterthought.

Public tours

The general public is invited to guided tours at the Rufe Jordan Prison Unit from 9 a.m. to 5 p.m. Saturday and from 1 p.m. to 5 p.m. Sunday. Residents are asked to park their vehicles at Recreation Park off of U.S. 60 East. Buses will transport visitors to the prison from Recreation Park.

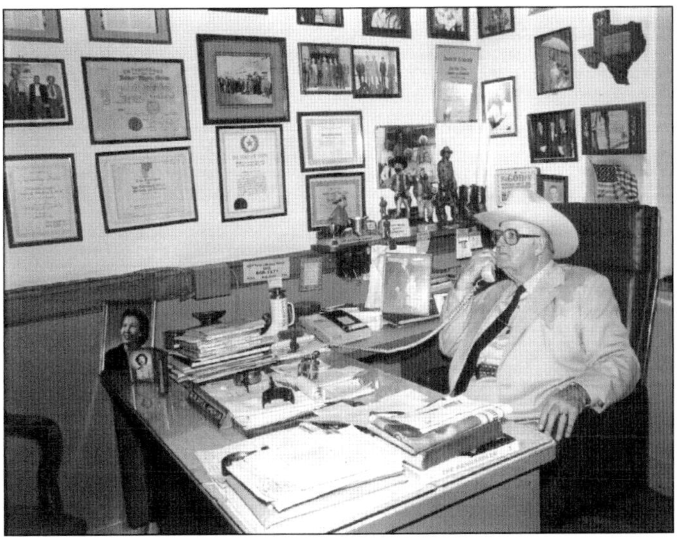

The office of Sheriff Jordan became an attraction to the residents of Gray County. He had pictures of his grandchildren, a 1950 Boys Ranch calendar, and awards from fellow officers. In 1983, Jordan was awarded the coveted Tom Tellepsen Award, which reads, "for an outstanding advancement in law enforcement and a contribution to the criminal justice system." Behind Jordan's chair is a plaque that says, "God couldn't be everywhere, so He made Grandfathers."

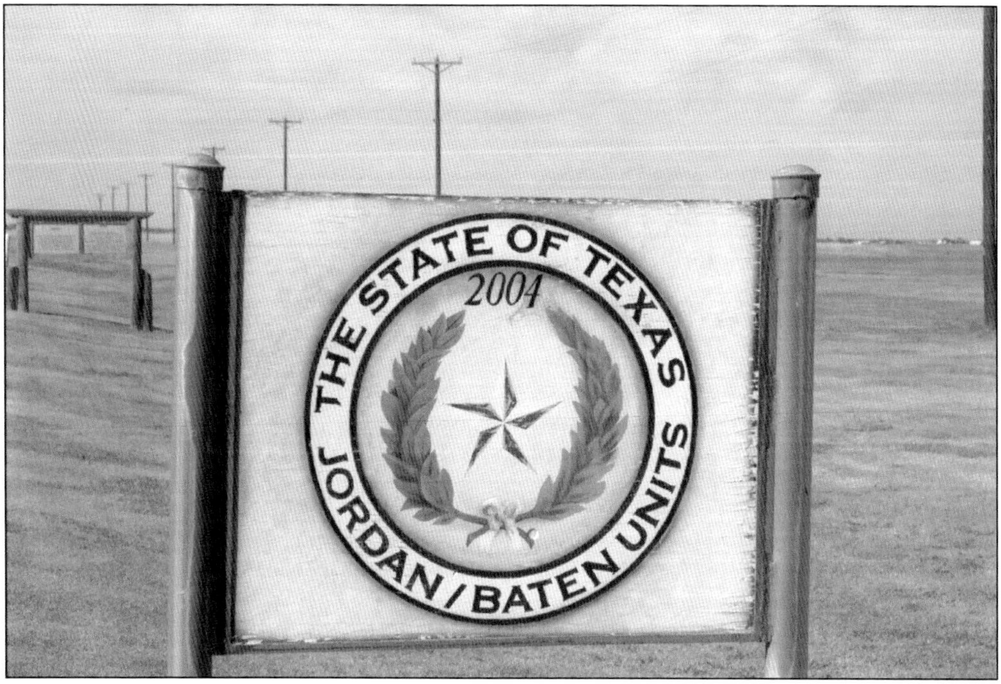

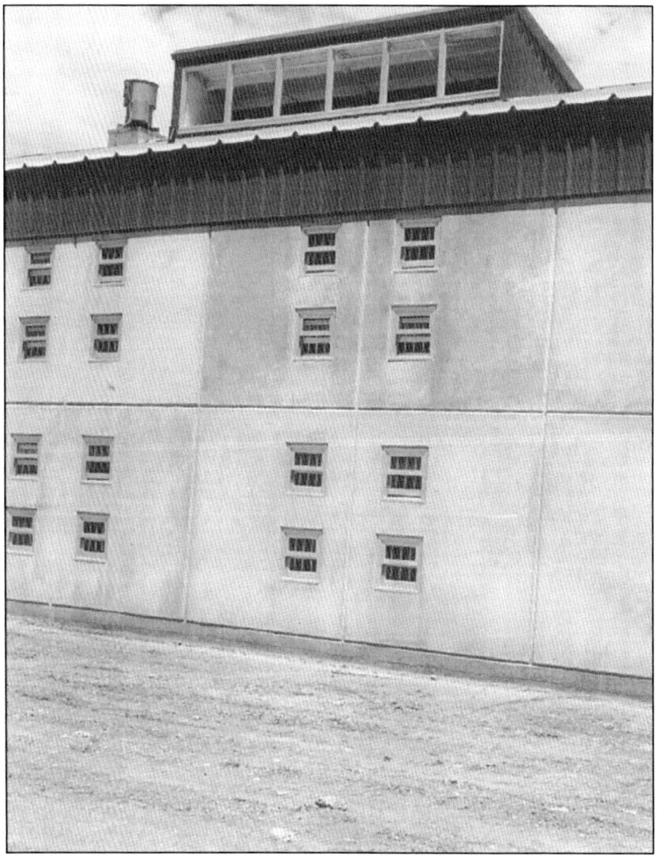

These photographs show the entry to the prison and a wall that houses 1,000 offenders. This is a minimum-security unit. Rufe Jordan has been dubbed by various writers as, "The Dean of Texas Sheriffs," "The Law West of the Pecos," and "The Patriarch of Texas Sheriffs." Jordan is the father of one of this book's authors, Anne Davidson.

Eight

Look at Us Now

Industry began to flourish during World War II in Pampa and Gray County. The Pampa Army Air Force (PAAF) Base opened in 1942, eleven miles east of Pampa. It closed in 1945 after graduating 6,292 aviation cadets and training 3,500 mechanics. There was a German Prisoner of War camp at McLean, 24 miles from Pampa.

Gray County did their part in the war effort. Carbon black plants, gasoline plants, and oil field supply companies were operating at full speed. This prosperity caused our city fathers to support more cultural centers in the community. The people built hospitals, a library, a junior college branch, new bank buildings, new hotels, and a civic center. The Celanese Corporation, a multimillion dollar chemical plant, came into Pampa in 1951 and, with a million-dollar payroll, eventually added 400 jobs.

Pampa has many beautiful city parks, good golf courses, and a lovely country club. There are four museums in the county—a military museum, a large barbed wire museum, and two history museums. Pampa is home to garden clubs, federated womens clubs, the Pampa Fine Arts Association, and a host of other educational organizations. The 14 pieces of outdoor sculpture are outstanding.

The White Deer Land Museum will be 40 years old in 2010. The first director, Clotille Thompson, in 1970, did a wonderful job of collecting and preserving the artifacts for 20 years. She retired in 1990, and Anne Davidson took her job. Two buildings have now been added, one that houses museum offices and one that contains showcases of the Red River War and early Gray County settlement. The original building, constructed in 1916, has two floors and contains the office of the White Deer Land Company, which was their third office in Pampa. It is an interesting old building that contains wonderful furnishings, period clothing, and the best arrowhead collection in the Panhandle.

This museum staff believes that the museum is an intricate part of Pampa and the history of the settlers who came to make their home here.

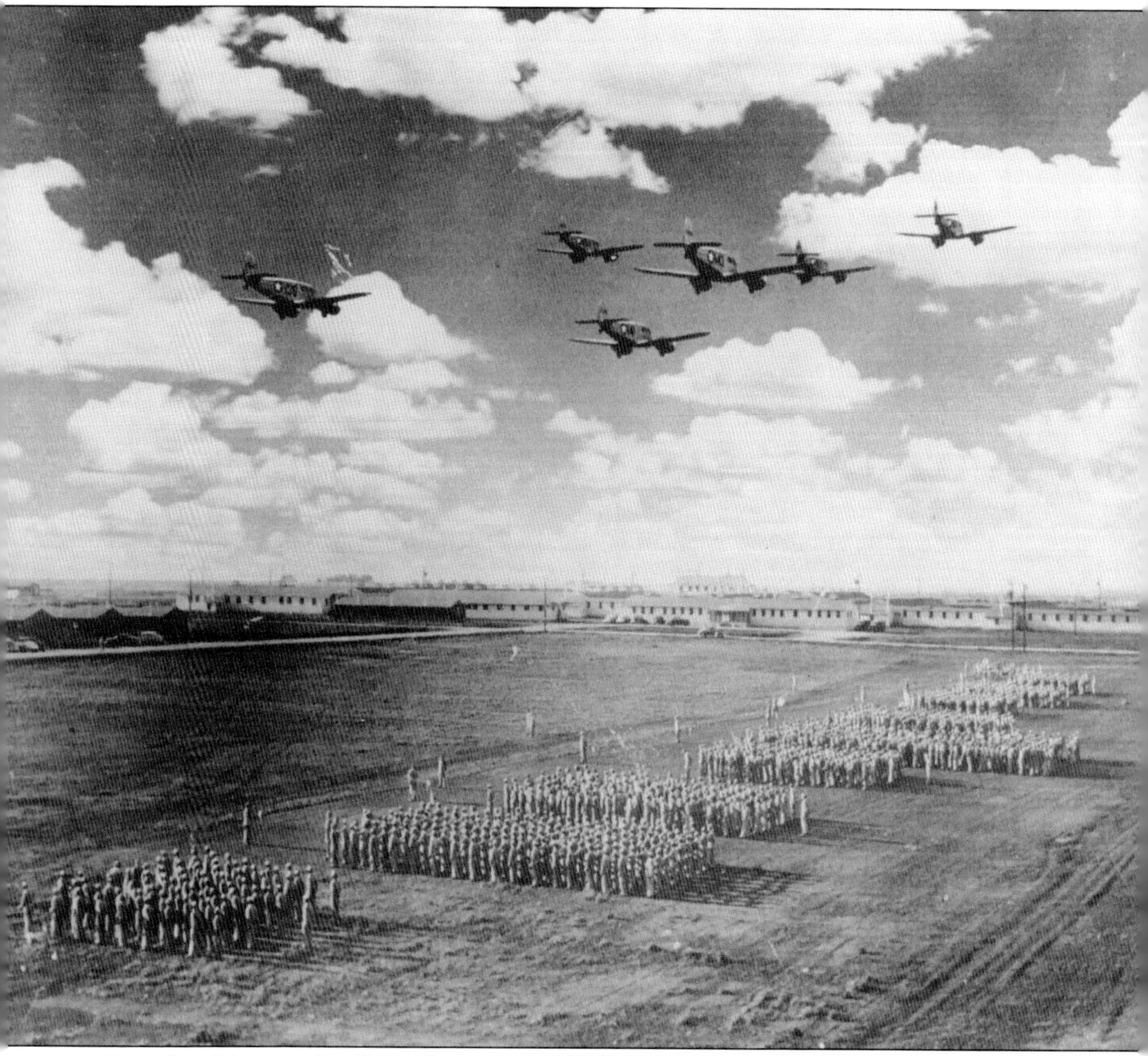

Less than 30 years after the oil boom came World War II. Pampa had the foresight to bid for an army air force base and they got it. It opened in 1942, and this view is from the tower. This site was chosen to train pilots for the war, and the first group of cadets arrived in December. The base stayed open three years and three months, graduated 6,292 aviation cadets, and trained 3,500 aircraft mechanics. It boosted the local economy greatly, and the people of Pampa opened their homes to the personnel, officers, and cadets at the base. M. K. Brown, comanager of the White Deer Land Company, fixed some of the second-floor rooms in the building to accommodate the girls who were working at the Base Post Exchange.

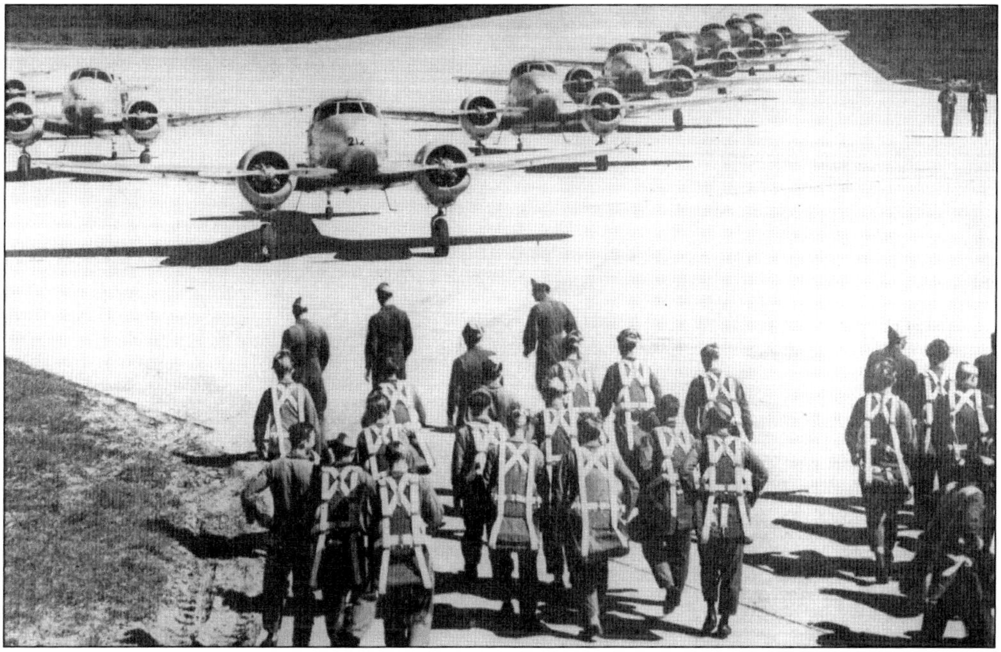

Instructors and students were just about to start an early day at PAAF Base. The cadets were first instructed in the B-25 Mitchell.

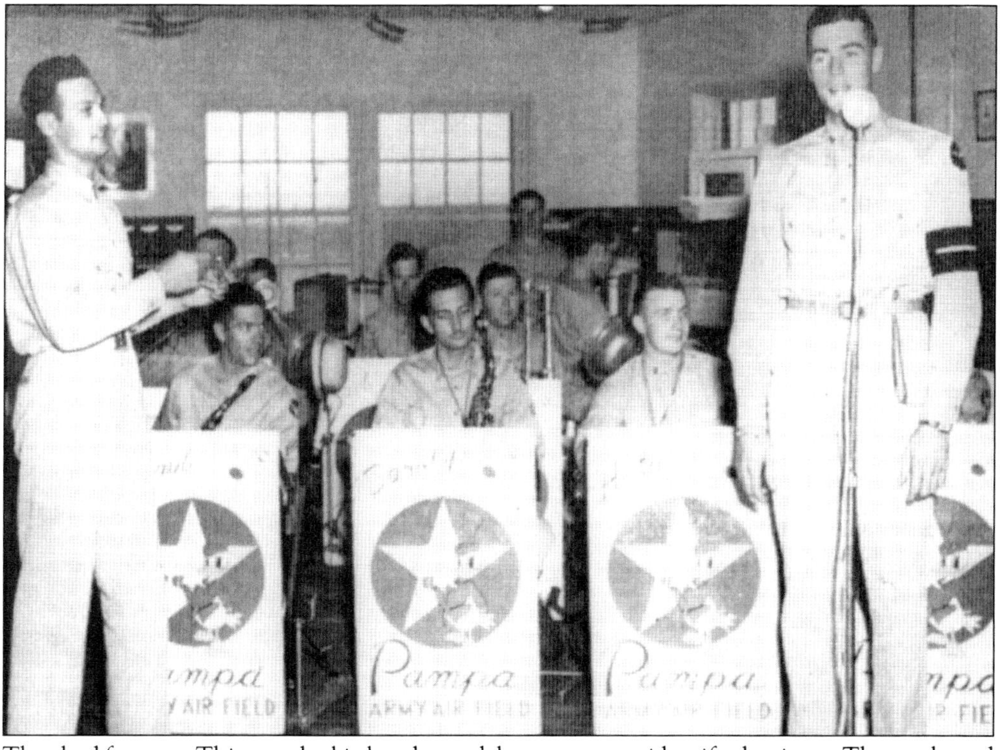

They had fun, too. This was the big band sound, but we cannot identify the singer. These talented boys came to Pampa from all over the United States, and a few chose to live here after the war was over.

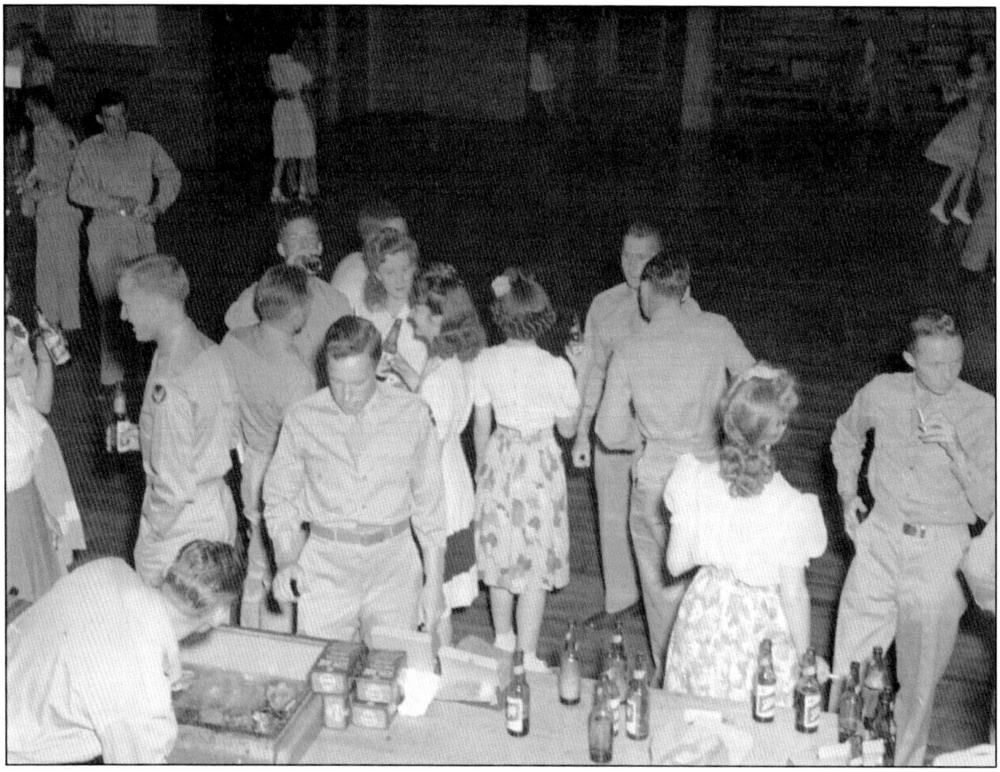

These ladies were called "Wilco Girls." They got their name from the moniker that pilots used, "Wilco, over and out." Wilco means "will comply." They entertained, wrote letters home, danced, and talked to the guys about their families. This looks like an average Friday night at the base.

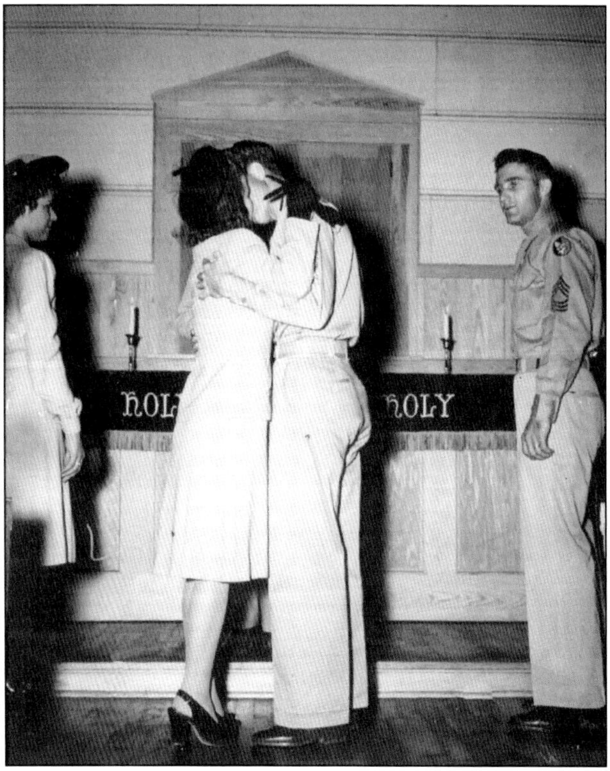

This was the first couple married at the air base. They were S.Sgt James G. Baird and Elveda Judkins. The wedding date was September 10, 1943, and the lady on the left is the bride's sister, Doris Smith. The man on the right, Lewis Epps, would later become their brother-in-law by marrying one of Elveda's other sisters. These folks still live in Pampa.

International opera star Mary Jane Rose Johnson graduated from Pampa High School and received a master's degree at West Texas A&M University. She was discovered by Pavarotti in 1981. Her career took her all over the world. She has performed at the Metropolitan Opera, the Opera Bastille in Paris, La Sala in Milan, and Tel Aviv. Mary Jane taught at Amarillo College and has performed with the Santa Fe Opera Company in Taos, New Mexico.

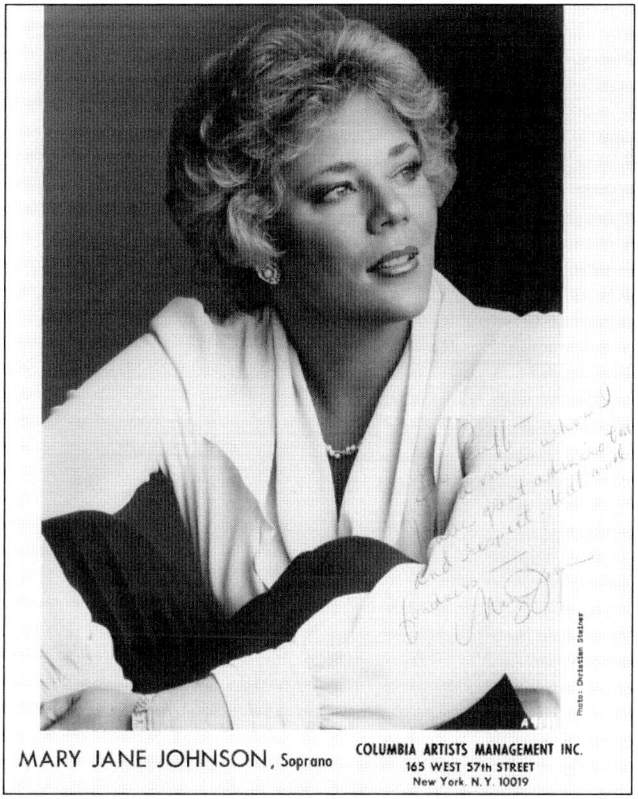

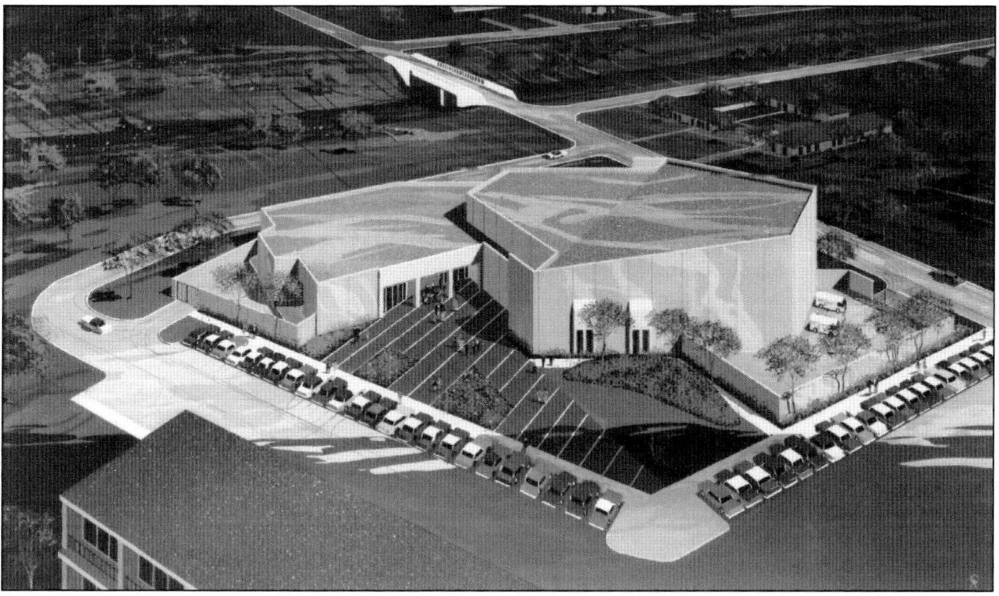

In 1970, the directors of the M. K. Brown Foundation gave the city of Pampa $400,000 to establish the beginning of funds for a memorial auditorium. The citizens of Pampa approved the issue of $800,000 in bonds. After much hard work on the part of Pampa citizens and a wonderful gift by Brown, a uniquely designed auditorium was built. It seats 1,500 and is 35,000 square feet. The building has been praised by many visiting celebrities.

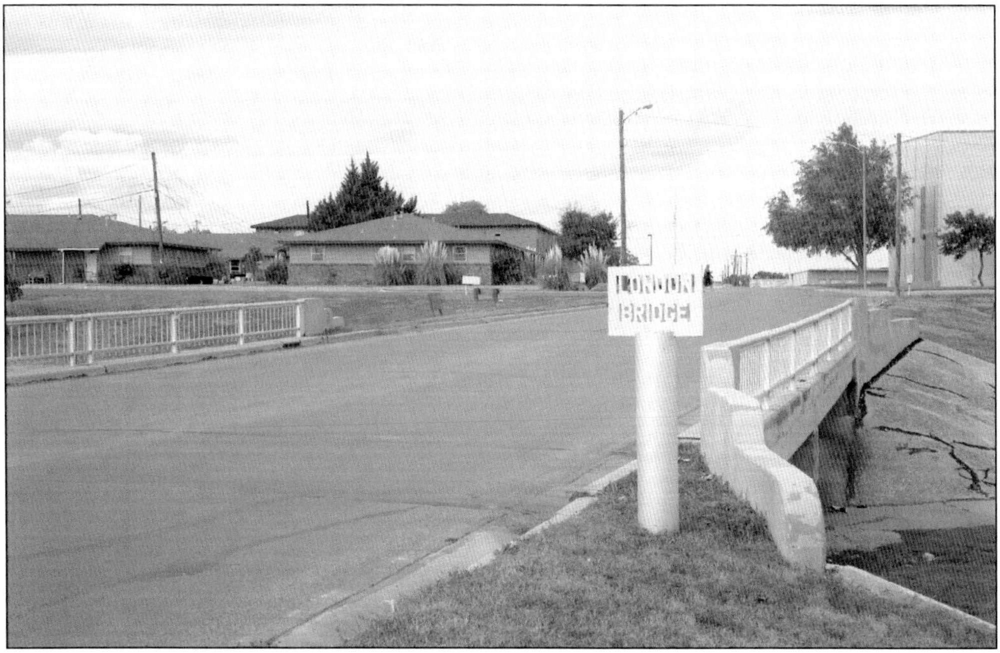

This bridge was named for the real London Bridge. Being an Englishman, M. K. Brown believed that everyone should have one. After building this attraction, Brown led the Pampa Harvester band as the first to parade across it.

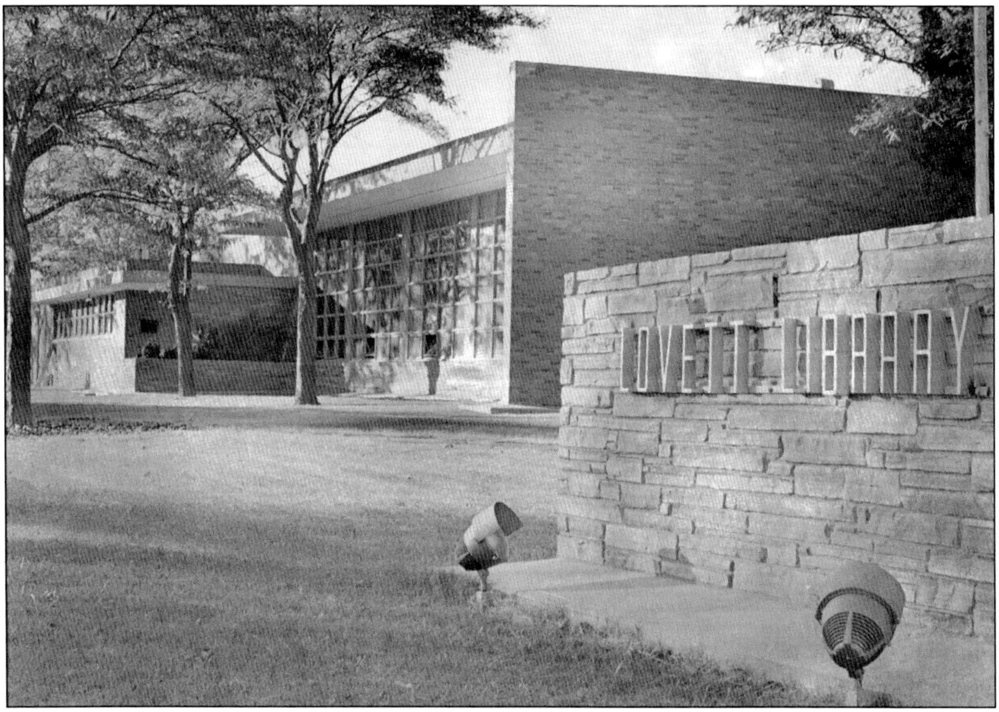

Lovett Library bears its name from Henry and Fannie Lovett, who came to this country in the late 1880s. Henry Lovett had been a buffalo-hide skinner. The Lovetts lost their only daughter to typhoid. This is a state-of-the-art library. A smaller Lovett Library was built in McLean.

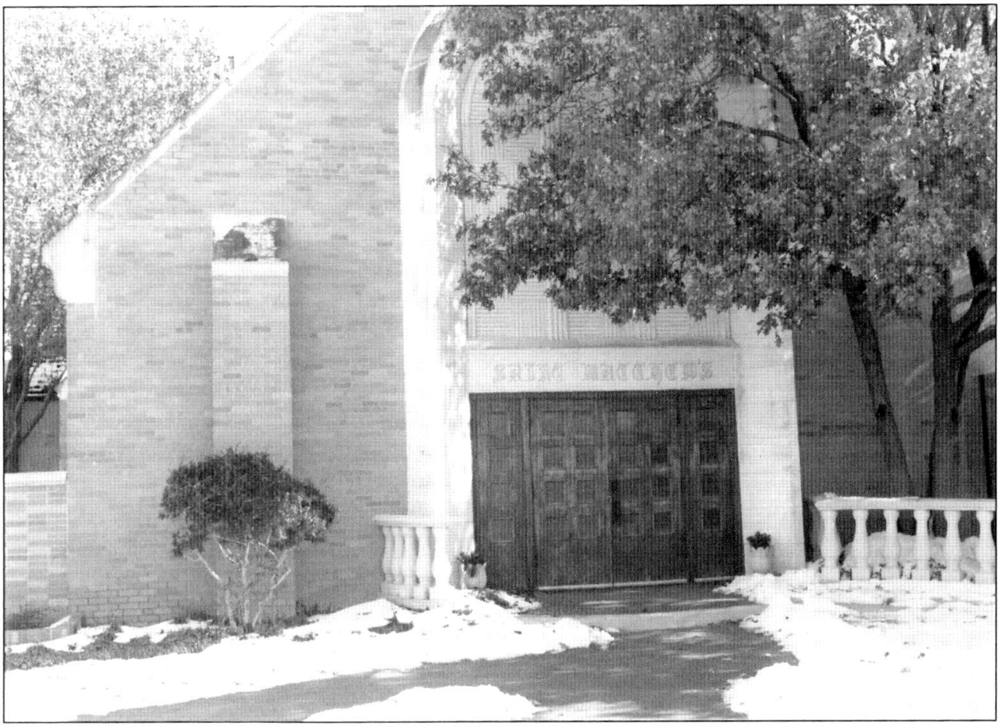

Saint Matthews Episcopal Church was funded generously by M. K. Brown. There are about 55 churches in Pampa.

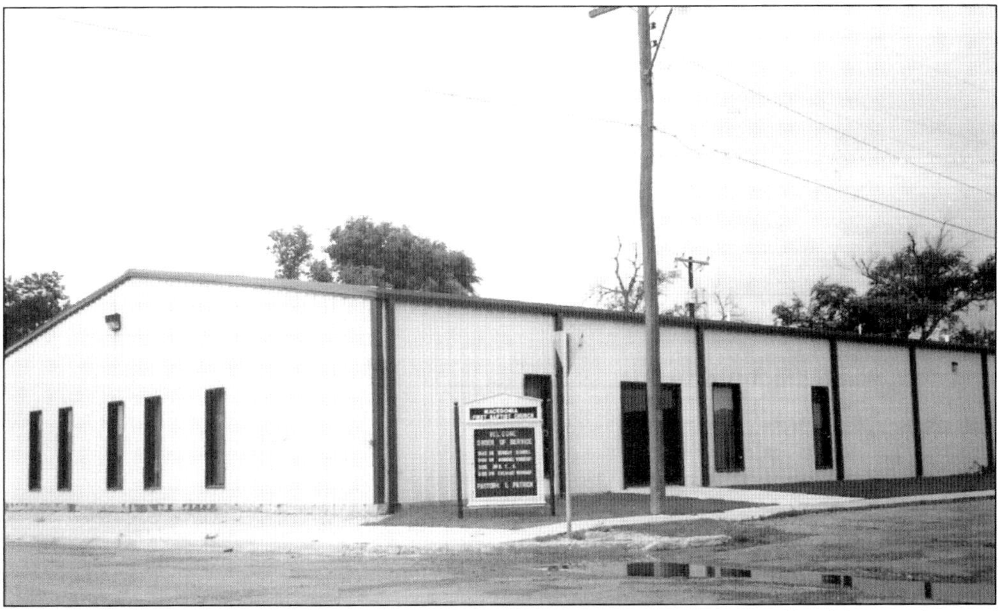

The Macedonian Baptist Church was rebuilt in 1998 and is now a metal building with good heating and air and an adequate PA system. This church was the first African American Baptist church in Pampa, organized in 1927. Macedonian Baptist Church has a talented group of singers in their choir.

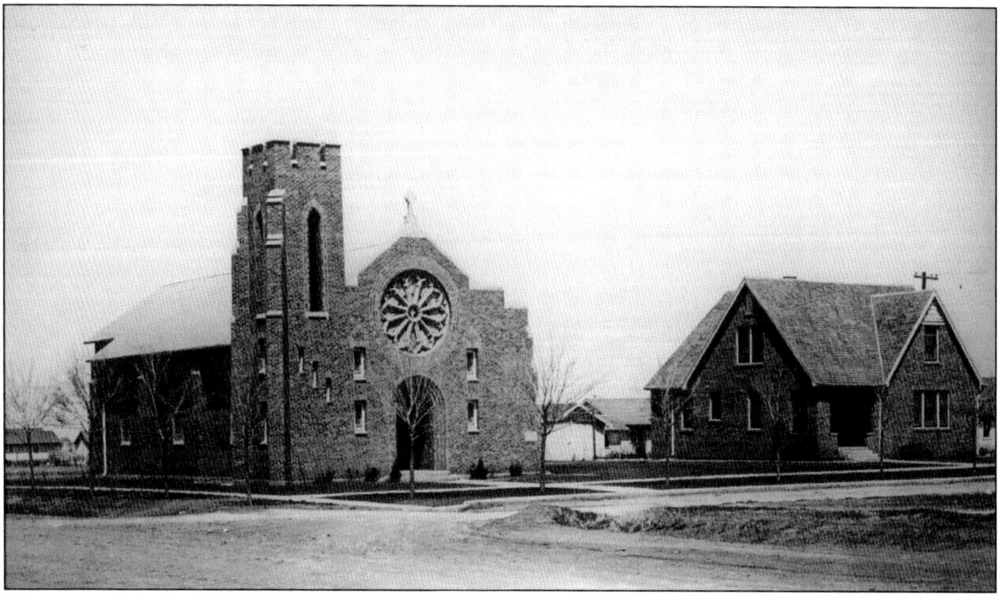

This was Holy Souls Catholic Church and rectory in Pampa. Immediately after the Spanish explorers left the area, the first martyr was killed in the Palo Duro Canyon. He was a Franciscan monk. One hundred years later, many Catholics began to come to this area. They came with the railroads and with the farming and ranching industry. The Catholic Church has played a large part in the history of Pampa.

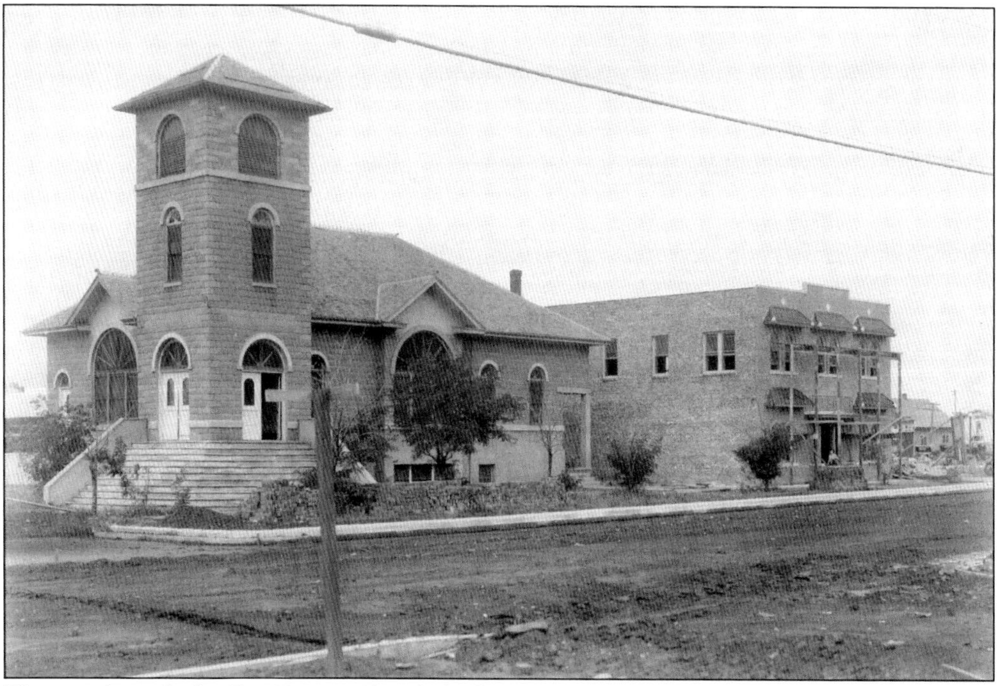

This was the early-day First Baptist Church, built in 1915. It was sometimes called the Rock Church and was located in downtown Pampa. When the new courthouse did not reach the completion date, the church basement was leased to the county for about a year. Pampa now has 11 other Baptist churches in the community.

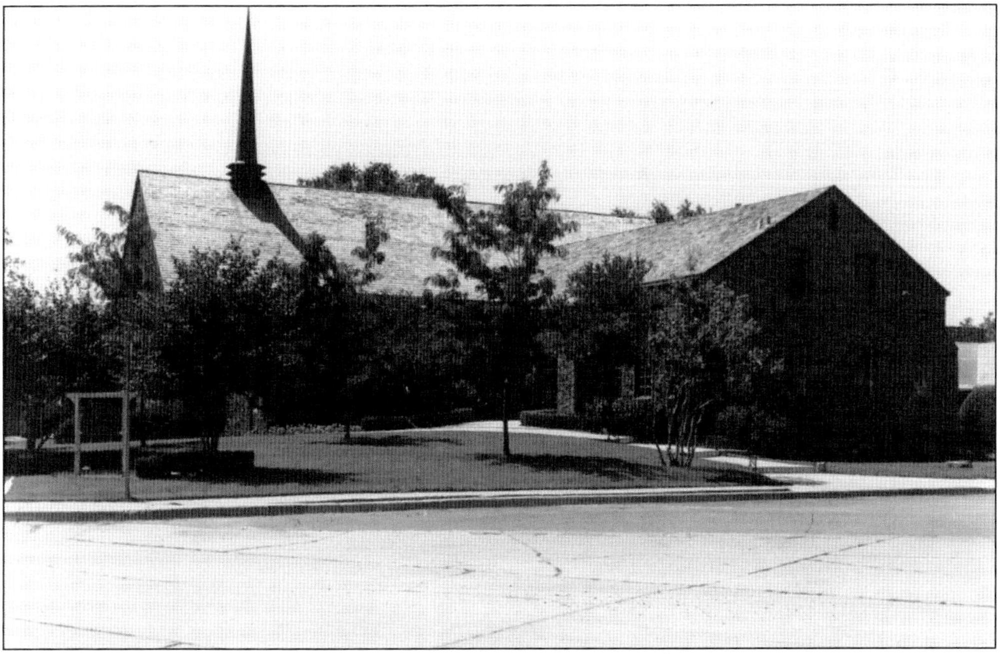

The attractive Presbyterian Church was built in 1940. The members have supported or organized several community services, including the Sheltered Workshop, Tralee Crises Center, Latchkey program, and Good Samaritan Counseling Service.

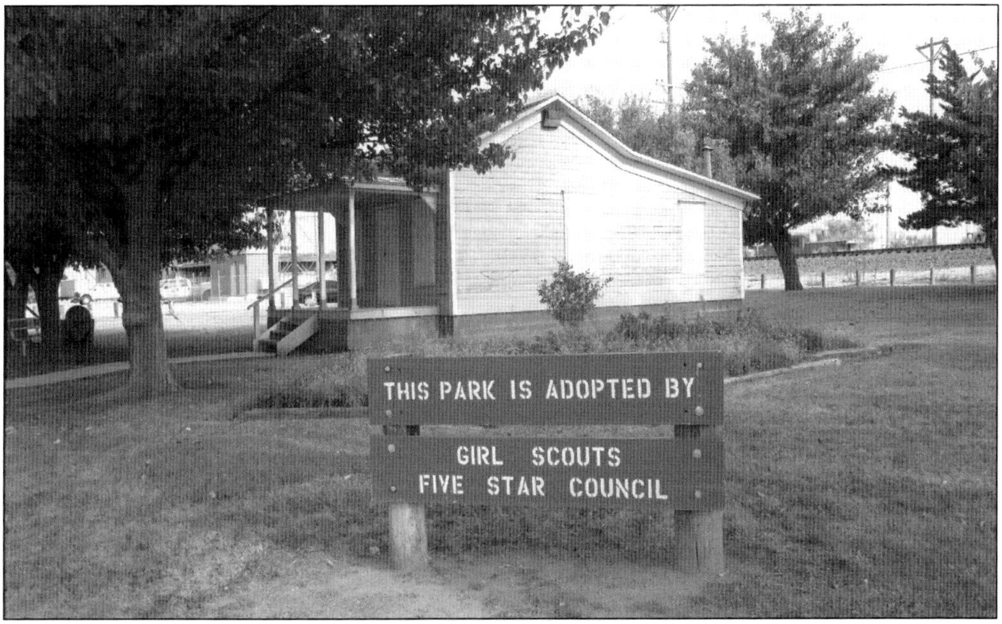

Pampa's oldest home, the Pioneer Cottage, built in 1903, bears a Texas Historical Commission marker. The cottage was moved back near its original site as a project of the Gray County Centennial–2002 and the Gray County Historical Commission. The small oak tree in the trefoil garden west of the building was brought to Pampa by Sam Houston IV and was grown from an acorn from the live oak at the site of Stephen F. Austin's death. The Travis school fourth graders helped plant the tree on San Jacinto Day 2004.

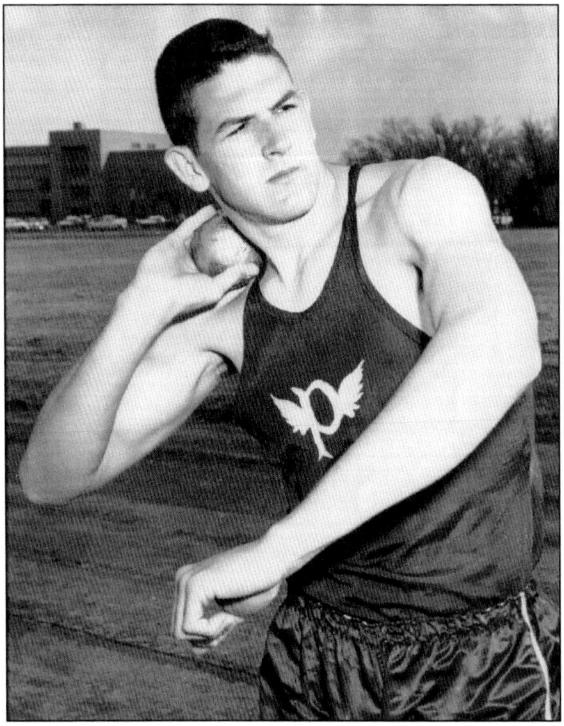

One of Pampa's prize athletes is Randy Matson. He won the Olympic silver in 1964 in the shot put. Then he won the gold in 1968 in the same event. The *Randy Matson Story* was written in 1971. Matson now lives in College Station, Texas.

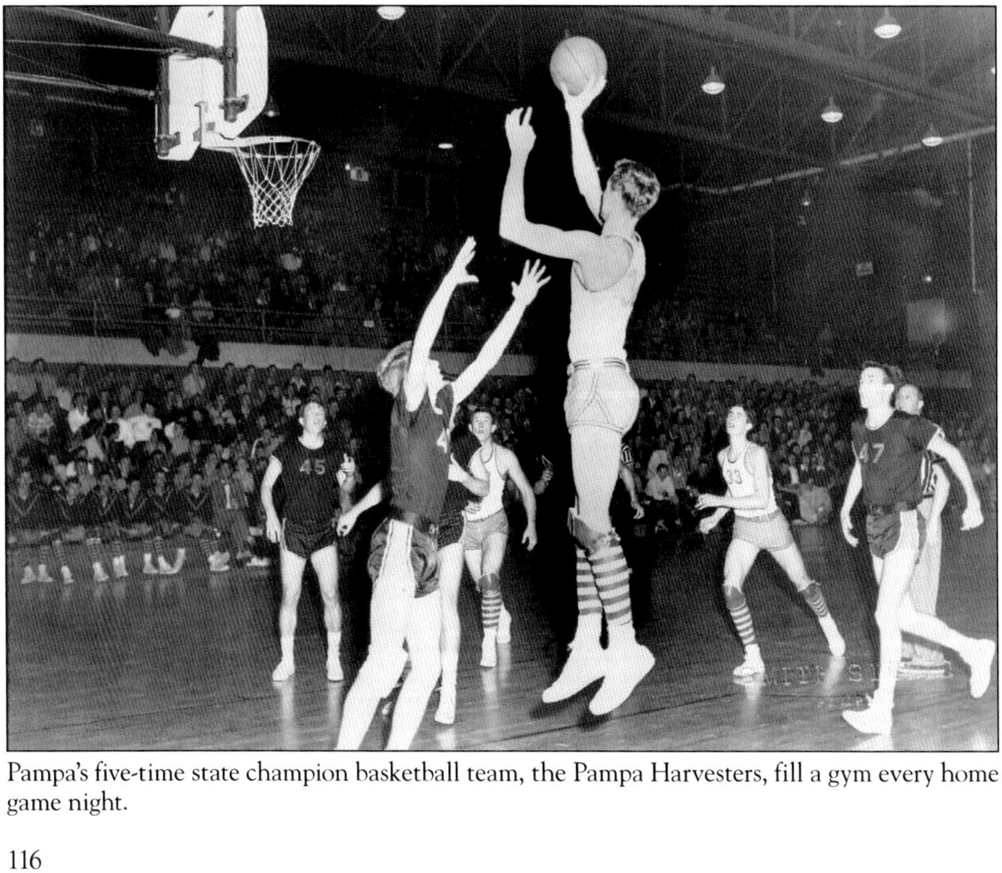

Pampa's five-time state champion basketball team, the Pampa Harvesters, fill a gym every home game night.

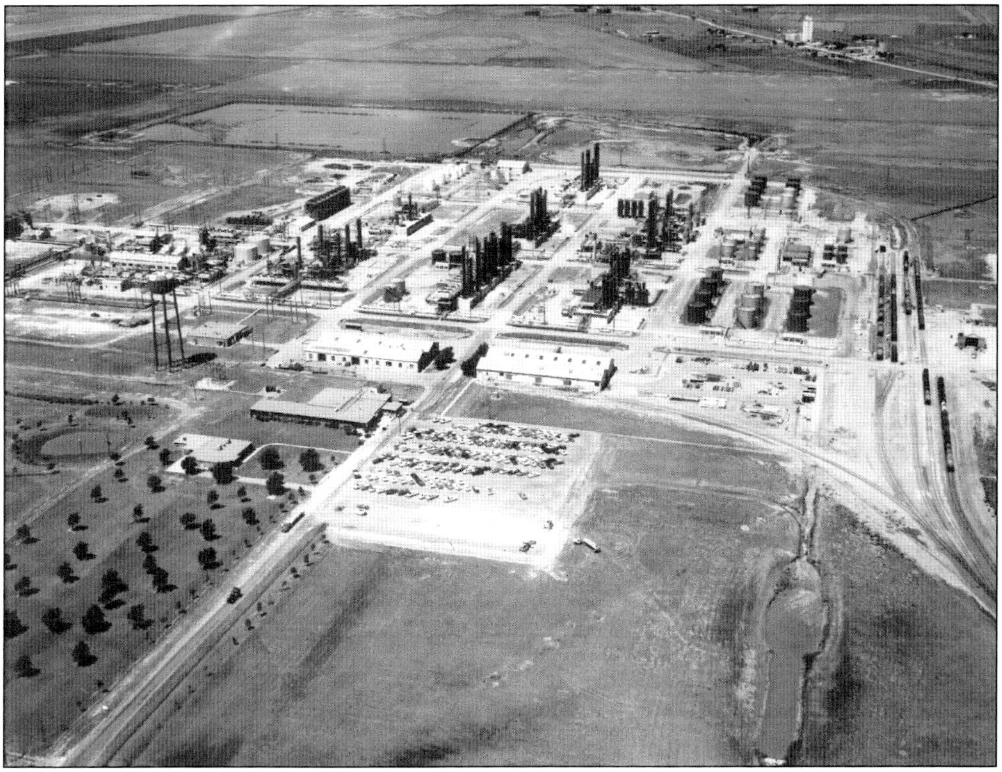

The Celanese Corporation plant came to Pampa in 1951. Celanese is a producer of industrial chemicals used in the manufacture of synthetic rubber, explosives, pharmaceuticals, and many other products. The newspaper article shows that a huge explosion left three dead and several injured in 1987. They recovered from the damage and went back into production. Their work force has been cut considerably since 2005. Celanese has been a large supporter in every facet of the Pampa Community.

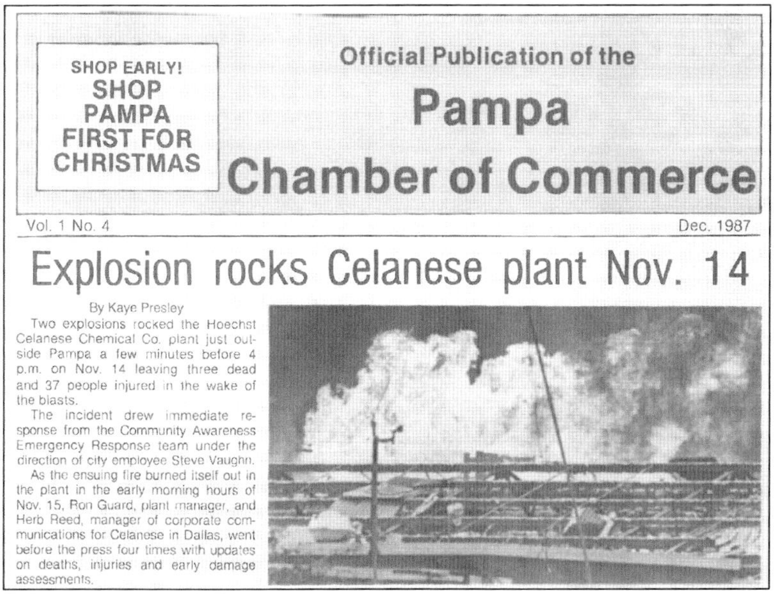

SHOP EARLY!
SHOP PAMPA FIRST FOR CHRISTMAS

Official Publication of the
Pampa
Chamber of Commerce

Vol. 1 No. 4 Dec. 1987

Explosion rocks Celanese plant Nov. 14

By Kaye Presley

Two explosions rocked the Hoechst Celanese Chemical Co. plant just outside Pampa a few minutes before 4 p.m. on Nov. 14 leaving three dead and 37 people injured in the wake of the blasts.

The incident drew immediate response from the Community Awareness Emergency Response team under the direction of city employee Steve Vaughn.

As the ensuing fire burned itself out in the plant in the early morning hours of Nov. 15, Ron Guard, plant manager, and Herb Reed, manager of corporate communications for Celanese in Dallas, went before the press four times with updates on deaths, injuries and early damage assessments.

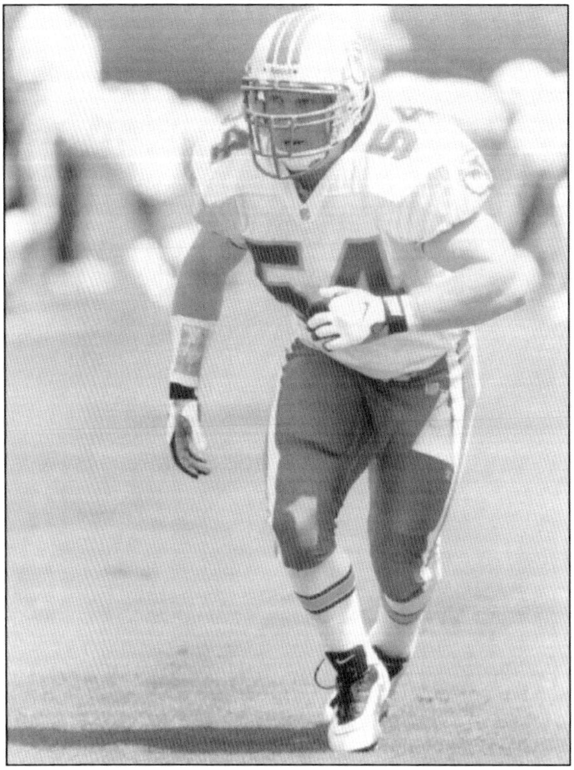

Zach Thomas was an all-state football player from Pampa High School. After graduation, he went to Texas Tech, where he was drafted by the Miami Dolphins in a three-year contract. He played for 12 years with the Dolphins, until 2007. He signed with the Dallas Cowboys in 2008 and the Kansas City Chiefs for one year in 2009. Zach currently holds the record for more tackles than any linebacker in the Pro Football Hall of Fame. Zach, his brother Bart, and their sister, Katina, are great-grandchildren of Pampa's first mayor, J. N. Duncan (Photographs courtesy of the Thomas family.)

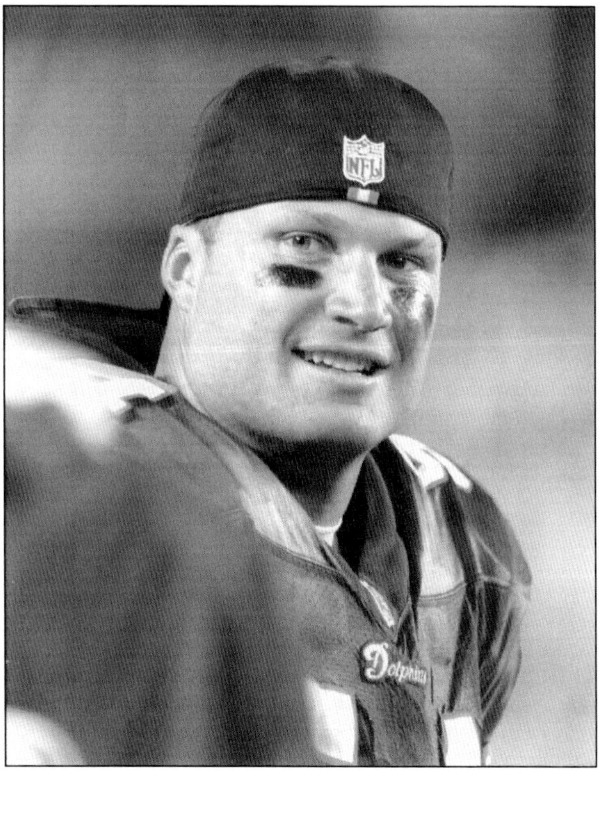

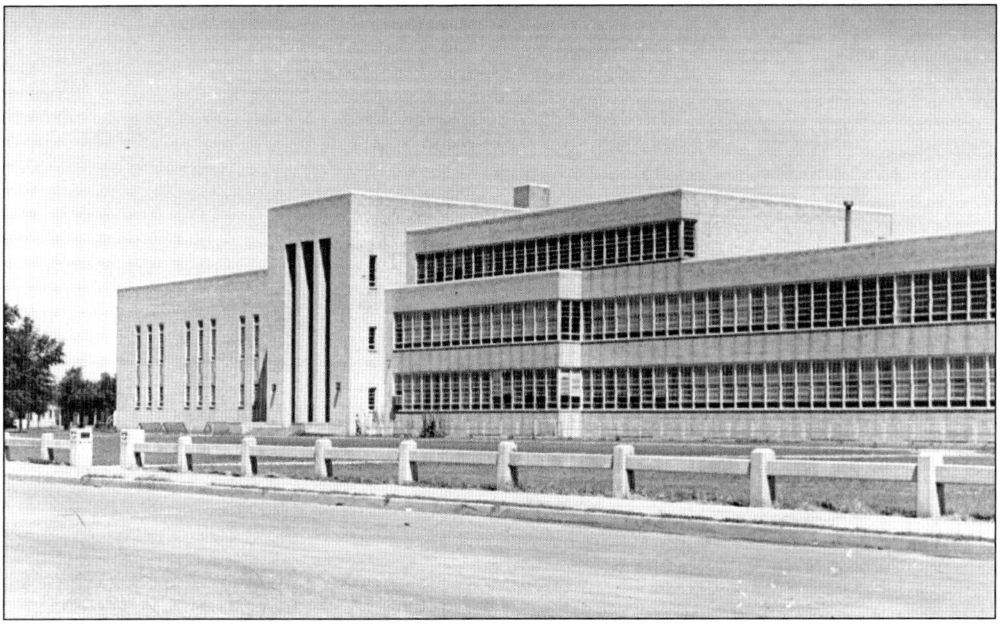

The first senior class of the new Pampa High School graduated in 1942. Some of the construction was slowed down because of the war. The fence in front was built by the Federal Works Progress Administration. The building was completely remodeled in 2009, is fully landscaped, and has a beautiful rotunda with the Pampa Harvester bronze sculpture inside the entrance. Pampa High School now graduates approximately 230 seniors each year.

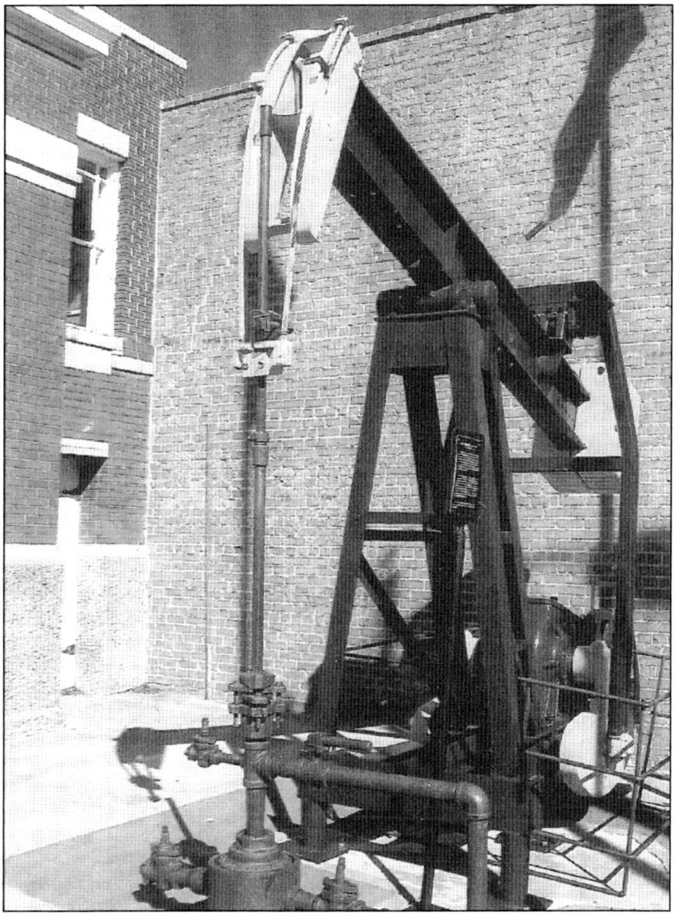

This pump jack is sitting on the south side of the Holland Wing of the museum. It is one of the green and gold 1929 Cabot pump jacks. This one was donated and installed at the museum by Curtis Well Service.

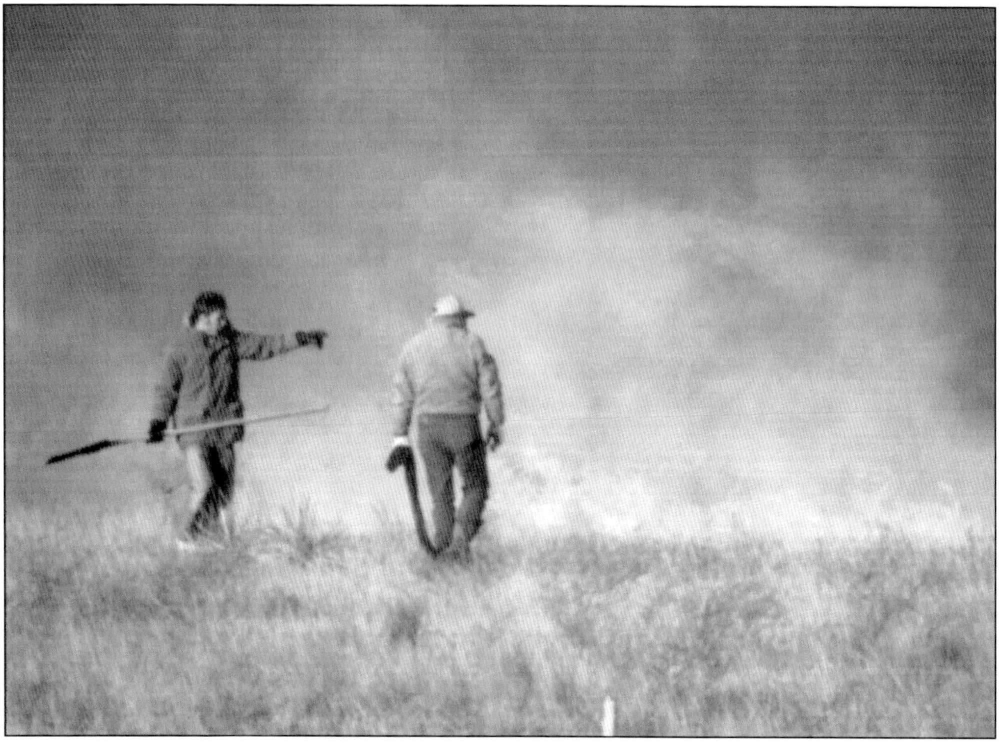

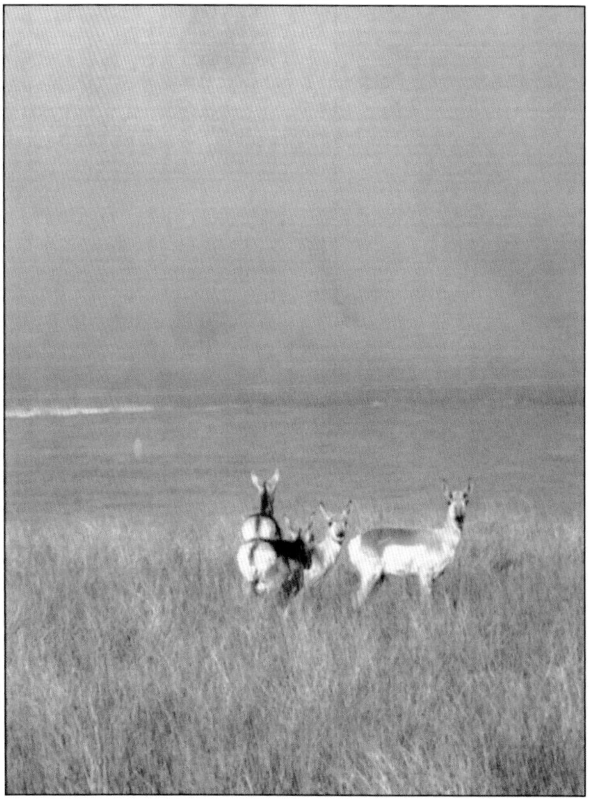

Wildfires swept across the prairie north, south, west, and some east of Pampa in 2006. They burned thousands of acres of grass, killed many cattle and other wildlife, threatened homes, and nearly sent farmers and ranchers into bankruptcy. The fires burned for many days and were a tragic event for Pampa and the other towns of Gray County. These two photographs show some of the fires burning. The homeowners above are beating out fires with blankets and shovels.

Antelope are watching the fire north of Pampa in March 2006.

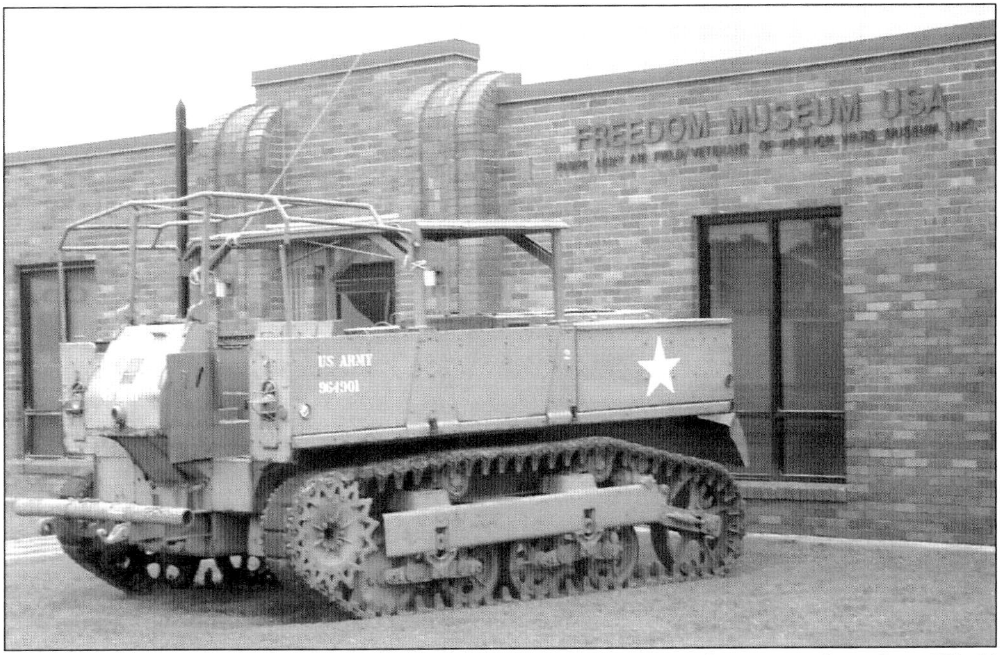

The Freedom Museum USA in Pampa is a specialty museum that houses artifacts from World War I, World War II, Korea, Vietnam, Operation Desert Storm, Operation Iraqi Freedom, and now from Afghanistan. The museum is a great educational tool for Pampa schoolchildren.

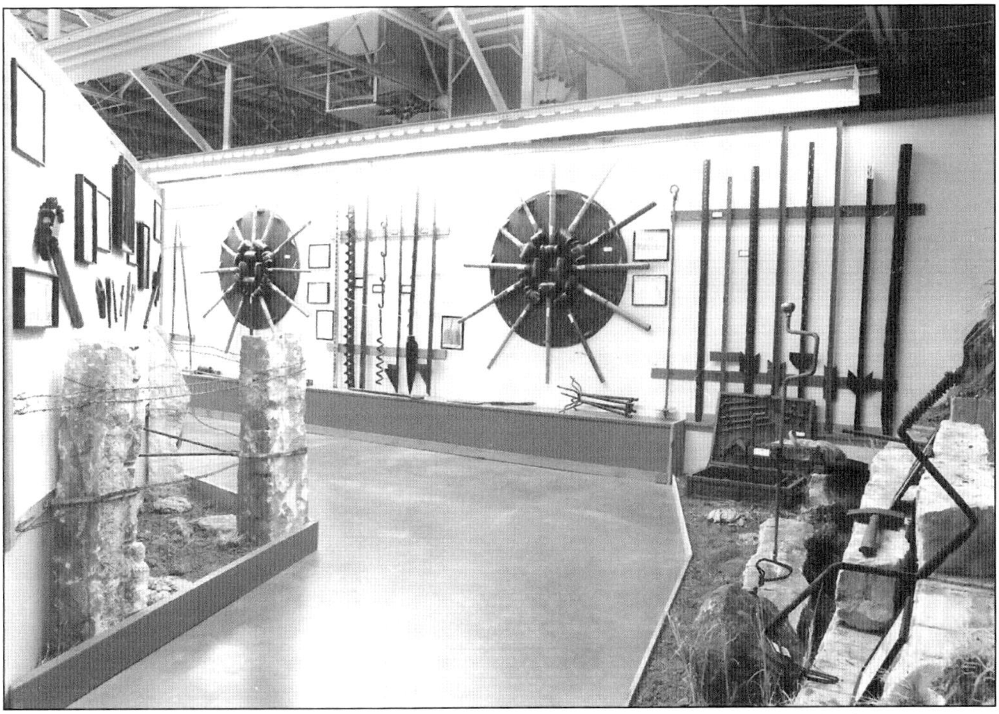

The Devil's Rope Museum is at McLean, 34 miles from Pampa. It is the largest barbed wire museum in the world. It also contains artifacts from the old Route 66 and Panhandle ranching history. Delbert and Ruth Trew, residents of Alanreed, developed the museum.

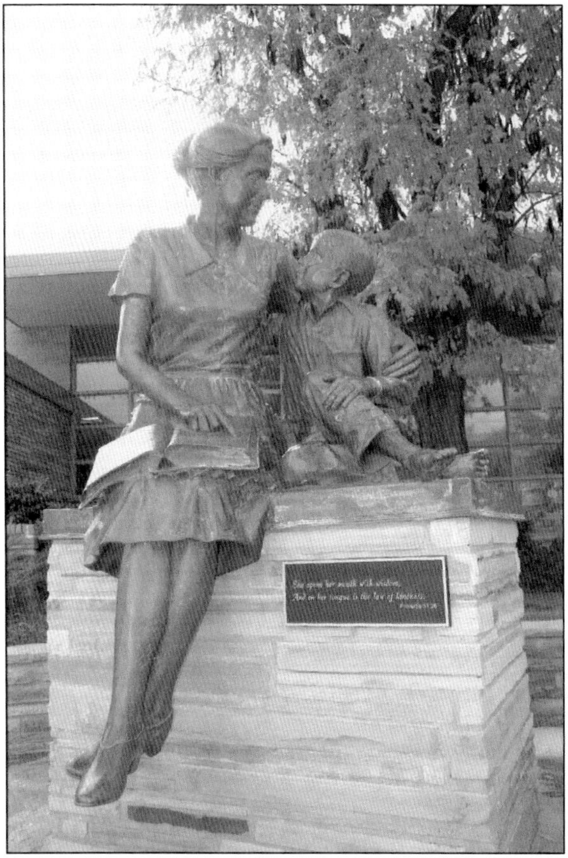

The influence of the Pampa Area Foundation for Outdoor Art is visible throughout the city. *The Lesson*, by Don Ray, was a gift from R. L. Franklin to the Lovett Library.

The Book of Knowledge is located at Clarendon College, Pampa Center. It was cast by Paul Coronis and financed by Las Pampas Koi and Water Garden Society.

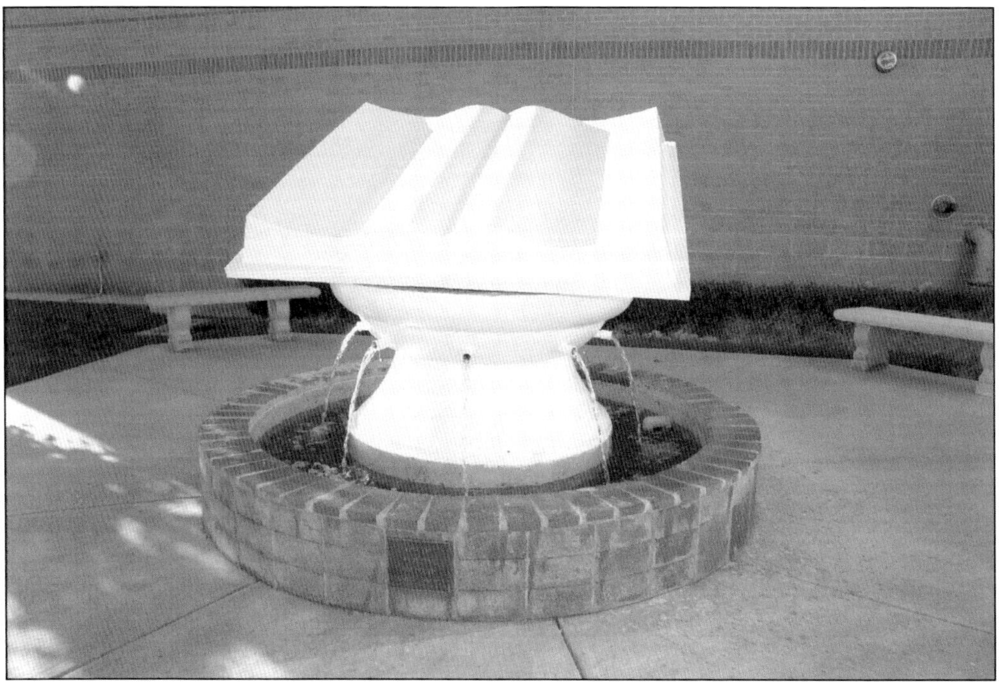

Perry Lefors, buffalo hunter and rancher, overlooks the traffic at 1100 North Hobart Street (U.S. Highway 70). The town of Lefors and Perry Lefors Air Field northwest of Pampa are named for this pioneer who came in 1876 and promoted the organization of Gray County. The bronze statue was commissioned by son Emmett Lefors. Perry and his four children died in the typhoid epidemic of 1909.

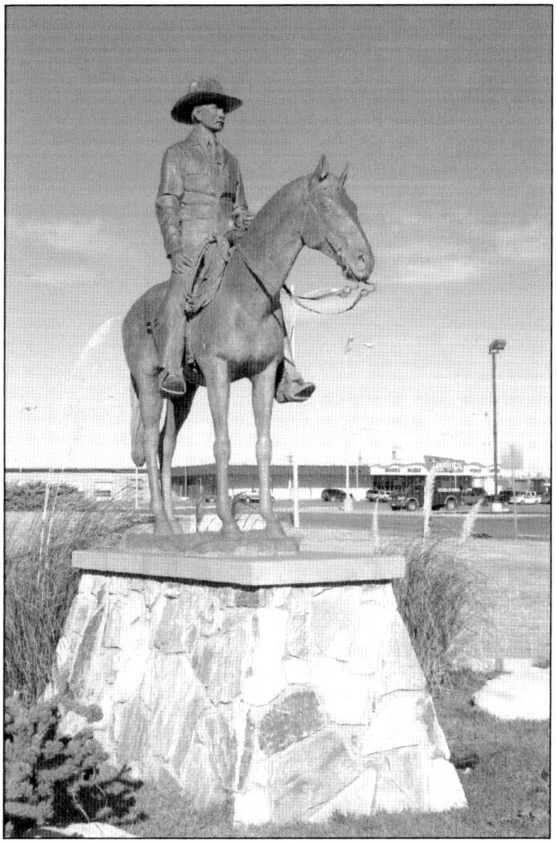

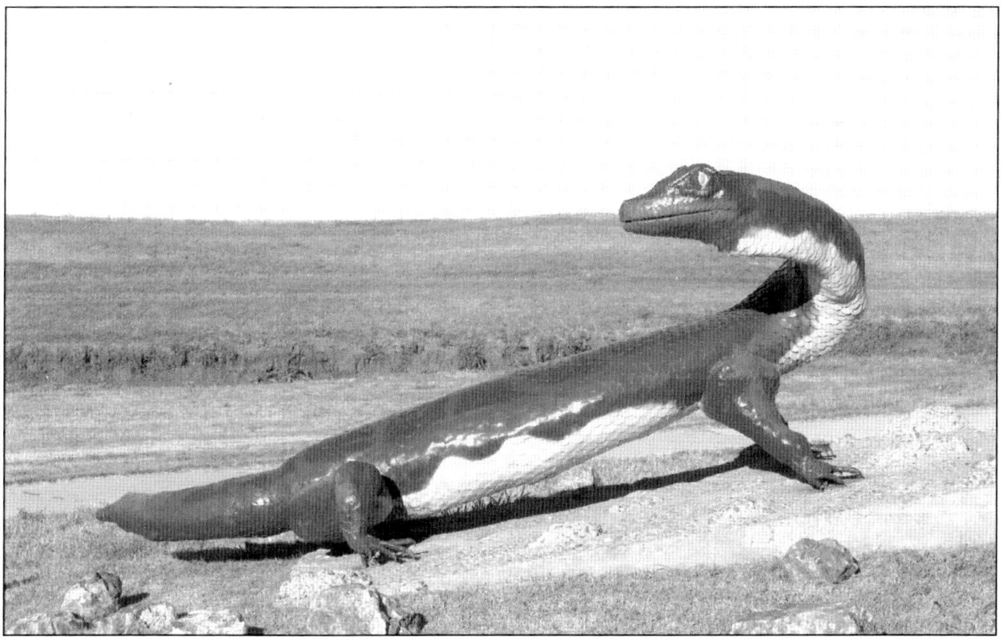

The Loch Ness Lizard was made by the Pampa High School metal trades class, supervised by teacher Warren Smith. It is a real source of entertainment for the younger children.

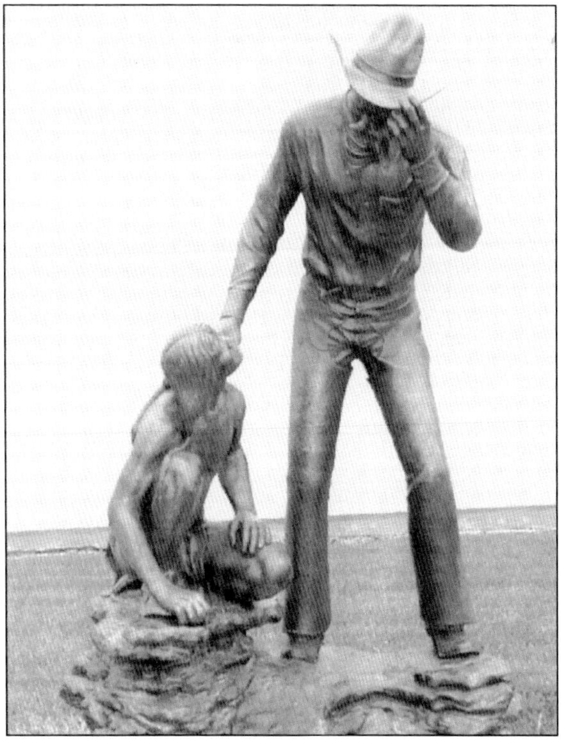

Grandfather's Vision was done by renowned Pampa artist Gerald Sanders. It is located at Brunow Park on Cuyler Street. It depicts a cowboy and his Indian friend puzzling over markings on the stone of an oil derrick—a sign of the future?

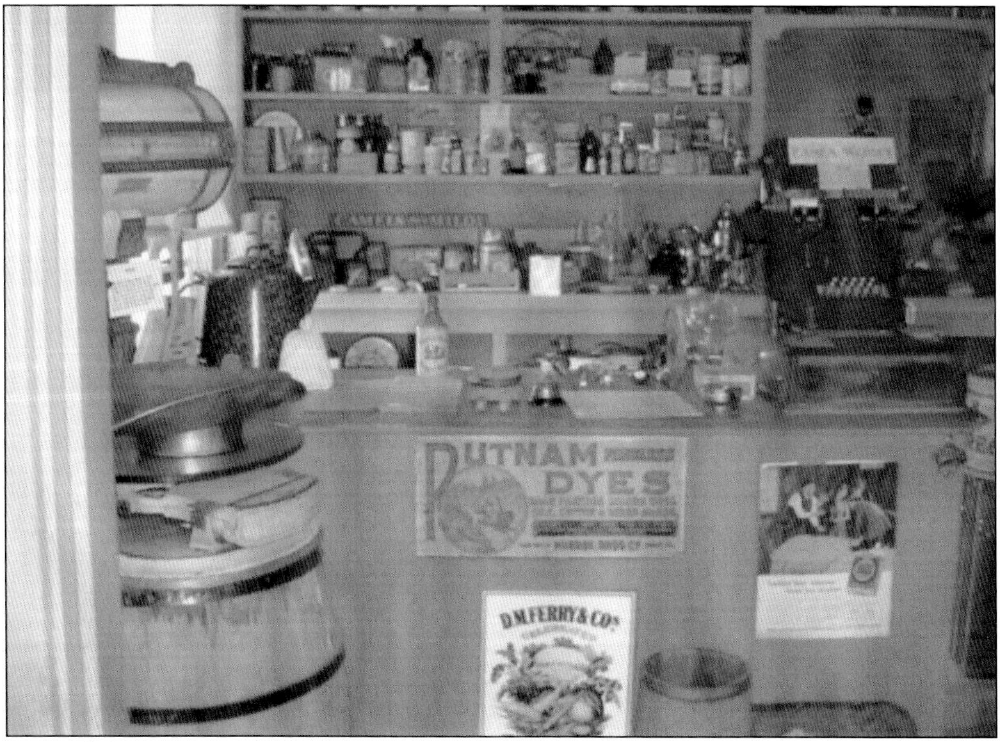

This exhibit is an antique grocery store in the museum. The store served the settlers of Pampa very well until 1930-1940, when larger markets became available.

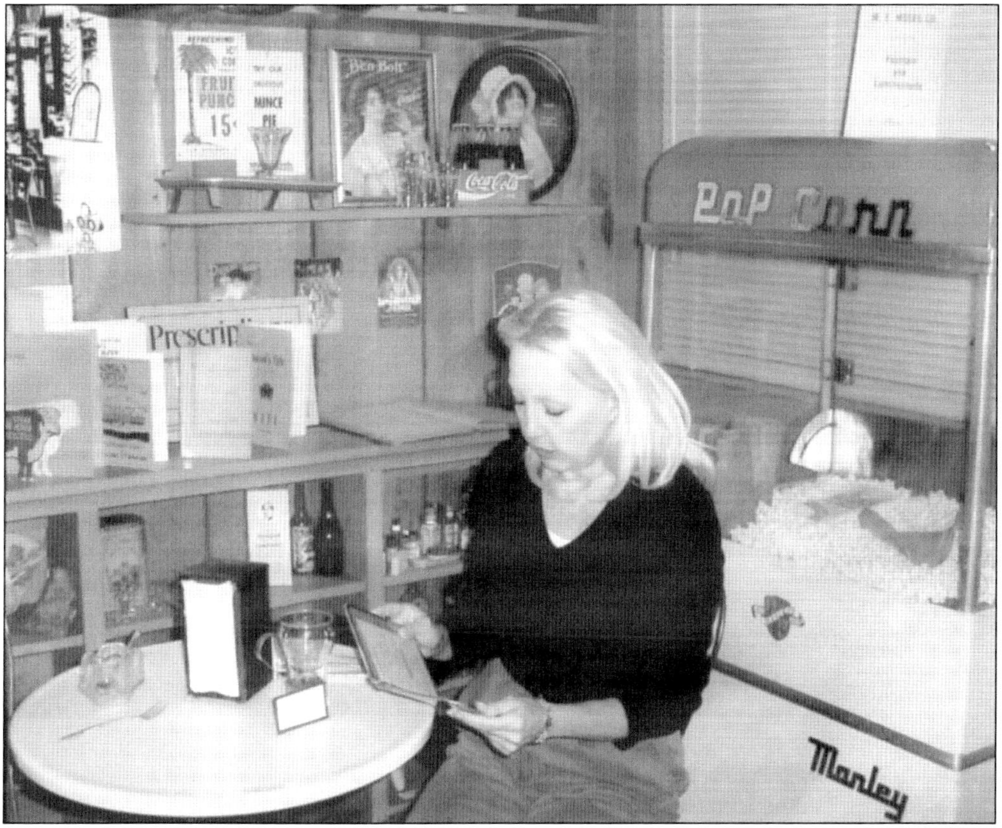

One of the coauthors of this book, Deborah Chambers, is reading the menu of Pampa's old drugstore fountain, and behind her is the general store's popcorn machine. This is one of the museum's favorite displays.

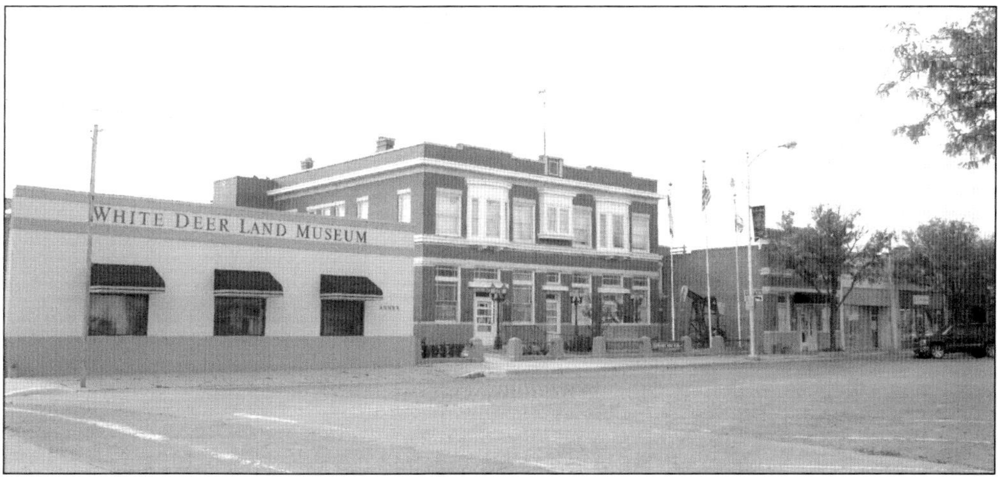

We are very proud to have worked on this book at the White Deer Land Museum in Pampa. This museum will be 40 years old in 2010 and now occupies three buildings with thousands of artifacts. In the museum are beautiful textiles, furnishings, a large collection of arrowheads donated by the R. J. Sailor family. The annex (left) showcases the Red River War of 1874–1875 and early settlement.

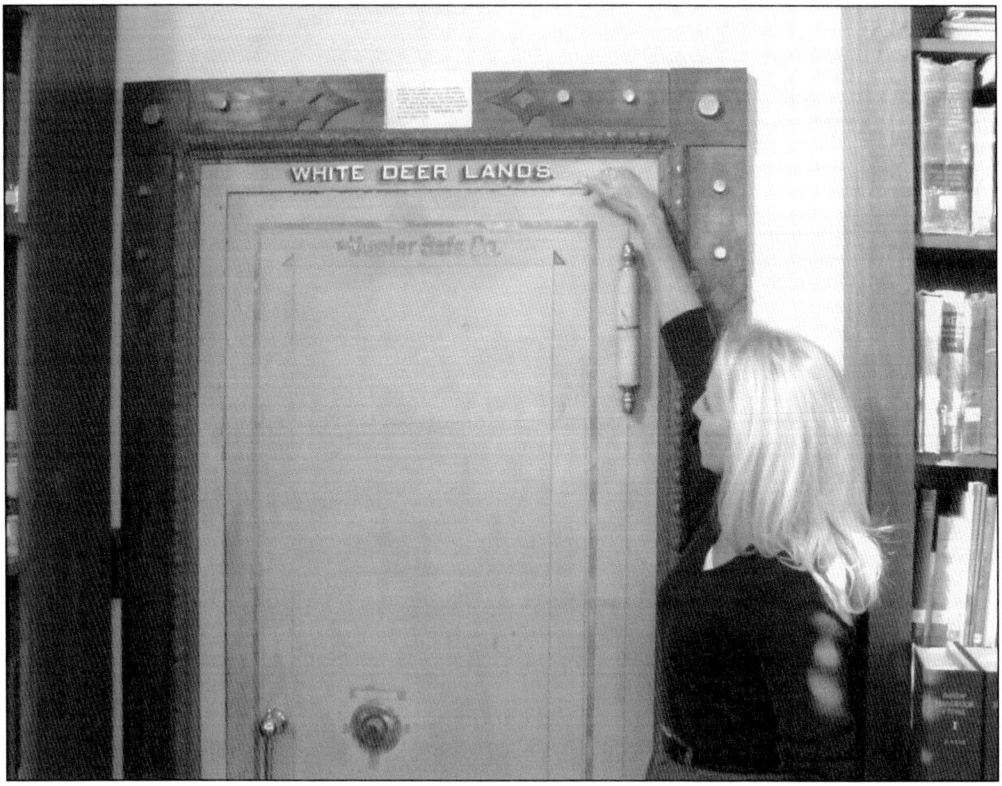

This is the museum's assistant director showing the vault in the office of the White Deer Lands. This vault was built by the Mosler Safe and Vault Company, one of the oldest builders of safes and jails in the United States. This is now an exhibit area, but the vault is still in use by the staff.

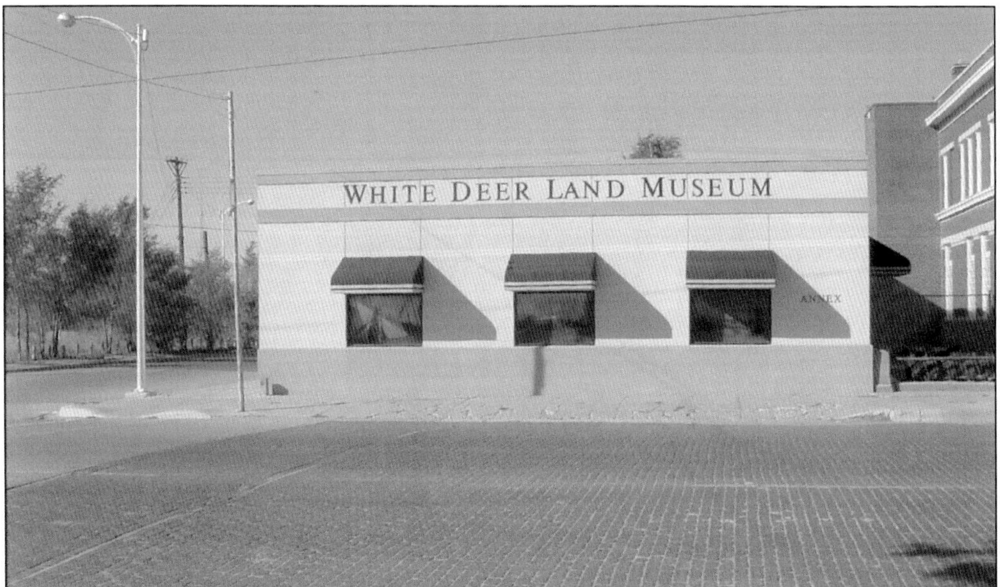

The annex building was completely renovated in 2008. It houses the Red River War exhibits and depicts early Pampa settlement.

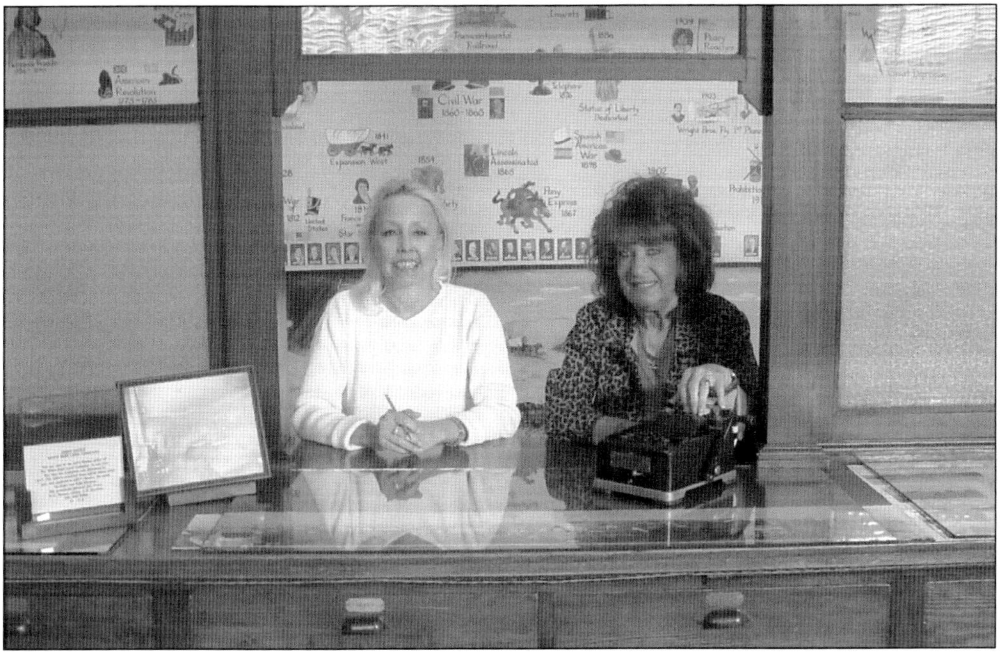

Deborah Chambers and Anne Davidson are getting ready to start another workday at the White Deer Land Museum. This is the office where thousands of acres of land were sold in four counties. Behind them is a hand-painted timeline of Gray County, Texas, and the United States. This museum is preserving history for many generations to come.

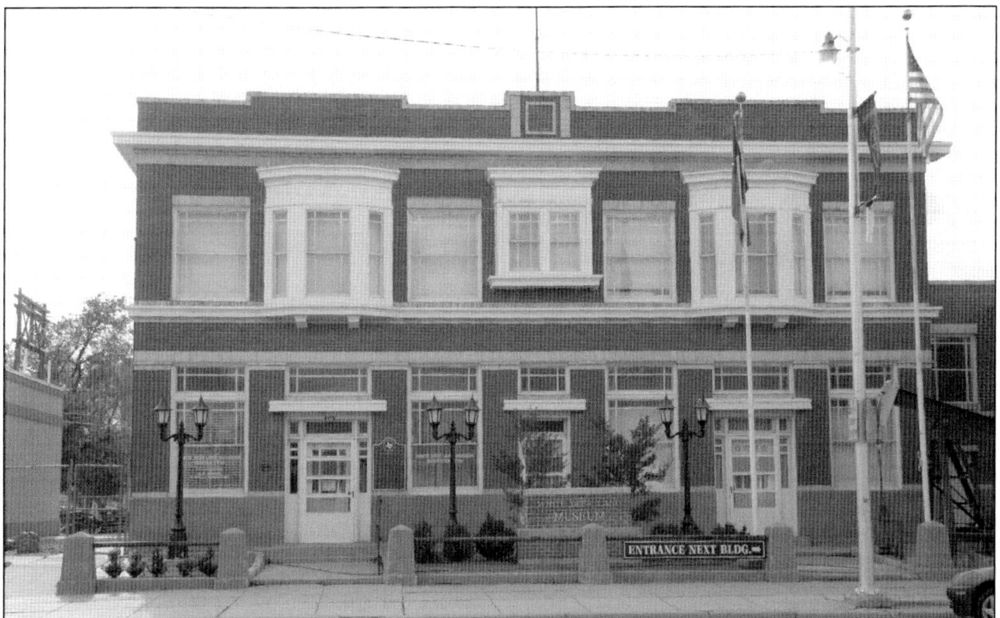

The White Deer Land building, located behind the old brick streets of Pampa, will be 93 years old in 2010. It is still very beautiful. The building has seen much take place in Pampa and will see much more. This museum and the two adjoining buildings belong to Gray County. Pampa has been blessed by this historic landmark.

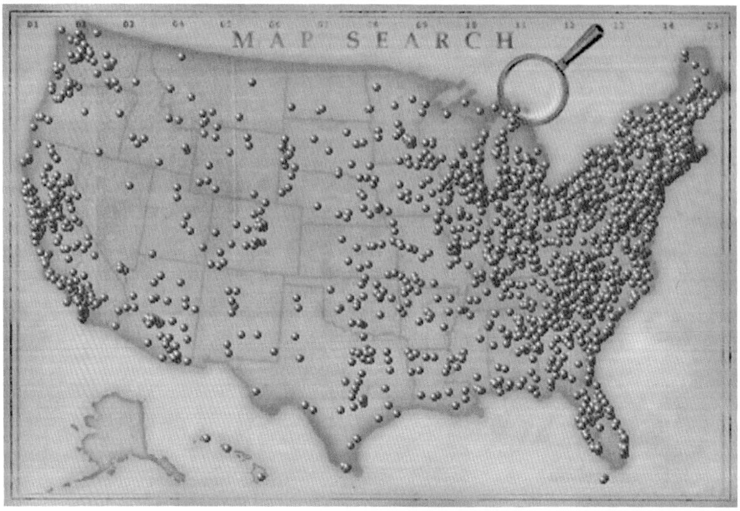
MAP SEARCH